The Annotated ANSI C Standard

American National Standard for Programming Languages—C

ANSI/ISO 9899-1990

Herbert Schildt

The Annotated ANSI C Standard

American National Standard for Programming Languages—C

ANSI/ISO 9899-1990

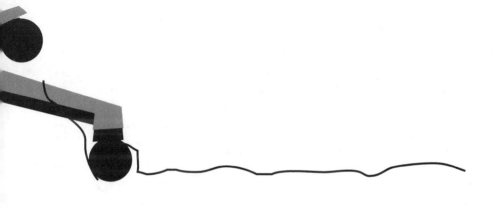

Osborne **McGraw-Hill**
2600 Tenth Street
Berkeley, California 94710
U.S.A.

For information on software, translations, or book distributors outside of
the U.S.A., please write to Osborne **McGraw-Hill** at the above address.

The Annotated ANSI C Standard
American National Standard for Programming Languages—C
ANSI/ISO 9899-1990

ACQUISITIONS EDITOR
Jeffrey M. Pepper

ASSOCIATE EDITOR
Vicki Van Ausdall

TECHNICAL EDITOR
Robert Goosey

PROJECT EDITOR
Madhu Prasher

COPY EDITOR
Carol Henry

PROOFREADER
Judith Brown

COMPUTER DESIGNERS
Fred Lass
Lance Ravella

COVER DESIGN
Compass Marketing

Copyright Notice

Contents

Annexes

Acknowledgments

Special thanks to Robert Goosey for his time, effort, and attention to detail while reviewing my annotations for technical accuracy. Robert is an extraordinary programmer and author and his comments were deeply appreciated.

Introduction

This book contains the full text of the ANSI/ISO Standard for the C programming language, which is commonly called the *ANSI C Standard*. (ANSI stands for American National Standards Institute, and ISO stands for International Organization for Standardization.) Since the ANSI C standard is the definitive reference source for the C language, it is a document that every C (or C++) programmer should have easy access to. To make the text of the standard more generally accessible and easier to understand, I have provided explanations, comments, and examples on the pages that face the pages of the standard.

I have written several books about C (and its progeny, C++), including introductory tutorials, reference guides, and advanced programming studies. *The Annotated ANSI C Standard*, however, represents the attainment of a longtime personal goal. Having started programming in C in the 1970s, I have watched the development and evolution of C with keen interest and greeted its acceptance and expanded use with substantial delight. The standardization of C in 1989 was a major milestone in programming. With the completion of the standard, it seemed to me important to make the standard available to as many programmers as possible. This annotated version of the ANSI C standard is the culmination of nearly two decades of programming in and writing about my favorite computer language: C.

From the start, I liked C because it was—first and foremost—a *programmer's* language! It was not designed by a committee nor developed to please an arbitrary administrative scheme. Rather, C was designed to enable real, wage-earning programmers to write efficient, portable code with a minimum of effort and without the language itself getting in the way. Put differently, C lets programmers be the best they can be.

C combines two things: freedom and power. The language has few restraints, and instantiates the assumption that the "programmer knows what he or she is doing." In addition, C is a language that is close to the hardware, making it especially good for the creation of systems code, which is still C's forte.

With power comes responsibility, however. C gives the programmer virtually total control over the machine and how a program executes, and so it is possible—in fact, easy—to create incorrect code that can cause substantial problems. It is the responsibility of every C programmer to exercise proper care and attention to detail.

In the years since I first learned C, it has become the most important programming language in the world. The ANSI C standard contained in this book is C's definitive description. It fully describes and defines the language in a formal way, providing the answers to all questions concerning C's use and implementation. The standard is the "court of last resort" in matters of the C language. And, because C++ is built upon ANSI-standard C, the standard is a guiding document for C++ as well.

The Creation of the Standard

The C language was invented by Dennis Ritchie in the 1970s and was described in *The C Programming Language,* by Brian Kernighan and Dennis Ritchie (Englewood Cliffs, NJ: Prentice-Hall, 1978). Known as "K&R" to C programmers, this book served for many years as the de facto standard for the language. (In fact, it is the base document for the ANSI C standard.) Because of C's rapid acceptance and popularity, many different implementations were created, including several for the use of the new (at the time) personal computer, or microcomputer as it was then called. Because the description of the C language was fairly detailed in K&R, most compilers were highly intercompatible; yet differences did exist, and a need for a C language standard was obvious to all involved.

The formal standardization process began in the summer of 1983, when the ANSI X3J11 committee was formed. The committee standardized the C language using these guidelines: use the K&R book as a basis, support existing programming practices whenever possible, and incorporate a few new features that were finding their way into the language. It is doubtful that many (if any) of the founding members thought, at the beginning, that the standardization process would take as long as it did—in the end, it took six years! The finished standard was approved by the American National Standards Institute (ANSI) on December 14, 1989, and the first copies of the standard became available early in 1990.

During the standardization process, many people played an important role. Though it is not possible to recognize everyone involved, listed below are the officers of the Technical Committee when the standard was finally submitted:

Chair	Jim Brodie
Vice-Chair	Thomas Plum
Secretary	P. J. Plauger
International Representative	P. J. Plauger (Previously, Steve Hersee)
Vocabulary Representative	Andrew Johnson
Draft Redactor	David F. Prosser (previously, Lawrence Rosler)

Rationale Redactor	Randy Hudson
Environment Subcommittee Chairs	Ralph Ryan, Ralph Phraner
Language Subcommittee Chair	Lawrence Rosler
Library Subcommittee Chair	P. J. Plauger

I was an Observing Member of the ANSI X3J11 committee throughout the standard's formation and adoption.

The ANSI C standard, once completed, was internationalized in 1990 and became the ANSI/ISO standard, which superseded the 1989 version. It is this 1990 version of the standard that is printed in this book.

The Purpose of My Annotations

The ANSI C standard is the definitive reference for the C language, but it is not easy reading! A language standard must describe the language in painstakingly precise and thorough detail, avoiding ambiguity and redundancy. As such, the best way to comprehend the ANSI C standard is to read the entire document, start to finish, several times.

While compiler implementors have the time and patience to read and thoroughly understand the ANSI C standard, most programmers do not. Rather, most programmers want quick, yet definitive answers to their questions about the language, its syntax, and its usage. This annotated version of the C standard addresses these needs. While containing, intact and unaltered, the complete ANSI C standard, it also includes explanations, comments, examples, and programming tips designed to make the standard easier to understand and use.

The purpose of my comments is to expand upon, amplify, or otherwise clarify the language and/or descriptions used in the standard. When a section is self-explanatory, I make no comment. Other sections have a longer response. I also offer usage hints and other practical advice where it seems appropriate.

Remember, none of my comments are intended to modify, alter, or otherwise rewrite the standard. Rather, they are presented to assist the reader in understanding this important C language document.

How to Use the Annotated C Standard

If you have the time, read the entire standard (including the annotations), start to finish, at least once. This will give you an overview of how the standard is organized, the definition of key terms, and an understanding of the relationships among the standard's parts. *Keep in mind that the complete and unaltered ANSI C Standard is printed on the left-hand page and my commentary appears on the right-hand page.*

To find an immediate answer to a question, begin with the main listing for the topic given in the index. Be sure to follow all cross-references (whether given in the standard or in the annotations). Often, an important piece of information is found in the cross-referenced sections. If a section of the standard seems especially confusing, try reading my commentary. It may help clarify the presentation in the standard.

One last point: Once you become familiar with the terms and format of the standard, you will find that it provides solid answers to all questions concerning the C language.

HS
6/3/93
Mahomet, IL

Programming languages — C

1 Scope

This International Standard specifies the form and establishes the interpretation of programs written in the C programming language.[1] It specifies

— the representation of C programs;

— the syntax and constraints of the C language;

— the semantic rules for interpreting C programs;

— the representation of input data to be processed by C programs;

— the representation of output data produced by C programs;

— the restrictions and limits imposed by a conforming implementation of C.

This International Standard does not specify

— the mechanism by which C programs are transformed for use by a data-processing system;

— the mechanism by which C programs are invoked for use by a data-processing system;

— the mechanism by which input data are transformed for use by a C program;

— the mechanism by which output data are transformed after being produced by a C program;

— the size or complexity of a program and its data that will exceed the capacity of any specific data-processing system or the capacity of a particular processor;

— all minimal requirements of a data-processing system that is capable of supporting a conforming implementation.

2 Normative references

The following standards contain provisions which, through reference in this text, constitute provisions of this International Standard. At the time of publication, the editions indicated were valid. All standards are subject to revision, and parties to agreements based on this International Standard are encouraged to investigate the possibility of applying the most recent editions of the standards indicated below. Members of IEC and ISO maintain registers of currently valid International Standards.

ISO 646:1983, *Information processing — ISO 7-bit coded character set for information interchange*.

ISO 4217:1987, *Codes for the representation of currencies and funds*.

---

[1] This International Standard is designed to promote the portability of C programs among a variety of data-processing systems. It is intended for use by implementors and programmers. It is accompanied by a Rationale document that explains many of the decisions of the Technical Committee that produced it.

Part 1   Scope

The ANSI/ISO C Standard formally describes the C language and sets forth the terms and conditions to which a compiler must comply to be called an "ANSI standard compiler." (Hereafter, the terms *ANSI standard* or simply *standard* will be used to refer to the ANSI/ISO C Standard.)

To put it simply and directly, the ANSI standard is a formal document that is not easy to understand upon first reading. However, the standard provides the "last word" on the C language and is always the court of last resort in any dispute regarding the language. If you learned to program in C in the normal way, then you learned the C language in a less formal and more intuitive manner than presented by the standard. Typically, programming books describe the language less strictly than the ANSI standard does. In other words, most programming books explain *how to use* the C language, but they do not fully *define* it. In contrast, the purpose of the standard is to fully define the C language. As such, the standard is a more precise document than you may be accustomed to.

The standard specifies several things about the C language: the form of a C program, the syntax of the language, the rules a compiler must follow when processing the language, the form of input and output that programs must accommodate, and various minimal limits that must be achieved. To this extent, the ANSI C standard is similar to any other language standard.

What the ANSI standard does not specify is how a program is compiled or executed. It does not even specify that the program will actually be compiled. For example, it is fully acceptable for a C program to be interpreted. More important is the fact that the standard does not completely specify the environment in which a C program will execute. This is particularly significant because C was designed to be a highly portable language.

A *conforming implementation* is a compiler that complies with the standard and is capable of compiling any program written in accordance with the standard. It is important to understand that many compilers that are loosely called "ANSI compatible" may not be fully compliant and, as such, are not technically conforming implementations. (The issue of conformance to the standard is discussed further in Part 4.)

Part 2   Normative references

In the *Normative references* section are listed two other standards that are referenced by the ANSI C standard. The first describes the 7-bit character codes. These are the standard codes used to represent characters within a computer and are commonly called the ASCII character codes. The second standard specifies how currency values are represented in various languages.

3 Definitions and conventions

In this International Standard, "shall" is to be interpreted as a requirement on an implementation or on a program; conversely, "shall not" is to be interpreted as a prohibition.

For the purposes of this International Standard, the following definitions apply. Other terms are defined at their first appearance, indicated by *italic* type. Terms explicitly defined in this International Standard are not to be presumed to refer implicitly to similar terms defined elsewhere. Terms not defined in this International Standard are to be interpreted according to ISO 2382.

3.1 alignment: A requirement that objects of a particular type be located on storage boundaries with addresses that are particular multiples of a byte address.

3.2 argument: An expression in the comma-separated list bounded by the parentheses in a function call expression, or a sequence of preprocessing tokens in the comma-separated list bounded by the parentheses in a function-like macro invocation. Also known as "actual argument" or "actual parameter."

3.3 bit: The unit of data storage in the execution environment large enough to hold an object that may have one of two values. It need not be possible to express the address of each individual bit of an object.

3.4 byte: The unit of data storage large enough to hold any member of the basic character set of the execution environment. It shall be possible to express the address of each individual byte of an object uniquely. A byte is composed of a contiguous sequence of bits, the number of which is implementation-defined. The least significant bit is called the *low-order* bit; the most significant bit is called the *high-order* bit.

3.5 character: A bit representation that fits in a byte. The representation of each member of the basic character set in both the source and execution environments shall fit in a byte.

3.6 constraints: Syntactic and semantic restrictions by which the exposition of language elements is to be interpreted.

3.7 diagnostic message: A message belonging to an implementation-defined subset of the implementation's message output.

3.8 forward references: References to later subclauses of this International Standard that contain additional information relevant to this subclause.

3.9 implementation: A particular set of software, running in a particular translation environment under particular control options, that performs translation of programs for, and supports execution of functions in, a particular execution environment.

3.10 implementation-defined behavior: Behavior, for a correct program construct and correct data, that depends on the characteristics of the implementation and that each implementation shall document.

3.11 implementation limits: Restrictions imposed upon programs by the implementation.

3.12 locale-specific behavior: Behavior that depends on local conventions of nationality, culture, and language that each implementation shall document.

3.13 multibyte character: A sequence of one or more bytes representing a member of the extended character set of either the source or the execution environment. The extended character set is a superset of the basic character set.

3.14 object: A region of data storage in the execution environment, the contents of which can represent values. Except for bit-fields, objects are composed of contiguous sequences of one or more bytes, the number, order, and encoding of which are either explicitly specified or implementation-defined. When referenced, an object may be interpreted as having a particular type; see 6.2.2.1.

Part 3   Definitions and conventions

Part 3 defines several terms used by the standard. Notice that the word *shall* is used in its imperative. That is, in the standard, the word *shall* means *must*. Conversely, *shall not* means *must not*.

Most of the definitions in this section are easy to understand and will already be familiar to most readers. However, a few clarifications are warranted, as noted here.

3.1   Alignment   The term *alignment* refers to the way variables are stored in memory. In some machine architectures, it is more efficient for certain types of values to be stored on word or paragraph boundaries. (A paragraph is 16 bytes.) In fact, in some situations, such an alignment may be required.

3.2   Argument   An *argument* is a value that is used in a call to a function. For example,

```
func(10, 20);
```

Here the values 10 and 20 are arguments that are passed to the function when it is called. (See *parameter* in paragraph 3.15.)

3.9   Implementation   In more straightforward terms, an *implementation* is a specific C compiler. For example, both Borland C and Microsoft C are implementations of the C language.

3.10   Implementation-defined behavior   *Implementation-defined behavior* refers to actions that are not defined by the standard but are, instead, related to the specific implementation and are left to the compiler. Put differently, in a correct C program situations may occur for which the response is left entirely to the discretion of the implementor of the compiler, based upon the specifics of the implementation. By allowing for implementation-defined behavior, the standard is, in essence, allowing C to be implemented in the widest range of environments and for the widest range of applications.

3.12   Locale-specific behavior   C is fully internationalized. As such, the behavior and implementation of certain elements of the language will depend upon the country in which the language is used. When such differences apply, they are referred to as *locale-specific behavior*.

3.13   Multibyte character   The basic character set of the C language (which is essentially the ASCII character set) is byte oriented. That is, each character in the basic character set fits in 1 byte. However, this limits the total character set to 255 characters. Although this is fine for many languages, such as English, French, and Russian, it cannot accommodate others, such as Chinese or Japanese. To solve this problem, C allows an extended character set composed of *multibyte characters*, which are used to hold additional characters.

3.15 parameter: An object declared as part of a function declaration or definition that acquires a value on entry to the function, or an identifier from the comma-separated list bounded by the parentheses immediately following the macro name in a function-like macro definition. Also known as "formal argument" or "formal parameter."

3.16 undefined behavior: Behavior, upon use of a nonportable or erroneous program construct, of erroneous data, or of indeterminately valued objects, for which this International Standard imposes no requirements. Permissible undefined behavior ranges from ignoring the situation completely with unpredictable results, to behaving during translation or program execution in a documented manner characteristic of the environment (with or without the issuance of a diagnostic message), to terminating a translation or execution (with the issuance of a diagnostic message).

If a "shall" or "shall not" requirement that appears outside of a constraint is violated, the behavior is undefined. Undefined behavior is otherwise indicated in this International Standard by the words "undefined behavior" or by the omission of any explicit definition of behavior. There is no difference in emphasis among these three; they all describe "behavior that is undefined."

3.17 unspecified behavior: Behavior, for a correct program construct and correct data, for which this International Standard explicitly imposes no requirements.

Examples

1. An example of unspecified behavior is the order in which the arguments to a function are evaluated.

2. An example of undefined behavior is the behavior on integer overflow.

3. An example of implementation-defined behavior is the propagation of the high-order bit when a signed integer is shifted right.

4. An example of locale-specific behavior is whether the `islower` function returns true for characters other than the 26 lowercase English letters.

Forward references: bitwise shift operators (6.3.7), expressions (6.3), function calls (6.3.2.2), the `islower` function (7.3.1.6), localization (7.4).

4 Compliance

A *strictly conforming program* shall use only those features of the language and library specified in this International Standard. It shall not produce output dependent on any unspecified, undefined, or implementation-defined behavior, and shall not exceed any minimum implementation limit.

The two forms of *conforming implementation* are hosted and freestanding. A *conforming hosted implementation* shall accept any strictly conforming program. A *conforming freestanding implementation* shall accept any strictly conforming program in which the use of the features specified in the library clause (clause 7) is confined to the contents of the standard headers `<float.h>`, `<limits.h>`, `<stdarg.h>`, and `<stddef.h>`. A conforming implementation may have extensions (including additional library functions), provided they do not alter the behavior of any strictly conforming program.[2]

A *conforming program* is one that is acceptable to a conforming implementation.[3]

---

2 This implies that a conforming implementation reserves no identifiers other than those explicitly reserved in this International Standard.

3 Strictly conforming programs are intended to be maximally portable among conforming implementations. Conforming programs may depend upon nonportable features of a conforming implementation.

3.14   *Object* The term *object* is used in the standard to denote something that occupies memory. An object is either a variable or a constant that resides at a physical memory address.

3.15   *Parameter* A function *parameter* is a local variable that receives the value of an argument when the function is called. For example,

```
void func(int a, int b) {
  /* ... */
}
/* ... */
func(4, 5);
```

Here **a** and **b** are parameters to **func().** They receive the values of the arguments 4 and 5 when the function is called.

3.16   *Undefined behavior* In the standard there are many references to *undefined behavior*. The standard uses this term to indicate that the compiler's response to an incorrect (or questionable) situation is not defined. In these instances, the compiler is free to respond to the situation as it sees fit, because the standard imposes no prescribed response.

The reason *undefined behavior* appears so frequently in the standard is because C was designed to give the programmer the greatest possible freedom and control over the machine. As such, C supports various constructs and standard library functions that can be used or misused. Since the misuse of a language element cannot be defined beforehand, the standard simply leaves it to the compiler implementor to respond appropriately.

3.17   *Unspecified behavior* *Unspecified behavior* is related to undefined behavior (defined just above), with the main difference being that unspecified behavior is not an action that results from an error. When the standard uses the term unspecified behavior, it means that what occurs is completely up to the implementation and not relevant to the standard.

Part 4   Compliance

The standard defines a *conforming implementation* as one that implements the C language as defined by the standard.

A *hosted implementation* must accept any type of program that is written in compliance with the standard. A hosted implementation represents the type of C

An implementation shall be accompanied by a document that defines all implementation-defined characteristics and all extensions.

Forward references: limits `<float.h>` and `<limits.h>` (7.1.5), variable arguments `<stdarg.h>` (7.8), common definitions `<stddef.h>` (7.1.6).

compilers with which you are probably familiar. A *freestanding implementation* must implement all language elements defined by the standard, but does not need to implement the entire standard library as defined by the standard. Most notably, a freestanding implementation does not need to implement the standard I/O library functions. Freestanding implementations are intended for special situations in which not all library functions are applicable.

For both the hosted and the freestanding implementations, a compiler is free to add extensions as long as standard features are not altered and the behavior of strictly conforming programs is not changed. The most common extensions added by compiler manufacturers are additional library functions. New keywords are not allowed extensions because they may alter the behavior of a strictly conforming program that uses such keywords as identifiers.

Note that it is common for compilers designed for the 8086 family of processors to add a set of keywords that accommodate the segmented architecture of these processors. For example, 8086-based compilers typically add the keywords *far* and *near*, which are used to specify intersegment and intrasegment pointers. However, by supporting such keyword extensions, the compilers become nonconforming implementations. For this reason, most of these compilers have a switch or option that turns off the non-ANSI keywords, thus allowing the compiler to become compliant.

The ANSI standard defines two types of C programs: *conforming* and *strictly conforming*. The difference between the two affects the program's portability. Specifically, a strictly conforming program uses only those language elements and library functions defined by the standard—this type of program is the most portable because it can be compiled by any conforming implementation. However, a strictly conforming program cannot use any extensions. In contrast, a conforming program can use any extensions—this means that the conforming program may not be portable.

The difference between conforming and strictly conforming is more pronounced in C than in many other languages, because C is designed to be inherently extensible due to its reliance on the library. Therefore, in practice, most programs are conforming rather than strictly conforming.

5 Environment

An implementation translates C source files and executes C programs in two data-processing-system environments, which will be called the *translation environment* and the *execution environment* in this International Standard. Their characteristics define and constrain the results of executing conforming C programs constructed according to the syntactic and semantic rules for conforming implementations.

Forward references: In the environment clause (clause 5), only a few of many possible forward references have been noted.

5.1 Conceptual models

5.1.1 Translation environment

5.1.1.1 Program structure

A C program need not all be translated at the same time. The text of the program is kept in units called *source files* in this International Standard. A source file together with all the headers and source files included via the preprocessing directive **#include**, less any source lines skipped by any of the conditional inclusion preprocessing directives, is called a *translation unit*. Previously translated translation units may be preserved individually or in libraries. The separate translation units of a program communicate by (for example) calls to functions whose identifiers have external linkage, manipulation of objects whose identifiers have external linkage, or manipulation of data files. Translation units may be separately translated and then later linked to produce an executable program.

Forward references: conditional inclusion (6.8.1), linkages of identifiers (6.1.2.2), source file inclusion (6.8.2).

5.1.1.2 Translation phases

The precedence among the syntax rules of translation is specified by the following phases.[4]

1. Physical source file characters are mapped to the source character set (introducing new-line characters for end-of-line indicators) if necessary. Trigraph sequences are replaced by corresponding single-character internal representations.

2. Each instance of a new-line character and an immediately preceding backslash character is deleted, splicing physical source lines to form logical source lines. A source file that is not empty shall end in a new-line character, which shall not be immediately preceded by a backslash character.

3. The source file is decomposed into preprocessing tokens[5] and sequences of white-space characters (including comments). A source file shall not end in a partial preprocessing token or comment. Each comment is replaced by one space character. New-line characters are retained. Whether each nonempty sequence of white-space characters other than new-line is retained or replaced by one space character is implementation-defined.

4. Preprocessing directives are executed and macro invocations are expanded. A **#include** preprocessing directive causes the named header or source file to be processed from phase 1 through phase 4, recursively.

---

4 Implementations must behave as if these separate phases occur, even though many are typically folded together in practice.

5 As described in 6.1, the process of dividing a source file's characters into preprocessing tokens is context-dependent. For example, see the handling of < within a **#include** preprocessing directive.

Part 5 Environment

Two factors affect the execution of your C program: the *translation environment* and the *execution environment*. The translation environment exists when your program is compiled, and the execution environment exists when your program is executed. Since the two environments may differ, the standard describes characteristics of each. Much of the information in this section is of interest primarily to compiler implementors, but some is valuable for all C programmers.

The exact nature of a C environment will affect the performance of a program; that is, differences in the translation and execution environments may affect the way a program behaves. (For example, the size of an integer may vary between environments.) It is in Part 5, Environment, that the standard defines the minimal constraints that apply. Keep in mind that it is, in most cases, permissible for the compiler or the execution platform to exceed these constraints. The standard simply sets a lower bound.

5.1.1.1 Program structure A *translation unit* is, essentially, a source file. As you probably know, C programs may be composed of two or more source files, which may be compiled separately and linked together to form the final executable program. Therefore, a translation unit is one of these source files and all of the files that it includes using **#include**.

The term *external linkage* refers to the functions and variables that are accessible to all parts of your program. This applies to all nonstatic functions and global variables. Remember, if you use the **static** modifier on a function or global variable, then you are restricting that function or variable to *file scope*, and it will not have external linkage. Identifiers with external linkage may be accessed by all parts of your program, no matter what file (that is, translation unit) they reside in.

5.1.1.2 Translation phases Here is a synopsis of the translation (compilation) rules as described in Section 5.1.1.2: First, several character translations are performed. (Note: Trigraph characters are described in Section 5.2.1.1.) Next, the source file is tokenized, and comments are replaced by a single space. (The fact that comments must be replaced by a space explains why you cannot embed a comment within an identifier name.) Then, all preprocessing operations are performed. Once the preprocessor is done, further character translations are performed, and the final tokenization of the source file occurs. Finally, the compiler generates object code; this code is then linked with other translation units and the library to produce the executable program.

5. Each source character set member and escape sequence in character constants and string literals is converted to a member of the execution character set.

6. Adjacent character string literal tokens are concatenated and adjacent wide string literal tokens are concatenated.

7. White-space characters separating tokens are no longer significant. Each preprocessing token is converted into a token. The resulting tokens are syntactically and semantically analyzed and translated.

8. All external object and function references are resolved. Library components are linked to satisfy external references to functions and objects not defined in the current translation. All such translator output is collected into a program image which contains information needed for execution in its execution environment.

Forward references: lexical elements (6.1), preprocessing directives (6.8), trigraph sequences (5.2.1.1).

5.1.1.3 Diagnostics

A conforming implementation shall produce at least one diagnostic message (identified in an implementation-defined manner) for every translation unit that contains a violation of any syntax rule or constraint. Diagnostic messages need not be produced in other circumstances.[6]

5.1.2 Execution environments

Two execution environments are defined: *freestanding* and *hosted*. In both cases, *program startup* occurs when a designated C function is called by the execution environment. All objects in static storage shall be *initialized* (set to their initial values) before program startup. The manner and timing of such initialization are otherwise unspecified. *Program termination* returns control to the execution environment.

Forward references: initialization (6.5.7).

5.1.2.1 Freestanding environment

In a freestanding environment (in which C program execution may take place without any benefit of an operating system), the name and type of the function called at program startup are implementation-defined. There are otherwise no reserved external identifiers. Any library facilities available to a freestanding program are implementation-defined.

The effect of program termination in a freestanding environment is implementation-defined.

5.1.2.2 Hosted environment

A hosted environment need not be provided, but shall conform to the following specifications if present.

5.1.2.2.1 Program startup

The function called at program startup is named **main**. The implementation declares no prototype for this function. It can be defined with no parameters:

```
int main(void) { /*...*/ }
```

or with two parameters (referred to here as **argc** and **argv**, though any names may be used, as they are local to the function in which they are declared):

---

6 The intent is that an implementation should identify the nature of, and where possible localize, each violation. Of course, an implementation is free to produce any number of diagnostics as long as a valid program is still correctly translated. It may also successfully translate an invalid program.

(*5.1.1.2 Translation phases,* continued)

In rule 5, the term *escape sequence* refers to a backslash character (\) constant.

5.1.1.3 Diagnostics The standard requires that a compiler issue error messages when an error in the source code is encountered. The standard also states that it is permissible for a compiler to issue warning messages for questionable, though syntactically correct, constructs. It simply stipulates that such warnings will not prevent an otherwise correct program from being compiled. For example, it is common for compilers to issue a warning message when no prototype is included before a function is called. Because prototypes are not technically necessary, the compiler cannot issue an error message, but it can issue a warning alerting you to this (possible) omission.

5.1.2 Execution environments All global variables and static local variables are initialized before program execution begins. The standard refers to these types of variables as being in *static storage*—this means memory that is not reused during program execution. For example, local variables are stored on the stack, which is dynamic (constantly changing). Static storage is fixed in its purpose throughout the duration of your program's execution.

5.1.2.1 Freestanding environment In a *freestanding* execution environment, how a program begins and ends execution is not specifically defined. Therefore, it is possible for a freestanding program to begin with a call to a function other than **main()**, for example.

5.1.2.2 Hosted environment A *hosted* execution environment, in contrast, must follow a well-defined set of rules. Most importantly, all C programs must begin execution with the **main()** function.

Interestingly, there is no prototype for **main()** declared by the compiler. You are therefore free to declare **main()** as required by your program. For example, here are three common methods of declaring **main()**:

```
void main(void) /* no return value, no parameters */

int main(void) /* return a value, no parameters */

/* return a value and include command-line parameters */
int main(int argc, char *argv[])
```

5.1.2.2.1 Program startup Remember, the names **argc** and **argv** are arbitrary. They could be any other legal identifiers you like. (However, using **argc** and **argv** follows generally accepted practice.)

```
int main(int argc, char *argv[]) { /*...*/ }
```

If they are defined, the parameters to the **main** function shall obey the following constraints:

— The value of **argc** shall be nonnegative.

— **argv[argc]** shall be a null pointer.

— If the value of **argc** is greater than zero, the array members **argv[0]** through **argv[argc-1]** inclusive shall contain pointers to strings, which are given implementation-defined values by the host environment prior to program startup. The intent is to supply to the program information determined prior to program startup from elsewhere in the hosted environment. If the host environment is not capable of supplying strings with letters in both uppercase and lowercase, the implementation shall ensure that the strings are received in lowercase.

— If the value of **argc** is greater than zero, the string pointed to by **argv[0]** represents the *program name*; **argv[0][0]** shall be the null character if the program name is not available from the host environment. If the value of **argc** is greater than one, the strings pointed to by **argv[1]** through **argv[argc-1]** represent the *program parameters*.

— The parameters **argc** and **argv** and the strings pointed to by the **argv** array shall be modifiable by the program, and retain their last-stored values between program startup and program termination.

5.1.2.2.2 Program execution

In a hosted environment, a program may use all the functions, macros, type definitions, and objects described in the library clause (clause 7).

5.1.2.2.3 Program termination

A return from the initial call to the **main** function is equivalent to calling the **exit** function with the value returned by the **main** function as its argument. If the **main** function executes a return that specifies no value, the termination status returned to the host environment is undefined.

Forward references: definition of terms (7.1.1), the **exit** function (7.10.4.3).

5.1.2.3 Program execution

The semantic descriptions in this International Standard describe the behavior of an abstract machine in which issues of optimization are irrelevant.

Accessing a volatile object, modifying an object, modifying a file, or calling a function that does any of those operations are all *side effects*, which are changes in the state of the execution environment. Evaluation of an expression may produce side effects. At certain specified points in the execution sequence called *sequence points*, all side effects of previous evaluations shall be complete and no side effects of subsequent evaluations shall have taken place.

In the abstract machine, all expressions are evaluated as specified by the semantics. An actual implementation need not evaluate part of an expression if it can deduce that its value is not used and that no needed side effects are produced (including any caused by calling a function or accessing a volatile object).

When the processing of the abstract machine is interrupted by receipt of a signal, only the values of objects as of the previous sequence point may be relied on. Objects that may be modified between the previous sequence point and the next sequence point need not have received their correct values yet.

An instance of each object with automatic storage duration is associated with each entry into its block. Such an object exists and retains its last-stored value during the execution of the block, and while the block is suspended (by a call of a function or receipt of a signal).

*(**5.1.2.2.1 Program startup,** continued)*

In most implementations, the return value from **main()**, if there is one, is returned to the operating system. Remember, if you don't explicitly return a value from **main()** then the value passed to the operating system is, technically, undefined. Though most compilers will automatically return 0 when no other return value is specified (even when **main()** is declared as **void**), you should not rely on this fact because it is not guaranteed by the standard.

5.1.2.3   Program execution   The standard uses the phrase "issues of optimization are irrelevant" when discussing program execution. This does not refer to your own coding practices—that is, whether you are an accomplished programmer or not. What the phrase refers to is optimizations performed by the compiler in order to produce faster and/or smaller object code.

In this section, the term *side effect* is not intended to have a negative connotation. Rather, it means, quite literally, that something has changed which may affect some event later in the program. The reason side effects are important has to do with the evaluation of an expression at run time. According to the standard, the compiler is free to ignore a subexpression if its value is not used and if it produces no side effects. The converse to this is that the compiler must fully evaluate a subexpression if it does (or may) produce a side effect. This implies that when a function is used in an expression, it must be executed because it may produce a side effect—even if its value is not important to the larger expression. In essence, this part of the standard simply guarantees that whenever a function is used in an expression, it will be executed.

The term *automatic storage,* for practical purposes, means the stack. In the last paragraph on page 7, the standard is stating that variables are local to the block and function in which they are declared, and that each entry into the block creates a unique set of variables. It also means that local variables will not have their values altered or overwritten by another block while the first block is still active.

The least requirements on a conforming implementation are:

— At sequence points, volatile objects are stable in the sense that previous evaluations are complete and subsequent evaluations have not yet occurred.

— At program termination, all data written into files shall be identical to the result that execution of the program according to the abstract semantics would have produced.

— The input and output dynamics of interactive devices shall take place as specified in 7.9.3. The intent of these requirements is that unbuffered or line-buffered output appear as soon as possible, to ensure that prompting messages actually appear prior to a program waiting for input.

What constitutes an interactive device is implementation-defined.

More stringent correspondences between abstract and actual semantics may be defined by each implementation.

Examples

1. An implementation might define a one-to-one correspondence between abstract and actual semantics: at every sequence point, the values of the actual objects would agree with those specified by the abstract semantics. The keyword **volatile** would then be redundant.

    Alternatively, an implementation might perform various optimizations within each translation unit, such that the actual semantics would agree with the abstract semantics only when making function calls across translation unit boundaries. In such an implementation, at the time of each function entry and function return where the calling function and the called function are in different translation units, the values of all externally linked objects and of all objects accessible via pointers therein would agree with the abstract semantics. Furthermore, at the time of each such function entry the values of the parameters of the called function and of all objects accessible via pointers therein would agree with the abstract semantics. In this type of implementation, objects referred to by interrupt service routines activated by the **signal** function would require explicit specification of **volatile** storage, as well as other implementation-defined restrictions.

2. In executing the fragment

    ```
    char c1, c2;
    /*...*/
    c1 = c1 + c2;
    ```

    the "integral promotions" require that the abstract machine promote the value of each variable to **int** size and then add the two **int**s and truncate the sum. Provided the addition of two **char**s can be done without creating an overflow exception, the actual execution need only produce the same result, possibly omitting the promotions.

3. Similarly, in the fragment

    ```
    float f1, f2;
    double d;
    /*...*/
    f1 = f2 * d;
    ```

    the multiplication may be executed using single-precision arithmetic if the implementation can ascertain that the result would be the same as if it were executed using double-precision arithmetic (for example, if **d** were replaced by the constant **2.0**, which has type **double**). Alternatively, an operation involving only **int**s or **float**s may be executed using double-precision operations if neither range nor precision is lost thereby.

4. To illustrate the grouping behavior of expressions, in the following fragment

(*5.1.2.3 Program execution, continued*)

From a programmer's point of view, and put into practical terms, the three points at the top of page 8 can be paraphrased as follows: First, one expression will be fully evaluated before the evaluation of the next expression begins. Second, when a program ends, any output file will contain what your program wrote to it. Third, I/O requests take place in the order in which they occur in your program. For example, given this sequence:

```
printf("Enter a string: ");
gets(s);
```

the output from **printf()** will occur before the request for input generated by **gets()**.

```
int a, b;
/*...*/
a = a + 32760 + b + 5;
```

the expression statement behaves exactly the same as

```
a = (((a + 32760) + b) + 5);
```

due to the associativity and precedence of these operators. Thus, the result of the sum `` (a + 32760) '' is next added to **b**, and that result is then added to **5** which results in the value assigned to **a**. On a machine in which overflows produce an exception and in which the range of values representable by an **int** is [-32768,+32767], the implementation cannot rewrite this expression as

```
a = ((a + b) + 32765);
```

since if the values for **a** and **b** were, respectively, -32754 and -15, the sum **a + b** would produce an exception while the original expression would not; nor can the expression be rewritten either as

```
a = ((a + 32765) + b);
```

or

```
a = (a + (b + 32765));
```

since the values for **a** and **b** might have been, respectively, 4 and -8 or -17 and 12. However on a machine in which overflows do not produce an exception and in which the results of overflows are reversible, the above expression statement can be rewritten by the implementation in any of the above ways because the same result will occur.

5. The grouping of an expression does not completely determine its evaluation. In the following fragment

```
#include <stdio.h>
int sum;
char *p;
/*...*/
sum = sum * 10 - '0' + (*p++ = getchar());
```

the expression statement is grouped as if it were written as

```
sum = (((sum * 10) - '0') + ((*(p++)) = (getchar())));
```

but the actual increment of **p** can occur at any time between the previous sequence point and the next sequence point (the ;), and the call to **getchar** can occur at any point prior to the need of its returned value.

Forward references: compound statement, or block (6.6.2), expressions (6.3), files (7.9.3), sequence points (6.3, 6.6), the **signal** function (7.7), type qualifiers (6.5.3).

There are no annotations for page 9.

5.2 Environmental considerations

5.2.1 Character sets

Two sets of characters and their associated collating sequences shall be defined: the set in which source files are written, and the set interpreted in the execution environment. The values of the members of the execution character set are implementation-defined; any additional members beyond those required by this subclause are locale-specific.

In a character constant or string literal, members of the execution character set shall be represented by corresponding members of the source character set or by *escape sequences* consisting of the backslash \ followed by one or more characters. A byte with all bits set to 0, called the *null character*, shall exist in the basic execution character set; it is used to terminate a character string literal.

Both the basic source and basic execution character sets shall have at least the following members: the 26 uppercase letters of the English alphabet

```
A  B  C  D  E  F  G  H  I  J  K  L  M
N  O  P  Q  R  S  T  U  V  W  X  Y  Z
```

the 26 lowercase letters of the English alphabet

```
a  b  c  d  e  f  g  h  i  j  k  l  m
n  o  p  q  r  s  t  u  v  w  x  y  z
```

the 10 decimal digits

```
0  1  2  3  4  5  6  7  8  9
```

the following 29 graphic characters

```
!  "  #  %  &  '  (  )  *  +  ,  -  .  /  :
;  <  =  >  ?  [  \  ]  ^  _  {  |  }  ~
```

the space character, and control characters representing horizontal tab, vertical tab, and form feed. In both the source and execution basic character sets, the value of each character after **0** in the above list of decimal digits shall be one greater than the value of the previous. In source files, there shall be some way of indicating the end of each line of text; this International Standard treats such an end-of-line indicator as if it were a single new-line character. In the execution character set, there shall be control characters representing alert, backspace, carriage return, and new line. If any other characters are encountered in a source file (except in a character constant, a string literal, a header name, a comment, or a preprocessing token that is never converted to a token), the behavior is undefined.

Forward references: character constants (6.1.3.4), preprocessing directives (6.8), string literals (6.1.4), comments (6.1.9).

5.2.1.1 Trigraph sequences

All occurrences in a source file of the following sequences of three characters (called *trigraph sequences*[7]) are replaced with the corresponding single character.

---

7 The trigraph sequences enable the input of characters that are not defined in the Invariant Code Set as described in ISO 646:1983, which is a subset of the seven-bit ASCII code set.

5.2   Environmental considerations The standard describes two character sets: the one in which your program's source file is written, and the one used when your program is executed. Both these character sets must contain the upper- and lowercase letters of the alphabet, the digits 0 through 9, and the common punctuation symbols. (In essence, C requires the ASCII character set.) The compiler implementor may define a larger character set, but all compilers must accept and provide at least this minimum if they are to be conforming implementations. This minimum character set is called the *basic character set*.

5.2.1.1   Trigraph sequences C was designed in English and assumes the common English-language character set, which includes symbols such as { and }, [and], and so on. Some other languages, however, do not have these (and other) characters, which are required by C. To solve this problem, the standard defines a set of *trigraph sequences*, which can be substitutes for the symbols and which will work in any situation. If you program in English or most other Western languages, you will not need to use the trigraph sequences.

```
??=    #
??(    [
??/    \
??)    ]
??'    ^
??<    {
??!    |
??>    }
??-    ~
```

No other trigraph sequences exist. Each **?** that does not begin one of the trigraphs listed above is not changed.

Example

The following source line

```
printf("Eh???/n");
```

becomes (after replacement of the trigraph sequence **??/**)

```
printf("Eh?\n");
```

5.2.1.2 Multibyte characters

The source character set may contain multibyte characters, used to represent members of the extended character set. The execution character set may also contain multibyte characters, which need not have the same encoding as for the source character set. For both character sets, the following shall hold:

— The single-byte characters defined in 5.2.1 shall be present.

— The presence, meaning, and representation of any additional members is locale-specific.

— A multibyte character may have a *state-dependent encoding*, wherein each sequence of multibyte characters begins in an *initial shift state* and enters other implementation-defined *shift states* when specific multibyte characters are encountered in the sequence. While in the initial shift state, all single-byte characters retain their usual interpretation and do not alter the shift state. The interpretation for subsequent bytes in the sequence is a function of the current shift state.

— A byte with all bits zero shall be interpreted as a null character independent of shift state.

— A byte with all bits zero shall not occur in the second or subsequent bytes of a multibyte character.

For the source character set, the following shall hold:

— A comment, string literal, character constant, or header name shall begin and end in the initial shift state.

— A comment, string literal, character constant, or header name shall consist of a sequence of valid multibyte characters.

5.2.1.2 *Multibyte characters* Multibyte characters are used to extend the basic character set. The *extended character set* is a superset of the basic character set. The extended character set is used to represent the character sets of languages other than English (and other Western languages) in which there are more than 255 characters. (Examples include Chinese and Japanese.) Therefore, a multibyte character is a character that requires more than one byte.

There are two interesting aspects to multibyte characters. First, the null character may not be used except in the first byte of a multibyte sequence. This restriction allows multibyte characters to be used in and manipulated by the standard string functions. (Remember that the string functions assume that a null terminates the string.) Second, it is permissible for the meaning of a multibyte character to be altered by the current shift state.

Later in this standard, a few multibyte character functions are defined that allow multibyte characters to be fully integrated into the C environment.

Unless you are writing in or for a language that uses a very large character set that requires multibyte characters, you are unlikely to need to worry about multibyte characters.

5.2.2 Character display semantics

The *active position* is that location on a display device where the next character output by the **fputc** function would appear. The intent of writing a printable character (as defined by the **isprint** function) to a display device is to display a graphic representation of that character at the active position and then advance the active position to the next position on the current line. The direction of writing is locale-specific. If the active position is at the final position of a line (if there is one), the behavior is unspecified.

Alphabetic escape sequences representing nongraphic characters in the execution character set are intended to produce actions on display devices as follows:

\a (*alert*) Produces an audible or visible alert. The active position shall not be changed.

\b (*backspace*) Moves the active position to the previous position on the current line. If the active position is at the initial position of a line, the behavior is unspecified.

\f (*form feed*) Moves the active position to the initial position at the start of the next logical page.

\n (*new line*) Moves the active position to the initial position of the next line.

\r (*carriage return*) Moves the active position to the initial position of the current line.

\t (*horizontal tab*) Moves the active position to the next horizontal tabulation position on the current line. If the active position is at or past the last defined horizontal tabulation position, the behavior is unspecified.

\v (*vertical tab*) Moves the active position to the initial position of the next vertical tabulation position. If the active position is at or past the last defined vertical tabulation position, the behavior is unspecified.

Each of these escape sequences shall produce a unique implementation-defined value which can be stored in a single **char** object. The external representations in a text file need not be identical to the internal representations, and are outside the scope of this International Standard.

Forward references: the **fputc** function (7.9.7.3), the **isprint** function (7.3.1.7).

5.2.3 Signals and interrupts

Functions shall be implemented such that they may be interrupted at any time by a signal, or may be called by a signal handler, or both, with no alteration to earlier, but still active, invocations' control flow (after the interruption), function return values, or objects with automatic storage duration. All such objects shall be maintained outside the *function image* (the instructions that comprise the executable representation of a function) on a per-invocation basis.

The functions in the standard library are not guaranteed to be reentrant and may modify objects with static storage duration.

5.2.4 Environmental limits

Both the translation and execution environments constrain the implementation of language translators and libraries. The following summarizes the environmental limits on a conforming implementation.

5.2.4.1 Translation limits

The implementation shall be able to translate and execute at least one program that contains at least one instance of every one of the following limits:[8]

---

8 Implementations should avoid imposing fixed translation limits whenever possible.

5.2.2   *Character display semantics*   The term *active position* refers to the location at which the next character will be written on a display device. For the console, this is the current cursor location. However, since the cursor may not always be visible (or even exist), the standard uses the term active position.

5.2.3   *Signals and interrupts*   This section specifies that functions may be interrupted and that such an interruption shall not alter the performance of the function.

One very important point is stated that may affect programs you write: Library functions need not be re-entrant. This implies that, when executing in a multitasking environment, each program must have and use its own copy of each library function. In other words, one copy of a library function in memory may not be used by two or more currently executing programs. This point is seldom an issue for most C programs, but it may apply if you are using C for some special purpose.

5.2.4   *Environmental limits*   The standard defines and describes a number of limits and constraints that a conforming implementation must meet. It is permissible for a compiler to exceed these limits. However, from a practical point of view, these limits may govern aspects of programs that you write. For example, since a conforming compiler need only accept 15 levels of nested **if** statements, you may not want to exceed that limit if you want your code to be portable.

— 15 nesting levels of compound statements, iteration control structures, and selection control structures

— 8 nesting levels of conditional inclusion

— 12 pointer, array, and function declarators (in any combinations) modifying an arithmetic, a structure, a union, or an incomplete type in a declaration

— 31 nesting levels of parenthesized declarators within a full declarator

— 32 nesting levels of parenthesized expressions within a full expression

— 31 significant initial characters in an internal identifier or a macro name

— 6 significant initial characters in an external identifier

— 511 external identifiers in one translation unit

— 127 identifiers with block scope declared in one block

— 1024 macro identifiers simultaneously defined in one translation unit

— 31 parameters in one function definition

— 31 arguments in one function call

— 31 parameters in one macro definition

— 31 arguments in one macro invocation

— 509 characters in a logical source line

— 509 characters in a character string literal or wide string literal (after concatenation)

— 32767 bytes in an object (in a hosted environment only)

— 8 nesting levels for **#include**d files

— 257 **case** labels for a **switch** statement (excluding those for any nested **switch** statements)

— 127 members in a single structure or union

— 127 enumeration constants in a single enumeration

— 15 levels of nested structure or union definitions in a single struct-declaration-list

5.2.4.2 Numerical limits

A conforming implementation shall document all the limits specified in this subclause, which shall be specified in the headers **<limits.h>** and **<float.h>**.

5.2.4.2.1 Sizes of integral types **<limits.h>**

The values given below shall be replaced by constant expressions suitable for use in **#if** preprocessing directives. Moreover, except for **CHAR_BIT** and **MB_LEN_MAX**, the following shall be replaced by expressions that have the same type as would an expression that is an object of the corresponding type converted according to the integral promotions. Their implementation-defined values shall be equal or greater in magnitude (absolute value) to those shown, with the same sign.

— number of bits for smallest object that is not a bit-field (byte)
  CHAR_BIT   **8**

— minimum value for an object of type **signed char**
  SCHAR_MIN   **-127**

— maximum value for an object of type **signed char**
  SCHAR_MAX   **+127**

5.2.4.1 Translation limits The following terms are used when defining compilation limits:

♦ A *compound statement* is a block of code.

♦ An *iteration control structure* is a loop.

♦ A *selection control statement* is either an **if** or a **switch** statement.

♦ A *declarator* is, in general terms, the portion of a declaration statement that follows the type name.

♦ An *internal identifier* is a name (such as a variable name) that is local to the file in which it is declared. This includes local variables and static global variables.

♦ An *external identifier* may be accessed by files other than the one in which the identifier is declared. This includes global variables and all nonstatic functions.

♦ A *translation unit* is, essentially, a file.

5.2.4.2 Numerical limits You can determine the exact numerical limits used by your compiler by examining the **limits.h** and the **float.h** header files. The standard requires that such limits be defined in these files.

— maximum value for an object of type **unsigned char**
   UCHAR_MAX   255

— minimum value for an object of type **char**
   CHAR_MIN   *see below*

— maximum value for an object of type **char**
   CHAR_MAX   *see below*

— maximum number of bytes in a multibyte character, for any supported locale
   MB_LEN_MAX   1

— minimum value for an object of type **short int**
   SHRT_MIN   -32767

— maximum value for an object of type **short int**
   SHRT_MAX   +32767

— maximum value for an object of type **unsigned short int**
   USHRT_MAX   65535

— minimum value for an object of type **int**
   INT_MIN   -32767

— maximum value for an object of type **int**
   INT_MAX   +32767

— maximum value for an object of type **unsigned int**
   UINT_MAX   65535

— minimum value for an object of type **long int**
   LONG_MIN   -2147483647

— maximum value for an object of type **long int**
   LONG_MAX   +2147483647

— maximum value for an object of type **unsigned long int**
   ULONG_MAX   4294967295

If the value of an object of type **char** is treated as a signed integer when used in an expression, the value of **CHAR_MIN** shall be the same as that of **SCHAR_MIN** and the value of **CHAR_MAX** shall be the same as that of **SCHAR_MAX**. Otherwise, the value of **CHAR_MIN** shall be 0 and the value of **CHAR_MAX** shall be the same as that of **UCHAR_MAX**.[9]

5.2.4.2.2 Characteristics of floating types <float.h>

The characteristics of floating types are defined in terms of a model that describes a representation of floating-point numbers and values that provide information about an implementation's floating-point arithmetic.[10] The following parameters are used to define the model for each floating-point type:

---

9 See 6.1.2.5.

10 The floating-point model is intended to clarify the description of each floating-point characteristic and does not require the floating-point arithmetic of the implementation to be identical.

(**5.2.4.2 Numerical limits,** *continued*)

You can use the macros described in Section 5.2.4.2 within your program (provided that you have included **limits.h** and **float.h**) to help make your program more portable.

Although the numerical limits for the integral types are self-explanatory, here are some interesting points: First, notice that a character is defined as 8 bits (1 byte). All other types may vary in size, but in C a character is always 1 byte long. Short integers and integers must be at least 16 bits long. This means that if you want to use a "very short" integer, you must use a character type. Long integers must be at least 32 bits long.

s	sign (± 1)
b	base or radix of exponent representation (an integer > 1)
e	exponent (an integer between a minimum e_{min} and a maximum e_{max})
p	precision (the number of base-b digits in the significand)
f_k	nonnegative integers less than b (the significand digits)

A normalized floating-point number x ($f_1 > 0$ if $x \neq 0$) is defined by the following model:

$$x = s \times b^e \times \sum_{k=1}^{p} f_k \times b^{-k} , \quad e_{min} \leq e \leq e_{max}$$

Of the values in the **<float.h>** header, **FLT_RADIX** shall be a constant expression suitable for use in **#if** preprocessing directives; all other values need not be constant expressions. All except **FLT_RADIX** and **FLT_ROUNDS** have separate names for all three floating-point types. The floating-point model representation is provided for all values except **FLT_ROUNDS**.

The rounding mode for floating-point addition is characterized by the value of **FLT_ROUNDS**:

-1	indeterminable
0	toward zero
1	to nearest
2	toward positive infinity
3	toward negative infinity

All other values for **FLT_ROUNDS** characterize implementation-defined rounding behavior.

The values given in the following list shall be replaced by implementation-defined expressions that shall be equal or greater in magnitude (absolute value) to those shown, with the same sign:

— radix of exponent representation, b

   FLT_RADIX   **2**

— number of base-**FLT_RADIX** digits in the floating-point significand, p

   FLT_MANT_DIG
   DBL_MANT_DIG
   LDBL_MANT_DIG

— number of decimal digits, q, such that any floating-point number with q decimal digits can be rounded into a floating-point number with p radix b digits and back again without change to

   the q decimal digits, $\left\lfloor (p - 1) \times \log_{10}b \right\rfloor + \begin{cases} 1 & \text{if } b \text{ is a power of 10} \\ 0 & \text{otherwise} \end{cases}$

   FLT_DIG   **6**
   DBL_DIG   **10**
   LDBL_DIG   **10**

— minimum negative integer such that **FLT_RADIX** raised to that power minus 1 is a normalized floating-point number, e_{min}

   FLT_MIN_EXP
   DBL_MIN_EXP
   LDBL_MIN_EXP

— minimum negative integer such that 10 raised to that power is in the range of normalized

   floating-point numbers, $\left\lceil \log_{10}b^{e_{min}-1} \right\rceil$

   FLT_MIN_10_EXP   **-37**
   DBL_MIN_10_EXP   **-37**
   LDBL_MIN_10_EXP   **-37**

(**5.2.4.2 Numerical limits,** *continued*)

The description of normalized floating-point numbers is primarily for compiler implementors, but several minimums are defined that may be of interest. For example, the minimum acceptable range for a floating point value of type **float** is

$$10^{-37} \text{ to } 10^{+37}$$

Keep in mind that the compiler is free to exceed the minimums described here (and most compilers do so). Be sure to check your compiler's documentation if the range of floating-point values is important to you.

— maximum integer such that **FLT_RADIX** raised to that power minus 1 is a representable finite floating-point number, e_{max}

```
FLT_MAX_EXP
DBL_MAX_EXP
LDBL_MAX_EXP
```

— maximum integer such that 10 raised to that power is in the range of representable finite floating-point numbers, $\left\lfloor \log_{10}((1 - b^{-p}) \times b^{c_{max}}) \right\rfloor$

FLT_MAX_10_EXP	+37
DBL_MAX_10_EXP	+37
LDBL_MAX_10_EXP	+37

The values given in the following list shall be replaced by implementation-defined expressions with values that shall be equal to or greater than those shown:

— maximum representable finite floating-point number, $(1 - b^{-p}) \times b^{c_{max}}$

FLT_MAX	1E+37
DBL_MAX	1E+37
LDBL_MAX	1E+37

The values given in the following list shall be replaced by implementation-defined expressions with values that shall be equal to or less than those shown:

— the difference between 1 and the least value greater than 1 that is representable in the given floating point type, b^{1-p}

FLT_EPSILON	1E-5
DBL_EPSILON	1E-9
LDBL_EPSILON	1E-9

— minimum normalized positive floating-point number, $b^{c_{min}-1}$

FLT_MIN	1E-37
DBL_MIN	1E-37
LDBL_MIN	1E-37

Examples

1. The following describes an artificial floating-point representation that meets the minimum requirements of this International Standard, and the appropriate values in a **<float.h>** header for type **float**:

$$x = s \times 16^{e} \times \sum_{k=1}^{6} f_k \times 16^{-k} , \quad -31 \le e \le +32$$

FLT_RADIX	16
FLT_MANT_DIG	6
FLT_EPSILON	9.53674316E-07F
FLT_DIG	6
FLT_MIN_EXP	-31
FLT_MIN	2.93873588E-39F
FLT_MIN_10_EXP	-38
FLT_MAX_EXP	+32
FLT_MAX	3.40282347E+38F
FLT_MAX_10_EXP	+38

There are no annotations for page 16.

2. The following describes floating-point representations that also meet the requirements for single-precision and double-precision normalized numbers in ANSI/IEEE 754-1985,[11] and the appropriate values in a **<float.h>** header for types **float** and **double**:

$$x_f = s \times 2^e \times \sum_{k=1}^{24} f_k \times 2^{-k}, \quad -125 \leq e \leq +128$$

$$x_d = s \times 2^e \times \sum_{k=1}^{53} f_k \times 2^{-k}, \quad -1021 \leq e \leq +1024$$

```
FLT_RADIX                          2
FLT_MANT_DIG                      24
FLT_EPSILON         1.19209290E-07F
FLT_DIG                            6
FLT_MIN_EXP                     -125
FLT_MIN             1.17549435E-38F
FLT_MIN_10_EXP                   -37
FLT_MAX_EXP                     +128
FLT_MAX             3.40282347E+38F
FLT_MAX_10_EXP                   +38
DBL_MANT_DIG                      53
DBL_EPSILON 2.2204460492503131E-16
DBL_DIG                           15
DBL_MIN_EXP                    -1021
DBL_MIN     2.2250738585072014E-308
DBL_MIN_10_EXP                  -307
DBL_MAX_EXP                    +1024
DBL_MAX     1.7976931348623157E+308
DBL_MAX_10_EXP                  +308
```

Forward references: conditional inclusion (6.8.1).

---

11 The floating-point model in that standard sums powers of *b* from zero, so the values of the exponent limits are one less than shown here.

There are no annotations for page 17.

6 Language

In the syntax notation used in the language clause (clause 6), syntactic categories (nonterminals) are indicated by *italic* type, and literal words and character set members (terminals) by **bold** type. A colon (:) following a nonterminal introduces its definition. Alternative definitions are listed on separate lines, except when prefaced by the words "one of." An optional symbol is indicated by the subscript "opt," so that

$$\{ \ expression_{opt} \ \}$$

indicates an optional expression enclosed in braces.

6.1 Lexical elements

Syntax

> *token:*
>> *keyword*
>> *identifier*
>> *constant*
>> *string-literal*
>> *operator*
>> *punctuator*
>
> *preprocessing-token:*
>> *header-name*
>> *identifier*
>> *pp-number*
>> *character-constant*
>> *string-literal*
>> *operator*
>> *punctuator*
>> each non-white-space character that cannot be one of the above

Constraints

Each preprocessing token that is converted to a token shall have the lexical form of a keyword, an identifier, a constant, a string literal, an operator, or a punctuator.

Semantics

A *token* is the minimal lexical element of the language in translation phases 7 and 8. The categories of tokens are: *keywords, identifiers, constants, string literals, operators,* and *punctuators.* A *preprocessing token* is the minimal lexical element of the language in translation phases 3 through 6. The categories of preprocessing token are: *header names, identifiers, preprocessing numbers, character constants, string literals, operators, punctuators,* and single non-white-space characters that do not lexically match the other preprocessing token categories. If a ' or a " character matches the last category, the behavior is undefined. Preprocessing tokens can be separated by *white space;* this consists of comments (described later), or *white-space characters* (space, horizontal tab, new-line, vertical tab, and form-feed), or both. As described in 6.8, in certain circumstances during translation phase 4, white space (or the absence thereof) serves as more than preprocessing token separation. White space may appear within a preprocessing token only as part of a header name or between the quotation characters in a character constant or string literal.

If the input stream has been parsed into preprocessing tokens up to a given character, the next preprocessing token is the longest sequence of characters that could constitute a preprocessing token.

Part 6 Language

This section of the standard formally describes the C language. It does so two ways: First, using syntax notation, it states what a language element is composed of. Second, in the text, it describes the elements of the syntax.

The syntax consists of an element followed by that element's definition. Much of the syntax description is made up of *syntactic categories,* which are not actually part of the C language. (For example, the term *token* is not a keyword or an operator in C.) Syntactic categories are terms that are used to describe the C syntax, and are displayed in italic. When a part of the C language, such as an actual keyword, is used in a syntax description, it is shown in boldface.

Sometimes a syntactic category can have more than one definition. When this happens, each definition is listed on a separate line. Optional elements are flagged by the subscript *opt* indicator.

6.1 Lexical elements In simple terms, a *token* is an indivisible piece of a program. The standard defines six types of tokens: keywords, identifiers, constants, strings, operators, and punctuation. (The precise definition of these tokens is given later in this section.) Thus every C program can be decomposed into a stream of tokens, with each token being of one of these six types. For example, given this fragment

```
int x;
x = 10;
```

the token stream is **int, x, ;, x, =, 10, ;**.

In the Semantics section, it is stated that a comment is a *white space,* which may separate preprocessing tokens. Remember, comments are turned into a single space by translation phase 3. Therefore, comments become white-space characters.

Examples

1. The program fragment **1Ex** is parsed as a preprocessing number token (one that is not a valid floating or integer constant token), even though a parse as the pair of preprocessing tokens **1** and **Ex** might produce a valid expression (for example, if **Ex** were a macro defined as **+1**). Similarly, the program fragment **1E1** is parsed as a preprocessing number (one that is a valid floating constant token), whether or not **E** is a macro name.

2. The program fragment **x+++++y** is parsed as **x ++ ++ + y**, which violates a constraint on increment operators, even though the parse **x ++ + ++ y** might yield a correct expression.

Forward references: character constants (6.1.3.4), comments (6.1.9), expressions (6.3), floating constants (6.1.3.1), header names (6.1.7), macro replacement (6.8.3), postfix increment and decrement operators (6.3.2.4), prefix increment and decrement operators (6.3.3.1), preprocessing directives (6.8), preprocessing numbers (6.1.8), string literals (6.1.4).

6.1.1 Keywords

Syntax

keyword: one of

auto	double	int	struct
break	else	long	switch
case	enum	register	typedef
char	extern	return	union
const	float	short	unsigned
continue	for	signed	void
default	goto	sizeof	volatile
do	if	static	while

Semantics

The above tokens (entirely in lowercase) are reserved (in translation phases 7 and 8) for use as keywords, and shall not be used otherwise.

6.1.2 Identifiers

Syntax

identifier:
    nondigit
    identifier nondigit
    identifier digit

nondigit: one of

_	a	b	c	d	e	f	g	h	i	j	k	l	m
	n	o	p	q	r	s	t	u	v	w	x	y	z
	A	B	C	D	E	F	G	H	I	J	K	L	M
	N	O	P	Q	R	S	T	U	V	W	X	Y	Z

digit: one of
    0 1 2 3 4 5 6 7 8 9

Description

An identifier is a sequence of nondigit characters (including the underscore _ and the lowercase and uppercase letters) and digits. The first character shall be a nondigit character.

Constraints

In translation phases 7 and 8, an identifier shall not consist of the same sequence of characters as a keyword.

6.1.1   **Keywords**   The 32 keywords that constitute the C language are listed here. No other keywords are allowed in a conforming program.

Remember that your compiler may contain an extended set of keywords to support certain implementation-specific features. For example, compilers for the 8086 family of processors typically contain the extended keywords **near** and **far**, to specify segment addresses. However, the use of such extensions will cause your program to be nonstandard.

6.1.2   **Identifiers**   An *identifier* is a name of something that you define in your program, such as a variable or a function. A conforming compiler guarantees that at least the first 31 characters will be significant for those identifiers that have internal linkage, and 6 characters will be significant for those identifiers that have external linkage. Most compilers will allow at least 31 significant characters for any type of identifier.

Semantics

An identifier denotes an object, a function, or one of the following entities that will be described later: a tag or a member of a structure, union, or enumeration; a typedef name; a label name; a macro name; or a macro parameter. A member of an enumeration is called an *enumeration constant*. Macro names and macro parameters are not considered further here, because prior to the semantic phase of program translation any occurrences of macro names in the source file are replaced by the preprocessing token sequences that constitute their macro definitions.

There is no specific limit on the maximum length of an identifier.

Implementation limits

The implementation shall treat at least the first 31 characters of an *internal name* (a macro name or an identifier that does not have external linkage) as significant. Corresponding lowercase and uppercase letters are different. The implementation may further restrict the significance of an *external name* (an identifier that has external linkage) to six characters and may ignore distinctions of alphabetical case for such names.[12] These limitations on identifiers are all implementation-defined.

Any identifiers that differ in a significant character are different identifiers. If two identifiers differ in a nonsignificant character, the behavior is undefined.

Forward references: linkages of identifiers (6.1.2.2), macro replacement (6.8.3).

6.1.2.1 Scopes of identifiers

An identifier is *visible* (i.e., can be used) only within a region of program text called its *scope*. There are four kinds of scopes: function, file, block, and function prototype. (A *function prototype* is a declaration of a function that declares the types of its parameters.)

A label name is the only kind of identifier that has *function scope*. It can be used (in a **goto** statement) anywhere in the function in which it appears, and is declared implicitly by its syntactic appearance (followed by a : and a statement). Label names shall be unique within a function.

Every other identifier has scope determined by the placement of its declaration (in a declarator or type specifier). If the declarator or type specifier that declares the identifier appears outside of any block or list of parameters, the identifier has *file scope*, which terminates at the end of the translation unit. If the declarator or type specifier that declares the identifier appears inside a block or within the list of parameter declarations in a function definition, the identifier has *block scope*, which terminates at the } that closes the associated block. If the declarator or type specifier that declares the identifier appears within the list of parameter declarations in a function prototype (not part of a function definition), the identifier has *function prototype scope*, which terminates at the end of the function declarator. If an outer declaration of a lexically identical identifier exists in the same name space, it is hidden until the current scope terminates, after which it again becomes visible.

Two identifiers have the same scope if and only if their scopes terminate at the same point.

Structure, union, and enumeration tags have scope that begins just after the appearance of the tag in a type specifier that declares the tag. Each enumeration constant has scope that begins just after the appearance of its defining enumerator in an enumerator list. Any other identifier has scope that begins just after the completion of its declarator.

---

12 See "future language directions" (6.9.1).

6.1.2.1   Scopes of identifiers   The standard defines four types of scopes: function, file, block, and function prototype. Here in simple terms is what they mean:

◆   *Function scope* begins with the opening { of a function and ends with its closing }. Function scope applies only to labels. Recall that a label is used as the target of a **goto** and that the label must be within the same function as the **goto**. Therefore, the label has function scope.

◆   *File scope* begins with the beginning of the file and ends with the end of the file, and refers only to those identifiers that are declared outside of all functions. For example, global variables and function names have file scope.

◆   *Block scope* begins with the opening { of a block and ends with its associated closing }. However, block scope also extends to function parameters in a function definition; that is, function parameters are included in the function's block scope.

◆   *Prototype scope* is the parameter declarations section of a function prototype.

Forward references: compound statement, or block (6.6.2), declarations (6.5), enumeration specifiers (6.5.2.2), function calls (6.3.2.2), function declarators (including prototypes) (6.5.4.3), function definitions (6.7.1), the **goto** statement (6.6.6.1), labeled statements (6.6.1), name spaces of identifiers (6.1.2.3), scope of macro definitions (6.8.3.5), source file inclusion (6.8.2), tags (6.5.2.3), type specifiers (6.5.2).

6.1.2.2 Linkages of identifiers

An identifier declared in different scopes or in the same scope more than once can be made to refer to the same object or function by a process called *linkage*. There are three kinds of linkage: external, internal, and none.

In the set of translation units and libraries that constitutes an entire program, each instance of a particular identifier with *external linkage* denotes the same object or function. Within one translation unit, each instance of an identifier with *internal linkage* denotes the same object or function. Identifiers with *no linkage* denote unique entities.

If the declaration of a file scope identifier for an object or a function contains the storage-class specifier **static**, the identifier has internal linkage.[13]

If the declaration of an identifier for an object or a function contains the storage-class specifier **extern**, the identifier has the same linkage as any visible declaration of the identifier with file scope. If there is no visible declaration with file scope, the identifier has external linkage.

If the declaration of an identifier for a function has no storage-class specifier, its linkage is determined exactly as if it were declared with the storage-class specifier **extern**. If the declaration of an identifier for an object has file scope and no storage-class specifier, its linkage is external.

The following identifiers have no linkage: an identifier declared to be anything other than an object or a function; an identifier declared to be a function parameter; a block scope identifier for an object declared without the storage-class specifier **extern**.

If, within a translation unit, the same identifier appears with both internal and external linkage, the behavior is undefined.

Forward references: compound statement, or block (6.6.2), declarations (6.5), expressions (6.3), external definitions (6.7).

6.1.2.3 Name spaces of identifiers

If more than one declaration of a particular identifier is visible at any point in a translation unit, the syntactic context disambiguates uses that refer to different entities. Thus, there are separate *name spaces* for various categories of identifiers, as follows:

— *label names* (disambiguated by the syntax of the label declaration and use);

— the *tags* of structures, unions, and enumerations (disambiguated by following any[14] of the keywords **struct**, **union**, or **enum**);

— the *members* of structures or unions; each structure or union has a separate name space for its members (disambiguated by the type of the expression used to access the member via the . or -> operator);

---

13 A function declaration can contain the storage-class specifier **static** only if it is at file scope; see 6.5.1.

14 There is only one name space for tags even though three are possible.

6.1.2.2   Linkages of identifiers   Here is a summary of the C linkages:

◆   Identifiers with *external linkage* are accessible by your entire program, and include global variables and functions so long as neither has been declared as **static**.

◆   Identifiers with *internal linkage* are accessible only within the file in which they are declared, and they have file scope. Such items include **static** global variables and functions.

◆   Identifiers with *no linkage* are items that have neither external nor internal linkage. No-linkage items include parameters and local variables. (In essence, an identifier with no linkage must have block, function, or prototype scope.) No-linkage items are typically allocated storage on the stack.

6.1.2.3   Name spaces of identifiers   The standard defines four types of identifiers: labels, tags, structure or union members, and ordinary identifiers (such as variable names). What this section says is that the name spaces for these identifiers are separate, meaning that the same identifier can be used in the same program four different ways without conflict, as long as the name spaces are different for each usage. For example, **count** can be used both as the name of a variable and as the name of a structure member, because the name spaces differ. Put differently, the identifiers that are part of one name space will not conflict with identifiers of the same name that are part of another. This program illustrates the separation of the name spaces:

```
/* This program is correct and demonstrates the
   separation of the name spaces. */

#include <stdio.h>

struct name {  /* tag name */
  float name;  /* member name */
};

void main(void)
{
  int name = 10; /* variable name */
  struct name s; /* tag name */

  goto name; /* label name */
    printf("This won't print.");
  name: /* label name */

  s.name = 200.88;  /* member name */
  printf("%d %f", name, s.name); /* variable and member names */
}
```

— all other identifiers, called *ordinary identifiers* (declared in ordinary declarators or as enumeration constants).

Forward references: enumeration specifiers (6.5.2.2), labeled statements (6.6.1), structure and union specifiers (6.5.2.1), structure and union members (6.3.2.3), tags (6.5.2.3).

6.1.2.4 Storage durations of objects

An object has a *storage duration* that determines its lifetime. There are two storage durations: static and automatic.

An object whose identifier is declared with external or internal linkage, or with the storage-class specifier **static** has *static storage duration*. For such an object, storage is reserved and its stored value is initialized only once, prior to program startup. The object exists and retains its last-stored value throughout the execution of the entire program.[15]

An object whose identifier is declared with no linkage and without the storage-class specifier **static** has *automatic storage duration*. Storage is guaranteed to be reserved for a new instance of such an object on each normal entry into the block with which it is associated, or on a jump from outside the block to a labeled statement in the block or in an enclosed block. If an initialization is specified for the value stored in the object, it is performed on each normal entry, but not if the block is entered by a jump to a labeled statement. Storage for the object is no longer guaranteed to be reserved when execution of the block ends in any way. (Entering an enclosed block suspends but does not end execution of the enclosing block. Calling a function suspends but does not end execution of the block containing the call.) The value of a pointer that referred to an object with automatic storage duration that is no longer guaranteed to be reserved is indeterminate.

Forward references: compound statement, or block (6.6.2), function calls (6.3.2.2), initialization (6.5.7).

6.1.2.5 Types

The meaning of a value stored in an object or returned by a function is determined by the *type* of the expression used to access it. (An identifier declared to be an object is the simplest such expression: the type is specified in the declaration of the identifier.) Types are partitioned into *object types* (types that describe objects), *function types* (types that describe functions), and *incomplete types* (types that describe objects but lack information needed to determine their sizes).

An object declared as type **char** is large enough to store any member of the basic execution character set. If a member of the required source character set enumerated in 5.2.1 is stored in a **char** object, its value is guaranteed to be positive. If other quantities are stored in a **char** object, the behavior is implementation-defined: the values are treated as either signed or nonnegative integers.

There are four *signed integer types*, designated as **signed char**, **short int**, **int**, and **long int**. (The signed integer and other types may be designated in several additional ways, as described in 6.5.2.)

An object declared as type **signed char** occupies the same amount of storage as a "plain" **char** object. A "plain" **int** object has the natural size suggested by the architecture of the execution environment (large enough to contain any value in the range **INT_MIN** to **INT_MAX** as defined in the header **<limits.h>**). In the list of signed integer types above, the range of values of each type is a subrange of the values of the next type in the list.

---

15 In the case of a volatile object, the last store may not be explicit in the program.

6.1.2.4   Storage duration of objects   The difference between *static storage duration* and *automatic storage duration* is easy to understand. Objects with static storage duration stay in existence the entire time that your program is executing. Static storage objects include global variables and **static** local variables. In contrast, an automatic storage object is created upon entry into the block in which it is declared, and is destroyed upon exit. Thus automatic storage objects are constantly being created and destroyed. In simplified terms, static storage objects are global variables, and automatic storage objects are local variables. Storage for automatic objects is generally the stack.

6.1.2.5   Types   The standard defines three terms that pertain to data types: *object types, function types,* and *incomplete types*. Object types apply to variable declarations; function types apply to functions; and incomplete types apply to objects of unknown size, such as an unsized array.

Notice that the standard formally states that **char** is both an integer type and a character type. This means it is perfectly valid to use **char** types as "little integers" when appropriate.

For each of the signed integer types, there is a corresponding (but different) *unsigned integer type* (designated with the keyword **unsigned**) that uses the same amount of storage (including sign information) and has the same alignment requirements. The range of nonnegative values of a signed integer type is a subrange of the corresponding unsigned integer type, and the representation of the same value in each type is the same.[16] A computation involving unsigned operands can never overflow, because a result that cannot be represented by the resulting unsigned integer type is reduced modulo the number that is one greater than the largest value that can be represented by the resulting unsigned integer type.

There are three *floating types*, designated as **float**, **double**, and **long double**. The set of values of the type **float** is a subset of the set of values of the type **double**; the set of values of the type **double** is a subset of the set of values of the type **long double**.

The type **char**, the signed and unsigned integer types, and the floating types are collectively called the *basic types*. Even if the implementation defines two or more basic types to have the same representation, they are nevertheless different types.

The three types **char**, **signed char**, and **unsigned char** are collectively called the *character types*.

An *enumeration* comprises a set of named integer constant values. Each distinct enumeration constitutes a different *enumerated type*.

The **void** type comprises an empty set of values; it is an incomplete type that cannot be completed.

Any number of *derived types* can be constructed from the object, function, and incomplete types, as follows:

— An *array type* describes a contiguously allocated nonempty set of objects with a particular member object type, called the *element type*.[17] Array types are characterized by their element type and by the number of elements in the array. An array type is said to be derived from its element type, and if its element type is T, the array type is sometimes called "array of T." The construction of an array type from an element type is called "array type derivation."

— A *structure type* describes a sequentially allocated nonempty set of member objects, each of which has an optionally specified name and possibly distinct type.

— A *union type* describes an overlapping nonempty set of member objects, each of which has an optionally specified name and possibly distinct type.

— A *function type* describes a function with specified return type. A function type is characterized by its return type and the number and types of its parameters. A function type is said to be derived from its return type, and if its return type is T, the function type is sometimes called "function returning T." The construction of a function type from a return type is called "function type derivation."

— A *pointer type* may be derived from a function type, an object type, or an incomplete type, called the *referenced type*. A pointer type describes an object whose value provides a reference to an entity of the referenced type. A pointer type derived from the referenced type T is sometimes called "pointer to T." The construction of a pointer type from a referenced type is called "pointer type derivation."

---

16 The same representation and alignment requirements are meant to imply interchangeability as arguments to functions, return values from functions, and members of unions.

17 Since object types do not include incomplete types, an array of incomplete type cannot be constructed.

(*6.1.2.5 Types,* continued)

The first paragraph on this page makes one point that is commonly overlooked, but obvious on inspection: An unsigned integer expression cannot overflow. This is because there is no way to represent such an overflow as an unsigned quantity.

The term *basic types* refers to data types that are built into the C language. They are **char, float, double, long double**, and all variations of **int**. Using the basic types, you, the programmer, may create *derived types*, which include arrays, structures, unions, pointers, and a function type. The function type encompasses its return types, as well as the type and number of its parameters; that is, a function type contains the type information described by the function's prototype.

These methods of constructing derived types can be applied recursively.

The type **char**, the signed and unsigned integer types, and the enumerated types are collectively called *integral types*. The representations of integral types shall define values by use of a pure binary numeration system.[18] The representations of floating types are unspecified.

Integral and floating types are collectively called *arithmetic types*. Arithmetic types and pointer types are collectively called *scalar types*. Array and structure types are collectively called *aggregate types*.[19]

An array type of unknown size is an incomplete type. It is completed, for an identifier of that type, by specifying the size in a later declaration (with internal or external linkage). A structure or union type of unknown content (as described in 6.5.2.3) is an incomplete type. It is completed, for all declarations of that type, by declaring the same structure or union tag with its defining content later in the same scope.

Array, function, and pointer types are collectively called *derived declarator types*. A *declarator type derivation* from a type *T* is the construction of a derived declarator type from *T* by the application of an array-type, a function-type, or a pointer-type derivation to *T*.

A type is characterized by its *type category*, which is either the outermost derivation of a derived type (as noted above in the construction of derived types), or the type itself if the type consists of no derived types.

Any type so far mentioned is an *unqualified type*. Each unqualified type has three corresponding *qualified versions* of its type:[20] a *const-qualified* version, a *volatile-qualified* version, and a version having both qualifications. The qualified or unqualified versions of a type are distinct types that belong to the same type category and have the same representation and alignment requirements.[16] A derived type is not qualified by the qualifiers (if any) of the type from which it is derived.

A pointer to **void** shall have the same representation and alignment requirements as a pointer to a character type. Similarly, pointers to qualified or unqualified versions of compatible types shall have the same representation and alignment requirements.[16] Pointers to other types need not have the same representation or alignment requirements.

Examples

1. The type designated as "**float ***" has type "pointer to **float**." Its type category is pointer, not a floating type. The const-qualified version of this type is designated as "**float * const**" whereas the type designated as "**const float ***" is not a qualified type — its type is "pointer to const-qualified **float**" and is a pointer to a qualified type.

2. The type designated as "**struct tag (*[5])(float)**" has type "array of pointer to function returning **struct tag**." The array has length five and the function has a single parameter of type **float**. Its type category is array.

Forward references: character constants (6.1.3.4), compatible type and composite type (6.1.2.6), declarations (6.5), tags (6.5.2.3), type qualifiers (6.5.3).

---

18 A positional representation for integers that uses the binary digits 0 and 1, in which the values represented by successive bits are additive, begin with 1, and are multiplied by successive integral powers of 2, except perhaps the bit with the highest position. (Adapted from the *American National Dictionary for Information Processing Systems.*)

19 Note that aggregate type does not include union type because an object with union type can only contain one member at a time.

20 See 6.5.3 regarding qualified array and function types.

(*6.1.2.5 Types,* continued)

There are several important terms defined here that are used extensively elsewhere in the standard.

◆ *Integral types* include characters, integers, and enumerations.

◆ *Arithmetic types* include the integral and floating types.

◆ *Scalar types* are the combination of the arithmetic and pointer types. Therefore, scalar types include all basic types plus pointer types.

◆ An *aggregate type* is either an array or a structure, and contains more than one member. (Structures are also commonly referred to as conglomerate types.) Since a union contains only one object at any one time, a union is not an aggregate type.

◆ A *const-qualified* type creates a **const** object.

◆ A *volatile-qualified* type creates a **volatile** object (**const** and **volatile** are *type qualifiers*). The standard states that a qualified type is different and distinct from an otherwise equivalent unqualified type. That is, preceding a type with either (or both) **const** or **volatile** specifies a different type.

The point being made in Example 1 is that **float * const** creates a **const** pointer to a **float** object. The object is not a **const** object; the pointer is. However, **const float *** creates a pointer to a **const** object. The pointer, itself, is not **const**.

6.1.2.6 Compatible type and composite type

Two types have *compatible type* if their types are the same. Additional rules for determining whether two types are compatible are described in 6.5.2 for type specifiers, in 6.5.3 for type qualifiers, and in 6.5.4 for declarators.[21] Moreover, two structure, union, or enumeration types declared in separate translation units are compatible if they have the same number of members, the same member names, and compatible member types; for two structures, the members shall be in the same order; for two structures or unions, the bit-fields shall have the same widths; for two enumerations, the members shall have the same values.

All declarations that refer to the same object or function shall have compatible type; otherwise, the behavior is undefined.

A *composite type* can be constructed from two types that are compatible; it is a type that is compatible with both of the two types and satisfies the following conditions:

— If one type is an array of known size, the composite type is an array of that size.

— If only one type is a function type with a parameter type list (a function prototype), the composite type is a function prototype with the parameter type list.

— If both types are function types with parameter type lists, the type of each parameter in the composite parameter type list is the composite type of the corresponding parameters.

These rules apply recursively to the types from which the two types are derived.

For an identifier with external or internal linkage declared in the same scope as another declaration for that identifier, the type of the identifier becomes the composite type.

Example

Given the following two file scope declarations:

```
int f(int (*)(), double (*)[3]);
int f(int (*)(char *), double (*)[]);
```

The resulting composite type for the function is:

```
int f(int (*)(char *), double (*)[3]);
```

Forward references: declarators (6.5.4), enumeration specifiers (6.5.2.2), structure and union specifiers (6.5.2.1), type definitions (6.5.6), type qualifiers (6.5.3), type specifiers (6.5.2).

6.1.3 Constants

Syntax

constant:
> *floating-constant*
> *integer-constant*
> *enumeration-constant*
> *character-constant*

Constraints

The value of a constant shall be in the range of representable values for its type.

---

21 Two types need not be identical to be compatible.

6.1.2.6   Compatible type and composite type   Here is a simplified definition for the terms *compatible type* and *composite type*. Two types are compatible if they specify the same type of object or if, in the case of array or function definitions, one type includes more information (for example, an array size or a parameter type) than the other. A composite type is a third type that is mutually compatible with two other compatible types.

6.1.3   Constants   As the Syntax section states, C defines four basic types of constants: integer, floating point, enumeration, and character. As you probably know, you can also define string constants, which are referred to later in the standard as *string literals*.

Semantics

Each constant has a type, determined by its form and value, as detailed later.

6.1.3.1 Floating constants

Syntax

> *floating-constant:*
> > *fractional-constant exponent-part$_{opt}$ floating-suffix$_{opt}$*
> > *digit-sequence exponent-part floating-suffix$_{opt}$*
>
> *fractional-constant:*
> > *digit-sequence$_{opt}$. digit-sequence*
> > *digit-sequence^{opt}*
>
> *exponent-part:*
> > **e** *sign$_{opt}$ digit-sequence*
> > **E** *sign$_{opt}$ digit-sequence*
>
> *sign:* one of
> > **+ -**
>
> *digit-sequence:*
> > *digit*
> > *digit-sequence digit*
>
> *floating-suffix:* one of
> > **f l F L**

Description

A floating constant has a *significand part* that may be followed by an *exponent part* and a suffix that specifies its type. The components of the significand part may include a digit sequence representing the whole-number part, followed by a period (.), followed by a digit sequence representing the fraction part. The components of the exponent part are an **e** or **E** followed by an exponent consisting of an optionally signed digit sequence. Either the whole-number part or the fraction part shall be present; either the period or the exponent part shall be present.

Semantics

The significand part is interpreted as a decimal rational number; the digit sequence in the exponent part is interpreted as a decimal integer. The exponent indicates the power of 10 by which the significand part is to be scaled. If the scaled value is in the range of representable values (for its type) the result is either the nearest representable value, or the larger or smaller representable value immediately adjacent to the nearest representable value, chosen in an implementation-defined manner.

An unsuffixed floating constant has type **double**. If suffixed by the letter **f** or **F**, it has type **float**. If suffixed by the letter **l** or **L**, it has type **long double**.

6.1.3.2 Integer constants

Syntax

> *integer-constant:*
> > *decimal-constant integer-suffix$_{opt}$*
> > *octal-constant integer-suffix$_{opt}$*
> > *hexadecimal-constant integer-suffix$_{opt}$*

6.1.3.1   *Floating constants* Standard C allows you to specify floating-point constants using either standard decimal notation or scientific notation. The choice is yours.

As you know, there are three types of floating-point values: **float, double**, and **long double**. By default, all floating-point constants are treated as type **double** by the compiler. To explicitly specify a **float**, you must follow the number with the suffix **F** or **f**. To explicitly specify a **long double**, you must use the **L** or **l** suffix. For example:

```
10.11 /* this is double by default */

10.11L /* this is now a long double constant */

10.11F /* this is now a float constant */
```

Because of the logical way that C handles type conversions, usually you can simply let floating-point constants default to type **double**, but if the specific type is important to your program, be sure to include the suffix when needed.

decimal-constant:
> *nonzero-digit*
> *decimal-constant digit*

octal-constant:
> **0**
> *octal-constant octal-digit*

hexadecimal-constant:
> **0x** *hexadecimal-digit*
> **0X** *hexadecimal-digit*
> *hexadecimal-constant hexadecimal-digit*

nonzero-digit: one of
> 1   2   3   4   5   6   7   8   9

octal-digit: one of
> 0   1   2   3   4   5   6   7

hexadecimal-digit: one of
> 0   1   2   3   4   5   6   7   8   9
> a   b   c   d   e   f
> A   B   C   D   E   F

integer-suffix:
> *unsigned-suffix long-suffix*$_{opt}$
> *long-suffix unsigned-suffix*$_{opt}$

unsigned-suffix: one of
> u   U

long-suffix: one of
> l   L

Description

An integer constant begins with a digit, but has no period or exponent part. It may have a prefix that specifies its base and a suffix that specifies its type.

A decimal constant begins with a nonzero digit and consists of a sequence of decimal digits. An octal constant consists of the prefix **0** optionally followed by a sequence of the digits **0** through **7** only. A hexadecimal constant consists of the prefix **0x** or **0X** followed by a sequence of the decimal digits and the letters **a** (or **A**) through **f** (or **F**) with values 10 through 15 respectively.

Semantics

The value of a decimal constant is computed base 10; that of an octal constant, base 8; that of a hexadecimal constant, base 16. The lexically first digit is the most significant.

The type of an integer constant is the first of the corresponding list in which its value can be represented. Unsuffixed decimal: **int, long int, unsigned long int**; unsuffixed octal or hexadecimal: **int, unsigned int, long int, unsigned long int**; suffixed by the letter **u** or **U**: **unsigned int, unsigned long int**; suffixed by the letter **l** or **L**: **long int, unsigned long int**; suffixed by both the letters **u** or **U** and **l** or **L**: **unsigned long int**.

6.1.3.2 *Integer constants* There are three things to note about integer constants. First, when an integer constant is specified, the compiler makes it into the smallest type that can hold the constant. Second, if you wish to explicitly specify a long integer, use the **l** or **L** suffix. Third, if you want to specify an unsigned integer, use the **u** or **U** suffix.

6.1.3.3 Enumeration constants

Syntax

> *enumeration-constant:*
>> *identifier*

Semantics

An identifier declared as an enumeration constant has type **int**.

Forward references: enumeration specifiers (6.5.2.2).

6.1.3.4 Character constants

Syntax

> *character-constant:*
>> *' c-char-sequence'*
>> **L***' c-char-sequence'*
>
> *c-char-sequence:*
>> *c-char*
>> *c-char-sequence c-char*
>
> *c-char:*
>>> any member of the source character set except
>>>> the single-quote ' , backslash \, or new-line character
>>> *escape-sequence*
>
> *escape-sequence:*
>> *simple-escape-sequence*
>> *octal-escape-sequence*
>> *hexadecimal-escape-sequence*
>
> *simple-escape-sequence:* one of
>> \'   \"   \?   \\
>> \a   \b   \f   \n   \r   \t   \v
>
> *octal-escape-sequence:*
>> \ *octal-digit*
>> \ *octal-digit octal-digit*
>> \ *octal-digit octal-digit octal-digit*
>
> *hexadecimal-escape-sequence:*
>> **\x** *hexadecimal-digit*
>> *hexadecimal-escape-sequence hexadecimal-digit*

Description

An integer character constant is a sequence of one or more multibyte characters enclosed in single-quotes, as in '**x**' or '**ab**'. A wide character constant is the same, except prefixed by the letter **L**. With a few exceptions detailed later, the elements of the sequence are any members of the source character set; they are mapped in an implementation-defined manner to members of the execution character set.

The single-quote ', the double-quote ", the question-mark ?, the backslash \, and arbitrary integral values, are representable according to the following table of escape sequences:

6.1.3.3 *Enumeration constants* Note that enumeration constants are integer types. In other words, an enumeration constant is a *named integer constant.*

6.1.3.4 *Character constants* For the most part, *character constants* are intuitive and are defined by the standard in a way compatible with how you normally use them in your C programs. Much of the description in this section has to do with explaining how multibyte characters are handled. If you don't need multibyte characters in your programs, most of this section will be of little interest.

Character constants are enclosed between single quotation marks. A single character is treated by the compiler as being of type **char**. However, in C, character constants are represented internally as integers. Therefore, the following fragment is perfectly correct:

```
int x;

x = 'A'; /* give x the value 65 */
```

In this example, the character constant **A** is assigned to the integer **x**. As the comment indicates, **x** will contain the value 65, which is the ASCII code for **A**.

An *integer character constant* is one or more multibyte characters. Remember, the multibyte characters include the basic (byte-oriented) character set.

A *wide character* is one or more multibyte characters, preceded by an **L**. A wide character has the type **wchar_t**, which is defined in **stddef.h**. The type **wchar_t** defines the type that is large enough to hold distinct values that represent each character in the extended character set (if it exists), including multibyte characters. Thus an object of type **wchar_t** can represent, as a single value, an encoded form of any value in the extended character set. (That is, there is a one-to-one correspondence between the characters defined by the extended character set and the encoded values of type **wchar_t**.)

single-quote '	\'
double-quote "	\"
question-mark ?	\?
backslash \	\\
octal integer	\octal digits
hexadecimal integer	\xhexadecimal digits

The double-quote " and question-mark ? are representable either by themselves or by the escape sequences \" and \?, respectively, but the single-quote ' and the backslash \ shall be represented, respectively, by the escape sequences \' and \\.

The octal digits that follow the backslash in an octal escape sequence are taken to be part of the construction of a single character for an integer character constant or of a single wide character for a wide character constant. The numerical value of the octal integer so formed specifies the value of the desired character or wide character.

The hexadecimal digits that follow the backslash and the letter **x** in a hexadecimal escape sequence are taken to be part of the construction of a single character for an integer character constant or of a single wide character for a wide character constant. The numerical value of the hexadecimal integer so formed specifies the value of the desired character or wide character.

Each octal or hexadecimal escape sequence is the longest sequence of characters that can constitute the escape sequence.

In addition, certain nongraphic characters are representable by escape sequences consisting of the backslash \ followed by a lowercase letter: \a, \b, \f, \n, \r, \t, and \v.[22] If any other escape sequence is encountered, the behavior is undefined.[23]

Constraints

The value of an octal or hexadecimal escape sequence shall be in the range of representable values for the type **unsigned char** for an integer character constant, or the unsigned type corresponding to **wchar_t** for a wide character constant.

Semantics

An integer character constant has type **int**. The value of an integer character constant containing a single character that maps into a member of the basic execution character set is the numerical value of the representation of the mapped character interpreted as an integer. The value of an integer character constant containing more than one character, or containing a character or escape sequence not represented in the basic execution character set, is implementation-defined. If an integer character constant contains a single character or escape sequence, its value is the one that results when an object with type **char** whose value is that of the single character or escape sequence is converted to type **int**.

A wide character constant has type **wchar_t**, an integral type defined in the **<stddef.h>** header. The value of a wide character constant containing a single multibyte character that maps into a member of the extended execution character set is the *wide character* (code) corresponding to that multibyte character, as defined by the **mbtowc** function, with an implementation-defined current locale. The value of a wide character constant containing more than one multibyte character, or containing a multibyte character or escape sequence not represented in the extended execution character set, is implementation-defined.

---

22 The semantics of these characters were discussed in 5.2.2.

23 See "future language directions" (6.9.2).

(6.1.3.4 Character constants, continued)

The term *escape sequence* refers to a *backslash character constant.*

If you wish to create a character constant that contains a value you cannot enter at the keyboard, enter the value as either an octal or hexadecimal constant. For example, this code assigns to **ch** the value 7:

```
char ch = '\07';
```

Examples

1. The construction `'\0'` is commonly used to represent the null character.

2. Consider implementations that use two's-complement representation for integers and eight bits for objects that have type **char**. In an implementation in which type **char** has the same range of values as **signed char**, the integer character constant `'\xFF'` has the value −1; if type **char** has the same range of values as **unsigned char**, the character constant `'\xFF'` has the value +255 .

3. Even if eight bits are used for objects that have type **char**, the construction `'\x123'` specifies an integer character constant containing only one character. (The value of this single-character integer character constant is implementation-defined and violates the above constraint.) To specify an integer character constant containing the two characters whose values are **0x12** and `'3'`, the construction `'\0223'` may be used, since a hexadecimal escape sequence is terminated only by a nonhexadecimal character. (The value of this two-character integer character constant is implementation-defined also.)

4. Even if 12 or more bits are used for objects that have type **wchar_t**, the construction **L**`'\1234'` specifies the implementation-defined value that results from the combination of the values **0123** and `'4'`.

Forward references: characters and integers (6.2.1.1) common definitions **<stddef.h>** (7.1.6), the **mbtowc** function (7.10.7.2).

6.1.4 String literals

Syntax

> *string-literal:*
>> `"`*s-char-sequence*$_{opt}$`"`
>> **L**`"`*s-char-sequence*$_{opt}$`"`
>
> *s-char-sequence:*
>> *s-char*
>> *s-char-sequence s-char*
>
> *s-char:*
>>> any member of the source character set except
>>>> the double-quote `"`, backslash `\`, or new-line character
>>> *escape-sequence*

Description

A character string literal is a sequence of zero or more multibyte characters enclosed in double-quotes, as in `"xyz"`. A wide string literal is the same, except prefixed by the letter **L**.

The same considerations apply to each element of the sequence in a character string literal or a wide string literal as if it were in an integer character constant or a wide character constant, except that the single-quote `'` is representable either by itself or by the escape sequence `\'`, but the double-quote `"` shall be represented by the escape sequence `\"`.

Semantics

In translation phase 6, the multibyte character sequences specified by any sequence of adjacent character string literal tokens, or adjacent wide string literal tokens, are concatenated into a single multibyte character sequence. If a character string literal token is adjacent to a wide string literal token, the behavior is undefined.

6.1.4   *String literals*   The term *string literal* essentially means *string constant*, and it refers to strings that you embed into your C programs. For example, in this fragment:

```
char s[80];
strcpy(s, "Hello there!");
```

the string "Hello there!" is a string literal.

As with character constants, there are two types of string literals: normal and wide. A normal string literal is enclosed between double quotation marks. A wide string literal is preceded by an **L**. The standard defines a string literal as a sequence of multibyte characters. Again, remember that multibyte characters include the basic character set. Thus, what you commonly think of as strings, such as "this is a test", are contained in this definition.

One important point relative to string literals that had been the subject of much contention prior to the completion of the standard is expressly defined here. The point is this: When two string literals are adjacent to each other in your source file, the compiler concatenates them into one single string literal. For example,

```
char s[] = "Hello " "there!";
```

initializes **s** with the string "Hello there!".

In translation phase 7. a byte or code of value zero is appended to each multibyte character sequence that results from a string literal or literals.[24] The multibyte character sequence is then used to initialize an array of static storage duration and length just sufficient to contain the sequence. For character string literals. the array elements have type **char**. and are initialized with the individual bytes of the multibyte character sequence; for wide string literals. the array elements have type **wchar_t**. and are initialized with the sequence of wide characters corresponding to the multibyte character sequence.

Identical string literals of either form need not be distinct. If the program attempts to modify a string literal of either form. the behavior is undefined.

Example

This pair of adjacent character string literals

```
"\x12" "3"
```

produces a single character string literal containing the two characters whose values are **\x12** and **'3'**. because escape sequences are converted into single members of the execution character set just prior to adjacent string literal concatenation.

Forward references: common definitions **<stddef.h>** (7.1.6).

6.1.5 Operators

Syntax

operator: one of

```
[  ]  (  )  .  ->
++  --  &  *  +  -  ~  !  sizeof
/  %  <<  >>  <  >  <=  >=  ==  !=  ^  |  &&  ||
?  :
=  *=  /=  %=  +=  -=  <<=  >>=  &=  ^=  |=
,  #  ##
```

Constraints

The operators **[ ]**. **( )**. and **? :** shall occur in pairs. possibly separated by expressions. The operators **#** and **##** shall occur in macro-defining preprocessing directives only.

Semantics

An operator specifies an operation to be performed (an *evaluation*) that yields a value. or yields a designator. or produces a side effect. or a combination thereof. An *operand* is an entity on which an operator acts.

Forward references: expressions (6.3). macro replacement (6.8.3).

---

24 A character string literal need not be a string (see 7.1.1). because a null character may be embedded in it by a \0 escape sequence.

(*6.1.4 String literals,* continued)

Here is the essence of the first paragraph on page 31: Character string literals are automatically null-terminated by the compiler, thus forming a string. The resulting string is stored in the string table associated with the executable form of your program. In other words, the executable version of a C program contains a table that contains the string literals used by the program.

The standard states that identical string literals need not be distinct. This means the compiler is free to make only one entry into the string table when two or more identical strings are specified within your program. Whether or not identical strings are collapsed into a single string depends on the implementation.

One final important point is made about string literals: Any modification of a string literal during the execution of your program is undefined. Because string literals are stored in a table that is, in most implementations, accessible during run time, it is often possible to modify the contents of the table. Doing so, however, may produce unexpected results. For example, if the compiler has collapsed identical strings into a single string, then modifying the table entry for one of these strings implies that the other strings are also altered. Further, the effect of changing the string literal table is implementation dependent. The best practice is to avoid altering the string table.

6.1.5 *Operators* Notice that the Semantics section explicitly states that an operation may produce a side effect. The term *side effect,* as used here, does not have a negative connotation. Rather, it simply means that the process performing an operation may cause an object to be modified or a file to be changed.

6.1.6 Punctuators

Syntax

> *punctuator:* one of
>
> [ ] ( ) { } * , : = ; ... #

Constraints

The punctuators **[ ]**, **( )**, and **{ }** shall occur (after translation phase 4) in pairs, possibly separated by expressions, declarations, or statements. The punctuator **#** shall occur in preprocessing directives only.

Semantics

A punctuator is a symbol that has independent syntactic and semantic significance but does not specify an operation to be performed that yields a value. Depending on context, the same symbol may also represent an operator or part of an operator.

Forward references: expressions (6.3), declarations (6.5), preprocessing directives (6.8), statements (6.6).

6.1.7 Header names

Syntax

> *header-name:*
>> *<h-char-sequence>*
>> *"q-char-sequence"*
>
> *h-char-sequence:*
>> *h-char*
>> *h-char-sequence h-char*
>
> *h-char:*
>> any member of the source character set except
>>> the new-line character and **>**
>
> *q-char-sequence:*
>> *q-char*
>> *q-char-sequence q-char*
>
> *q-char:*
>> any member of the source character set except
>>> the new-line character and **"**

Constraints

Header name preprocessing tokens shall only appear within a **#include** preprocessing directive.

Semantics

The sequences in both forms of header names are mapped in an implementation-defined manner to headers or external source file names as specified in 6.8.2.

If the characters ', \, ", or /* occur in the sequence between the **<** and **>** delimiters, the behavior is undefined. Similarly, if the characters ', \, or /* occur in the sequence between the **"** delimiters, the behavior is undefined.[25]

---

25 Thus, sequences of characters that resemble escape sequences cause undefined behavior.

6.1.6   Punctuators   In C, *punctuators* are symbols that separate one language element from another. Remember, however, that a symbol may have specific meanings in different contexts. For example, the comma is a punctuator when used in a parameter list but is an operator in certain other contexts.

6.1.7   Header names   C defines two means by which a header file may be included in your program using the **#include** preprocessing directive: First, the header file name may be enclosed within angle brackets. Second, the header file name may be enclosed within double quotation marks.

In a later section, the standard discusses the difference between these two methods. Briefly, however, it is this: When the file name is enclosed using angle brackets, the file is searched for in some implementation-defined manner; if the file is not found, the search fails. When the file name is enclosed in double quotation marks, the file is searched for in some other implementation-defined manner. If the file is not found, the search is repeated using the search method employed when a file name is enclosed between angle brackets. If both methods fail to find the file, the search fails.

Example

The following sequence of characters:

```
0x3<1/a.h>1e2
#include <1/a.h>
#define const.member@$
```

forms the following sequence of preprocessing tokens (with each individual preprocessing token delimited by a { on the left and a } on the right).

```
{0x3}{<}{1}{/}{a}{.}{h}{>}{1e2}
{#}{include} {<1/a.h>}
{#}{define} {const}{.}{member}{@}{$}
```

Forward references: source file inclusion (6.8.2).

6.1.8 Preprocessing numbers

Syntax

> *pp-number:*
> > *digit*
> > . *digit*
> > *pp-number digit*
> > *pp-number nondigit*
> > *pp-number **e** sign*
> > *pp-number **E** sign*
> > *pp-number .*

Description

A preprocessing number begins with a digit optionally preceded by a period (.) and may be followed by letters, underscores, digits, periods, and **e+**, **e-**, **E+**, or **E-** character sequences.

Preprocessing number tokens lexically include all floating and integer constant tokens.

Semantics

A preprocessing number does not have type or a value; it acquires both after a successful conversion (as part of translation phase 7) to a floating constant token or an integer constant token.

6.1.9 Comments

Except within a character constant, a string literal, or a comment, the characters **/*** introduce a comment. The contents of a comment are examined only to identify multibyte characters and to find the characters ***/** that terminate it.[26]

---

26 Thus, comments do not nest.

6.1.8   Preprocessing numbers   This section simply states formally the legal form of numbers. A *preprocessing number* does not have a type until it is given one by the compiler. Its type is determined by the context in which it is used.

6.1.9   Comments   This section states formally what you probably already know from your own programming experience: Comments may not be nested. Further, they may not occur within a string or character constant. If a comment is included within a string constant, it simply becomes part of the string. For example, this code:

```
printf("This /* will be */ printed.");
```

produces this display:

```
This /* will be */ printed.
```

Because comments are converted into spaces in translation phase 3, a comment cannot occur within an identifier. For example, as far as the compiler is concerned, this line:

```
whi/*comment*/le
```

looks like this:

```
whi le
```

6.2 Conversions

Several operators convert operand values from one type to another automatically. This subclause specifies the result required from such an *implicit conversion*, as well as those that result from a cast operation (an *explicit conversion*). The list in 6.2.1.5 summarizes the conversions performed by most ordinary operators; it is supplemented as required by the discussion of each operator in 6.3.

Conversion of an operand value to a compatible type causes no change to the value or the representation.

Forward references: cast operators (6.3.4).

6.2.1 Arithmetic operands

6.2.1.1 Characters and integers

A **char**, a **short int**, or an **int** bit-field, or their signed or unsigned varieties, or an enumeration type, may be used in an expression wherever an **int** or **unsigned int** may be used. If an **int** can represent all values of the original type, the value is converted to an **int**; otherwise, it is converted to an **unsigned int**. These are called the *integral promotions*.[27] All other arithmetic types are unchanged by the integral promotions.

The integral promotions preserve value including sign. As discussed earlier, whether a "plain" **char** is treated as signed is implementation-defined.

Forward references: enumeration specifiers (6.5.2.2), structure and union specifiers (6.5.2.1).

6.2.1.2 Signed and unsigned integers

When a value with integral type is converted to another integral type, if the value can be represented by the new type, its value is unchanged.

When a signed integer is converted to an unsigned integer with equal or greater size, if the value of the signed integer is nonnegative, its value is unchanged. Otherwise: if the unsigned integer has greater size, the signed integer is first promoted to the signed integer corresponding to the unsigned integer; the value is converted to unsigned by adding to it one greater than the largest number that can be represented in the unsigned integer type.[28]

When a value with integral type is demoted to an unsigned integer with smaller size, the result is the nonnegative remainder on division by the number one greater than the largest unsigned number that can be represented in the type with smaller size. When a value with integral type is demoted to a signed integer with smaller size, or an unsigned integer is converted to its corresponding signed integer, if the value cannot be represented the result is implementation-defined.

---

27 The integral promotions are applied only as part of the usual arithmetic conversions, to certain argument expressions, to the operands of the unary **+**, **-**, and **~** operators, and to both operands of the shift operators, as specified by their respective subclauses.

28 In a two's-complement representation, there is no actual change in the bit pattern except filling the high-order bits with copies of the sign bit if the unsigned integer has greater size.

6.2   Conversions The standard defines two sorts of type conversions: *implicit* and *explicit*.

In the C language, many type conversions are performed automatically and are not, in any sense, errors. These are implicit conversions and they occur most often in mixed-type expressions. (This differs from more strongly typed languages in which mixed-type expressions are not allowed.)

Explicit conversions use the cast operator. In C it is possible to cast one type into another. (Again, this differs from some other, strongly typed languages.) The rules governing such type conversions are discussed in this section.

6.2.1.1   Characters and integers This section states two important facts: First, characters and integers may be freely mixed in expressions. This sanctions the use of characters as "little integers." Second, in an integer expression, *integral promotions* will automatically occur. An integral promotion is a *type promotion* that occurs within an expression. It raises the original type so that it is compatible with an integer type.

6.2.1.2   Signed and unsigned integers Here is a summary of the conversions described in this section:

A conversion of one integral type into another produces no change of value if the target type can represent the value contained in the source. For example, the conversion of an **int** that contains the value 1 converted into an **unsigned char** produces no alteration of value, because both types can hold that value.

A conversion of an integer into an unsigned integer of equal or greater size causes no change in value if the original value is greater than or equal to zero. If the original value is negative, then, in a 2's complement implementation the sign bit of the integer is extended, but the resulting number is interpreted as a positive value.

The conversion of a larger signed integer into a smaller unsigned integer causes the high-order bytes of the signed integer to be lost. If a signed integer is converted into a smaller integer type, the result is defined by the implementation. Also, if an unsigned integer is converted into a signed integer, the result is defined by the implementation.

In the most general terms, when you convert from a larger integer type to a smaller type, high-order bytes are lost. When converting from a signed integer into an unsigned integer of equal (or greater) size, meaning may be altered.

6.2.1.3 Floating and integral

When a value of floating type is converted to integral type, the fractional part is discarded. If the value of the integral part cannot be represented by the integral type, the behavior is undefined.[29]

When a value of integral type is converted to floating type, if the value being converted is in the range of values that can be represented but cannot be represented exactly, the result is either the nearest higher or nearest lower value, chosen in an implementation-defined manner.

6.2.1.4 Floating types

When a **float** is promoted to **double** or **long double**, or a **double** is promoted to **long double**, its value is unchanged.

When a **double** is demoted to **float** or a **long double** to **double** or **float**, if the value being converted is outside the range of values that can be represented, the behavior is undefined. If the value being converted is in the range of values that can be represented but cannot be represented exactly, the result is either the nearest higher or nearest lower value, chosen in an implementation-defined manner.

6.2.1.5 Usual arithmetic conversions

Many binary operators that expect operands of arithmetic type cause conversions and yield result types in a similar way. The purpose is to yield a common type, which is also the type of the result. This pattern is called the *usual arithmetic conversions*:

First, if either operand has type **long double**, the other operand is converted to **long double**.

Otherwise, if either operand has type **double**, the other operand is converted to **double**.

Otherwise, if either operand has type **float**, the other operand is converted to **float**.

Otherwise, the integral promotions are performed on both operands. Then the following rules are applied:

If either operand has type **unsigned long int**, the other operand is converted to **unsigned long int**.

Otherwise, if one operand has type **long int** and the other has type **unsigned int**, if a **long int** can represent all values of an **unsigned int**, the operand of type **unsigned int** is converted to **long int**; if a **long int** cannot represent all the values of an **unsigned int**, both operands are converted to **unsigned long int**.

Otherwise, if either operand has type **long int**, the other operand is converted to **long int**.

Otherwise, if either operand has type **unsigned int**, the other operand is converted to **unsigned int**.

Otherwise, both operands have type **int**.

The values of floating operands and of the results of floating expressions may be represented in greater precision and range than that required by the type; the types are not changed thereby.[30]

---

29 The remaindering operation performed when a value of integral type is converted to unsigned type need not be performed when a value of floating type is converted to unsigned type. Thus, the range of portable floating values is $(-1, Utype\_\textbf{MAX}+1)$.

30 The cast and assignment operators still must perform their specified conversions, as described in 6.2.1.3 and 6.2.1.4.

6.2.1.3 Floating and integral If possible, the conversion of a floating-point value into an integral value will yield a result that contains the nonfractional part of the floating-point value. The standard also states that (because of the way floating-point values are represented by a specific implementation) an integral value may be converted into a floating-point approximation when no precise equivalent value is available.

6.2.1.4 Floating types In general, the conversion of a smaller floating-point type into a larger one causes no changes. When converting a larger type into a smaller one, if the value cannot be represented, information content may be lost. If the value can be represented by the smaller type, precision may be reduced.

6.2.1.5 Usual arithmetic conversions In simplified terms, this section states that in mixed-type expressions, smaller types are automatically converted into the larger type according to the specified rules. In general, this means promoting smaller types to that of the largest type used in the overall expression.

The type conversion rules may seem lengthy, but these automatic conversions are also intuitive. You have probably already taken advantage of them on several occasions, even if you have been programming in C for only a short while.

6.2.2 Other operands

6.2.2.1 Lvalues and function designators

An *lvalue* is an expression (with an object type or an incomplete type other than **void**) that designates an object.[31] When an object is said to have a particular type, the type is specified by the lvalue used to designate the object. A *modifiable lvalue* is an lvalue that does not have array type, does not have an incomplete type, does not have a const-qualified type, and if it is a structure or union, does not have any member (including, recursively, any member of all contained structures or unions) with a const-qualified type.

Except when it is the operand of the **sizeof** operator, the unary **&** operator, the **++** operator, the **--** operator, or the left operand of the **.** operator or an assignment operator, an lvalue that does not have array type is converted to the value stored in the designated object (and is no longer an lvalue). If the lvalue has qualified type, the value has the unqualified version of the type of the lvalue; otherwise, the value has the type of the lvalue. If the lvalue has an incomplete type and does not have array type, the behavior is undefined.

Except when it is the operand of the **sizeof** operator or the unary **&** operator, or is a character string literal used to initialize an array of character type, or is a wide string literal used to initialize an array with element type compatible with **wchar_t**, an lvalue that has type ''array of *type*'' is converted to an expression that has type ''pointer to *type*'' that points to the initial element of the array object and is not an lvalue.

A *function designator* is an expression that has function type. Except when it is the operand of the **sizeof** operator[32] or the unary **&** operator, a function designator with type ''function returning *type*'' is converted to an expression that has type ''pointer to function returning *type*.''

Forward references: address and indirection operators (6.3.3.2), assignment operators (6.3.16), common definitions **<stddef.h>** (7.1.6), initialization (6.5.7), postfix increment and decrement operators (6.3.2.4), prefix increment and decrement operators (6.3.3.1), the **sizeof** operator (6.3.3.4), structure and union members (6.3.2.3).

6.2.2.2 void

The (nonexistent) value of a *void expression* (an expression that has type **void**) shall not be used in any way, and implicit or explicit conversions (except to **void**) shall not be applied to such an expression. If an expression of any other type occurs in a context where a void expression is required, its value or designator is discarded. (A void expression is evaluated for its side effects.)

6.2.2.3 Pointers

A pointer to **void** may be converted to or from a pointer to any incomplete or object type. A pointer to any incomplete or object type may be converted to a pointer to **void** and back again; the result shall compare equal to the original pointer.

For any qualifier *q*, a pointer to a non-*q*-qualified type may be converted to a pointer to the *q*-qualified version of the type; the values stored in the original and converted pointers shall compare equal.

---

31 The name ''lvalue'' comes originally from the assignment expression **E1 = E2**, in which the left operand **E1** must be a (modifiable) lvalue. It is perhaps better considered as representing an object ''locator value.'' What is sometimes called ''rvalue'' is in this International Standard described as the ''value of an expression.''
An obvious example of an lvalue is an identifier of an object. As a further example, if **E** is a unary expression that is a pointer to an object, ***E** is an lvalue that designates the object to which **E** points.

32 Because this conversion does not occur, the operand of the **sizeof** operator remains a function designator and violates the constraint in 6.3.3.4.

6.2.2.1 Lvalues and function designators As stated in footnote 31 on this page, the term *lvalue* traditionally refers to objects that can occur on the left side of an assignment statement. That is, an lvalue refers to an object that can have its value modified. The standard, however, alters this definition slightly, stating that an lvalue is simply an expression that, when evaluated, describes an object.

A *modifiable lvalue* is an lvalue that can be modified. To understand the difference, consider the following definitions:

```
const int i;
int j;
```

Here, **i** is an lvalue, but it may not occur on the left side of an assignment statement (because a **const** object cannot be modified by the program). On the other hand, **j** is both an lvalue and may be modified; therefore, **j** is a modifiable lvalue.

A *function designator* describes a function.

Two other interesting points are stated in this section, which are restated plainly here: First, an array name without an index is a pointer to the first element of the array and is not an lvalue. Thus, an array name without an index cannot be modified. Second, a function name used by itself (that is, without any parameter list) is a pointer to the function and is not modifiable. That is, a pointer to a function is not an lvalue.

6.2.2.2 void A **void** expression has no value and may not be converted into any other type. Importantly, however, a **void** expression is fully evaluated so that all side effects are generated. That is, the compiler will execute any function call that is part of a **void** expression so that the function may perform its actions even though the expression containing the function generates no value.

6.2.2.3 Pointers This section specifies two fundamental C features: First, a **void *** pointer may point to any type of object or be assigned to any other type of pointer. For example, the standard library dynamic allocation function **malloc()** returns a **void *** pointer that may be assigned to any other type of pointer. Second, a null pointer is the same, regardless of the type of pointer involved. Thus the following fragment is valid, and the message "equivalent" is displayed:

```
int *ip = 0;
float *fp = 0;
if(ip==fp) printf("equivalent");
```

An integral constant expression with the value 0, or such an expression cast to type **void ***. is called a *null pointer constant*.[33] If a null pointer constant is assigned to or compared for equality to a pointer, the constant is converted to a pointer of that type. Such a pointer, called a *null pointer*, is guaranteed to compare unequal to a pointer to any object or function.

Two null pointers, converted through possibly different sequences of casts to pointer types, shall compare equal.

Forward references: cast operators (6.3.4), equality operators (6.3.9), simple assignment (6.3.16.1).

---

33 The macro **NULL** is defined in **<stddef.h>** as a null pointer constant; see 7.1.6.

There are no annotations for page 37.

6.3 Expressions

An *expression* is a sequence of operators and operands that specifies computation of a value, or that designates an object or a function, or that generates side effects, or that performs a combination thereof.

Between the previous and next sequence point an object shall have its stored value modified at most once by the evaluation of an expression. Furthermore, the prior value shall be accessed only to determine the value to be stored.[34]

Except as indicated by the syntax[35] or otherwise specified later (for the function-call operator `()`, `&&`, `||`, `?:`, and comma operators), the order of evaluation of subexpressions and the order in which side effects take place are both unspecified.

Some operators (the unary operator `~`, and the binary operators `<<`, `>>`, `&`, `^`, and `|`, collectively described as *bitwise operators*) shall have operands that have integral type. These operators return values that depend on the internal representations of integers, and thus have implementation-defined aspects for signed types.

If an *exception* occurs during the evaluation of an expression (that is, if the result is not mathematically defined or not in the range of representable values for its type), the behavior is undefined.

An object shall have its stored value accessed only by an lvalue that has one of the following types:[36]

— the declared type of the object,

— a qualified version of the declared type of the object,

— a type that is the signed or unsigned type corresponding to the declared type of the object,

— a type that is the signed or unsigned type corresponding to a qualified version of the declared type of the object,

— an aggregate or union type that includes one of the aforementioned types among its members (including, recursively, a member of a subaggregate or contained union), or

— a character type.

---

34 This paragraph renders undefined statement expressions such as

```
i = ++i + 1;
```

while allowing

```
i = i + 1;
```

35 The syntax specifies the precedence of operators in the evaluation of an expression, which is the same as the order of the major subclauses of this subclause, highest precedence first. Thus, for example, the expressions allowed as the operands of the binary `+` operator (6.3.6) shall be those expressions defined in 6.3.1 through 6.3.6. The exceptions are cast expressions (6.3.4) as operands of unary operators (6.3.3), and an operand contained between any of the following pairs of operators: grouping parentheses `()` (6.3.1), subscripting brackets `[]` (6.3.2.1), function-call parentheses `()` (6.3.2.2), and the conditional operator `?:` (6.3.15).

Within each major subclause, the operators have the same precedence. Left- or right-associativity is indicated in each subclause by the syntax for the expressions discussed therein.

36 The intent of this list is to specify those circumstances in which an object may or may not be aliased.

6.3 Expressions Notice that, in the C language, an *expression* is a syntactically valid combination of operators and operands that

◆ Yields a value, or

◆ Specifies an object or function, or

◆ Generates a side effect, or

◆ Accomplishes a combination of the above

The standard states that when an expression is evaluated, each object's value is modified only once. In theory, this means the compiler will not physically change the value of a variable in memory until the entire expression has been evaluated. In practice, however, you may not want to rely on this. (For example, most compilers will compile the examples in the footnote on this page in such a way that the value assigned to **i** in the first case is 1 greater than it is in the second case.)

A *sequence point* is essentially the end of an expression. (See Annex C, page 189.)

The rest of this section formally defines what type of lvalue can refer to an object. (Remember, a qualified type is one that contains either **const** or **volatile**.)

6.3.1 Primary expressions

Syntax

> *primary-expression:*
> > *identifier*
> > *constant*
> > *string-literal*
> > (*expression*)

Semantics

An identifier is a primary expression, provided it has been declared as designating an object (in which case it is an lvalue) or a function (in which case it is a function designator).

A constant is a primary expression. Its type depends on its form and value, as detailed in 6.1.3.

A string literal is a primary expression. It is an lvalue with type as detailed in 6.1.4.

A parenthesized expression is a primary expression. Its type and value are identical to those of the unparenthesized expression. It is an lvalue, a function designator, or a void expression if the unparenthesized expression is, respectively, an lvalue, a function designator, or a void expression.

Forward references: declarations (6.5).

6.3.2 Postfix operators

Syntax

> *postfix-expression:*
> > *primary-expression*
> > *postfix-expression* [*expression*]
> > *postfix-expression* (*argument-expression-list*$_{opt}$)
> > *postfix-expression* . *identifier*
> > *postfix-expression* -> *identifier*
> > *postfix-expression* ++
> > *postfix-expression* --
>
> *argument-expression-list:*
> > *assignment-expression*
> > *argument-expression-list* , *assignment-expression*

6.3.2.1 Array subscripting

Constraints

One of the expressions shall have type "pointer to object *type*," the other expression shall have integral type, and the result has type "*type*."

Semantics

A postfix expression followed by an expression in square brackets [] is a subscripted designation of an element of an array object. The definition of the subscript operator [] is that **E1[E2]** is identical to **(*(E1+(E2)))**. Because of the conversion rules that apply to the binary + operator, if **E1** is an array object (equivalently, a pointer to the initial element of an array object) and **E2** is an integer, **E1[E2]** designates the **E2**-th element of **E1** (counting from zero).

Successive subscript operators designate an element of a multidimensional array object. If **E** is an *n*-dimensional array ($n \geq 2$) with dimensions $i \times j \times \ldots \times k$, then **E** (used as other than an lvalue) is converted to a pointer to an $(n-1)$-dimensional array with dimensions $j \times \ldots \times k$. If the unary * operator is applied to this pointer explicitly, or implicitly as a result of subscripting, the

6.3.1   Primary expressions A *primary expression* is either an identifier, a constant, a string constant, or a parenthesized expression. This category is meaningful mostly to compiler implementors and does not, in general, influence how you write programs.

6.3.2   Postfix operators C contains these *postfix operators*:

◆ Array subscripting: [ ]

◆ Argument list: ( )

◆ Structure member access: .

◆ Pointer to structure member access: ->

◆ Increment: ++

◆ Decrement: - -

A postfix operator is one that follows an expression. Though this seems straight-forward, you might wonder why the **.** and **->** operators are called postfix, since they seem to be used with two operands (the expression that designates the structure or union, and the member referred to). The answer is that the member name must be an identifier; it cannot be anything else (that is, it cannot be an expression). In essence, the identifier constitutes a special type of operand. Thus, the **.** and the **->** postfix the expression that designates the structure (or union).

6.3.2.1   Array subscripting Relative to C programs, the most salient points from this section on array subscripting are these: Each dimension of an array is specified within its own set of square brackets. The dimensions are specified such that the rightmost index changes fastest when the array is accessed in the order in which the elements are stored in memory. A multidimensional array of n dimensions is equivalent to an array of arrays having n-1 dimensions.

result is the pointed-to $(n-1)$-dimensional array, which itself is converted into a pointer if used as other than an lvalue. It follows from this that arrays are stored in row-major order (last subscript varies fastest).

Example

Consider the array object defined by the declaration

```
int x[3][5];
```

Here **x** is a 3×5 array of **int**s; more precisely, **x** is an array of three element objects, each of which is an array of five **int**s. In the expression **x[i]**, which is equivalent to **(*(x+(i)))**, **x** is first converted to a pointer to the initial array of five **int**s. Then **i** is adjusted according to the type of **x**, which conceptually entails multiplying **i** by the size of the object to which the pointer points, namely an array of five **int** objects. The results are added and indirection is applied to yield an array of five **int**s. When used in the expression **x[i][j]**, that in turn is converted to a pointer to the first of the **int**s, so **x[i][j]** yields an **int**.

Forward references: additive operators (6.3.6), address and indirection operators (6.3.3.2), array declarators (6.5.4.2).

6.3.2.2 Function calls

Constraints

The expression that denotes the called function[37] shall have type pointer to function returning **void** or returning an object type other than an array type.

If the expression that denotes the called function has a type that includes a prototype, the number of arguments shall agree with the number of parameters. Each argument shall have a type such that its value may be assigned to an object with the unqualified version of the type of its corresponding parameter.

Semantics

A postfix expression followed by parentheses **()** containing a possibly empty, comma-separated list of expressions is a function call. The postfix expression denotes the called function. The list of expressions specifies the arguments to the function.

If the expression that precedes the parenthesized argument list in a function call consists solely of an identifier, and if no declaration is visible for this identifier, the identifier is implicitly declared exactly as if, in the innermost block containing the function call, the declaration

```
extern int identifier();
```

appeared.[38]

An argument may be an expression of any object type. In preparing for the call to a function, the arguments are evaluated, and each parameter is assigned the value of the corresponding argument.[39] The value of the function call expression is specified in 6.6.6.4.

---

37 Most often, this is the result of converting an identifier that is a function designator.

38 That is, an identifier with block scope declared to have external linkage with type function without parameter information and returning an **int**. If in fact it is not defined as having type "function returning **int**," the behavior is undefined.

39 A function may change the values of its parameters, but these changes cannot affect the values of the arguments. On the other hand, it is possible to pass a pointer to an object, and the function may change the value of the object pointed to. A parameter declared to have array or function type is converted to a parameter with a pointer type as described in 6.7.1.

6.3.2.2 Function calls This section specifies several important attributes of functions.

A function cannot return an array. It may, however, return a pointer type that may be referenced by the calling code as an array.

If a function is called for which no prototype has been defined, then it is assumed to return an integer and have an unknown number of parameters. The reason for this assumption is to provide compatibility with older C programs created before the modern function prototype existed. In older programs, there is no way for the compiler to check the type or number of arguments to a function.

At the end of this page, it is formally stated that C uses *call-by-value* parameter passing, meaning that a parameter to a function receives a copy of the value of the argument used to call the function. Thus, changes made to the parameter do not affect the argument. As the note states, however, pointers can be passed that can be used to alter the objects pointed to by the pointers.

If the expression that denotes the called function has a type that does not include a prototype, the integral promotions are performed on each argument and arguments that have type **float** are promoted to **double**. These are called the *default argument promotions*. If the number of arguments does not agree with the number of parameters, the behavior is undefined. If the function is defined with a type that does not include a prototype, and the types of the arguments after promotion are not compatible with those of the parameters after promotion, the behavior is undefined. If the function is defined with a type that includes a prototype, and the types of the arguments after promotion are not compatible with the types of the parameters, or if the prototype ends with an ellipsis (, . . .), the behavior is undefined.

If the expression that denotes the called function has a type that includes a prototype, the arguments are implicitly converted, as if by assignment, to the types of the corresponding parameters. The ellipsis notation in a function prototype declarator causes argument type conversion to stop after the last declared parameter. The default argument promotions are performed on trailing arguments. If the function is defined with a type that is not compatible with the type (of the expression) pointed to by the expression that denotes the called function, the behavior is undefined.

No other conversions are performed implicitly; in particular, the number and types of arguments are not compared with those of the parameters in a function definition that does not include a function prototype declarator.

The order of evaluation of the function designator, the arguments, and subexpressions within the arguments is unspecified, but there is a sequence point before the actual call.

Recursive function calls shall be permitted, both directly and indirectly through any chain of other functions.

Example

In the function call

```
(*pf[f1()]) (f2(), f3() + f4())
```

the functions **f1**, **f2**, **f3**, and **f4** may be called in any order. All side effects shall be completed before the function pointed to by **pf[f1()]** is entered.

Forward references: function declarators (including prototypes) (6.5.4.3), function definitions (6.7.1), the **return** statement (6.6.6.4), simple assignment (6.3.16.1).

6.3.2.3 Structure and union members

Constraints

The first operand of the . operator shall have a qualified or unqualified structure or union type, and the second operand shall name a member of that type.

The first operand of the -> operator shall have type "pointer to qualified or unqualified structure" or "pointer to qualified or unqualified union," and the second operand shall name a member of the type pointed to.

Semantics

A postfix expression followed by a dot . and an identifier designates a member of a structure or union object. The value is that of the named member, and is an lvalue if the first expression is an lvalue. If the first expression has qualified type, the result has the so-qualified version of the type of the designated member.

(**6.3.2.2 Function calls,** *continued*)

Here is a synopsis of the information on the top of page 41.

When a function that does not have a prototype declared for it is called, default type promotions of the arguments take place. These promotions apply to integral and **float** arguments. For example, when a function without a prototype is called with a **char** argument, it is automatically elevated to **int**.

In the absence of a prototype, the compiler will not flag as an error a mismatch between the number or type of the arguments used to call a function and those defined by its parameters. (Many compilers will issue warning messages about this condition, however.)

When a function is called that includes a prototype, arguments are automatically converted into the types of their corresponding parameters, and the default type promotions are not applied. This means, for example, that when a parameter is declared as type **char** and the argument is of type **char**, no integral promotion will take place. (In essence, a prototype ensures that a function will receive the type of value it requires.) When a prototye includes an ellipsis (...), the remaining arguments are treated as if no prototype for them exists (which, in fact, it doesn't). This means the default type promotions will be applied to those arguments.

When no prototype for a function exists, it is not an error if the types and/or number of parameters and arguments differ. The reason for this seemingly strange rule is to provide compatibility with older C programs in which prototypes do not exist. (Prototypes were added to C during the establishment of the ANSI C standard and were not part of the original definition.)

This section also formally states that a conforming compiler must allow recursive functions.

6.3.2.3   *Structure and union members*   This section defines the structure and union operators. The key point is this: When the left operand is an expression that designates a structure or union, the dot (**.**) operator followed by a member name is used to access that member. If the left operand is a pointer to a structure or union, the arrow (**->**) operator followed by a member name is used to access that member.

A postfix expression followed by an arrow -> and an identifier designates a member of a structure or union object. The value is that of the named member of the object to which the first expression points, and is an lvalue.[40] If the first expression is a pointer to a qualified type, the result has the so-qualified version of the type of the designated member.

With one exception, if a member of a union object is accessed after a value has been stored in a different member of the object, the behavior is implementation-defined.[41] One special guarantee is made in order to simplify the use of unions: If a union contains several structures that share a common initial sequence (see below), and if the union object currently contains one of these structures, it is permitted to inspect the common initial part of any of them. Two structures share a *common initial sequence* if corresponding members have compatible types (and, for bit-fields, the same widths) for a sequence of one or more initial members.

Examples

1. If **f** is a function returning a structure or union, and **x** is a member of that structure or union, **f().x** is a valid postfix expression but is not an lvalue.

2. The following is a valid fragment:

```
union {
       struct {
              int       alltypes;
       } n;
       struct {
              int       type;
              int       intnode;
       } ni;
       struct {
              int       type;
              double    doublenode;
       } nf;
} u;
u.nf.type = 1;
u.nf.doublenode = 3.14;
/*...*/
if (u.n.alltypes == 1)
       /*...*/ sin(u.nf.doublenode) /*...*/
```

Forward references: address and indirection operators (6.3.3.2), structure and union specifiers (6.5.2.1).

6.3.2.4 Postfix increment and decrement operators

Constraints

The operand of the postfix increment or decrement operator shall have qualified or unqualified scalar type and shall be a modifiable lvalue.

---

40 If **&E** is a valid pointer expression (where **&** is the "address-of" operator, which generates a pointer to its operand), the expression **(&E)->MOS** is the same as **E.MOS**.

41 The "byte orders" for scalar types are invisible to isolated programs that do not indulge in type punning (for example, by assigning to one member of a union and inspecting the storage by accessing another member that is an appropriately sized array of character type), but must be accounted for when conforming to externally imposed storage layouts.

(*6.3.2.3 Structure and union members,* continued)

The second paragraph on this page simply ensures that when a union contains two or more structures that have a common set of initial members, those members will "overlap" one another. This allows for, among other things, a common element to be used as a "selector" that determines what type of object the union is currently holding.

6.3.2.4 Postfix increment and decrement operators The postfix versions of the **++** and **- -** operators increment or decrement, respectively, their operand. The value of this operation, however, is the value of the operand *before* it is incremented or decremented. That is, when these operations are used as part of a larger expression, the value of the operand is obtained prior to alteration. For example, after this fragment:

```
int i, j = 1;
i = j++;
```

i has the value 1, not 2, because **j**'s value is obtained prior to being incremented.

Semantics

The result of the postfix **++** operator is the value of the operand. After the result is obtained, the value of the operand is incremented. (That is, the value 1 of the appropriate type is added to it.) See the discussions of additive operators and compound assignment for information on constraints, types, and conversions and the effects of operations on pointers. The side effect of updating the stored value of the operand shall occur between the previous and the next sequence point.

The postfix **--** operator is analogous to the postfix **++** operator, except that the value of the operand is decremented (that is, the value 1 of the appropriate type is subtracted from it).

Forward references: additive operators (6.3.6), compound assignment (6.3.16.2).

6.3.3 Unary operators

Syntax

> *unary-expression:*
>> *postfix-expression*
>> **++** *unary-expression*
>> **--** *unary-expression*
>> *unary-operator cast-expression*
>> **sizeof** *unary-expression*
>> **sizeof** (*type-name*)
>
> *unary-operator:* one of
>> **&   *   +   -   ~   !**

6.3.3.1 Prefix increment and decrement operators

Constraints

The operand of the prefix increment or decrement operator shall have qualified or unqualified scalar type and shall be a modifiable lvalue.

Semantics

The value of the operand of the prefix **++** operator is incremented. The result is the new value of the operand after incrementation. The expression **++E** is equivalent to **(E+=1)**. See the discussions of additive operators and compound assignment for information on constraints, types, side effects, and conversions and the effects of operations on pointers.

The prefix **--** operator is analogous to the prefix **++** operator, except that the value of the operand is decremented.

Forward references: additive operators (6.3.6), compound assignment (6.3.16.2).

6.3.3.2 Address and indirection operators

Constraints

The operand of the unary **&** operator shall be either a function designator or an lvalue that designates an object that is not a bit-field and is not declared with the **register** storage-class specifier.

The operand of the unary ***** operator shall have pointer type.

Semantics

The result of the unary **&** (address-of) operator is a pointer to the object or function designated by its operand. If the operand has type ''*type*,'' the result has type ''pointer to *type*.''

The unary ***** operator denotes indirection. If the operand points to a function, the result is a function designator; if it points to an object, the result is an lvalue designating the object. If the

6.3.3 Unary operators There are eight *unary operators*: **++, − −, &, *, +,−, ~,** and **!**. Unary operators have only one operand associated with them.

6.3.3.1 Prefix increment and decrement operators The prefix version of the **++** and **− −** operators increment or decrement, respectively, their operand. They differ from their postfix relatives in only one way: The value of the operation is the value of the operand *after* it is incremented or decremented. That is, when these operations are used as part of a larger expression, the value of the operand is obtained after its alteration. For example, after this fragment:

```
int i, j = 1;
i = ++j;
```

i has the value 2.

6.3.3.2 Address and indirection operators In straightforward language, the **&** obtains the address of the object it precedes. It can be remembered as the "address of" operator. For example, this statement:

```
p = &i;
```

can be verbalized as, "Assign p the *address of* i." You cannot obtain the address of a bit-field or of a register variable.

The ***** precedes an address and denotes the value at that address; in effect, it "de-references" a pointer. It can be remembered as the "at address" operator. For example, the last line in this fragment:

```
int i, *p;
p = &i;
*p = 10;
```

can be verbalized as, "At *address* p, put the value 10." It is your responsibility to make sure that you apply the ***** to valid addresses.

operand has type "pointer to *type*," the result has type "*type*." If an invalid value has been assigned to the pointer, the behavior of the unary * operator is undefined.[42]

Forward references: storage-class specifiers (6.5.1), structure and union specifiers (6.5.2.1).

6.3.3.3 Unary arithmetic operators

Constraints

The operand of the unary + or – operator shall have arithmetic type; of the ~ operator, integral type; of the ! operator, scalar type.

Semantics

The result of the unary + operator is the value of its operand. The integral promotion is performed on the operand, and the result has the promoted type.

The result of the unary – operator is the negative of its operand. The integral promotion is performed on the operand, and the result has the promoted type.

The result of the ~ operator is the bitwise complement of its operand (that is, each bit in the result is set if and only if the corresponding bit in the converted operand is not set). The integral promotion is performed on the operand, and the result has the promoted type. The expression **~E** is equivalent to **(ULONG_MAX-E)** if **E** is promoted to type **unsigned long**, to **(UINT_MAX-E)** if **E** is promoted to type **unsigned int**. (The constants **ULONG_MAX** and **UINT_MAX** are defined in the header **<limits.h>**.)

The result of the logical negation operator ! is 0 if the value of its operand compares unequal to 0, 1 if the value of its operand compares equal to 0. The result has type **int**. The expression **!E** is equivalent to **(0==E)**.

Forward references: limits **<float.h>** and **<limits.h>** (7.1.6).

6.3.3.4 The **sizeof** operator

Constraints

The **sizeof** operator shall not be applied to an expression that has function type or an incomplete type, to the parenthesized name of such a type, or to an lvalue that designates a bit-field object.

Semantics

The **sizeof** operator yields the size (in bytes) of its operand, which may be an expression or the parenthesized name of a type. The size is determined from the type of the operand, which is not itself evaluated. The result is an integer constant.

When applied to an operand that has type **char**, **unsigned char**, or **signed char**, (or a qualified version thereof) the result is 1. When applied to an operand that has array type, the result is the total number of bytes in the array.[43] When applied to an operand that has structure or union type, the result is the total number of bytes in such an object, including internal and trailing padding.

---

42 It is always true that if **E** is a function designator or an lvalue that is a valid operand of the unary **&** operator, ***&E** is a function designator or an lvalue equal to **E**. If ***P** is an lvalue and **T** is the name of an object pointer type, ***(T)P** is an lvalue that has a type compatible with that to which **T** points.

Among the invalid values for dereferencing a pointer by the unary * operator are a null pointer, an address inappropriately aligned for the type of object pointed to, and the address of an automatic storage duration object when execution of the block with which the object is associated has terminated.

43 When applied to a parameter declared to have array or function type, the **sizeof** operator yields the size of the pointer obtained by converting as in 6.2.2.1; see 6.7.1.

6.3.3.3   Unary arithmetic operators   These operators are straightforward. Here is a synopsis: The unary **+** has no effect. The unary **−** results in a value that has the opposite sign as the operand. The **~** produces a value in which the state of each bit is the reverse of that in its operand. The **!** results in a true value only if the value it precedes is zero.

6.3.3.4   The sizeof operator   The **sizeof** operator results in a value that is the size, in bytes, of the variable or type that it precedes. This operator has two forms. If it is applied to a type, then **sizeof** takes this form:

> sizeof (*type*)

That is, the type name must be enclosed within parentheses. If **sizeof** is applied to a variable, you may use this form:

> sizeof *var-name*

In this case, no parentheses are necessary.

The **sizeof** operator cannot be applied to functions, incomplete types, or bit–fields.

There is one interesting C feature defined in this section: The size of a character type is 1. Although the size of all other types is implementation dependent, the C language formally stipulates that character types are exactly 1 byte long.

The type of the value returned by **sizeof** is **size_t**. This type is guaranteed to hold the size of the largest object that can be created by the implementation.

The value of the result is implementation-defined, and its type (an unsigned integral type) is **size_t** defined in the **<stddef.h>** header.

Examples

1. A principal use of the **sizeof** operator is in communication with routines such as storage allocators and I/O systems. A storage-allocation function might accept a size (in bytes) of an object to allocate and return a pointer to **void**. For example:

    ```
    extern void *alloc(size_t);
    double *dp = alloc(sizeof *dp);
    ```

    The implementation of the **alloc** function should ensure that its return value is aligned suitably for conversion to a pointer to **double**.

2. Another use of the **sizeof** operator is to compute the number of elements in an array:

    ```
    sizeof array / sizeof array[0]
    ```

Forward references: common definitions **<stddef.h>** (7.1.6), declarations (6.5), structure and union specifiers (6.5.2.1), type names (6.5.5).

6.3.4 Cast operators

Syntax

> *cast-expression:*
> > *unary-expression*
> > (*type-name*) *cast-expression*

Constraints

Unless the type name specifies void type, the type name shall specify qualified or unqualified scalar type and the operand shall have scalar type.

Semantics

Preceding an expression by a parenthesized type name converts the value of the expression to the named type. This construction is called a *cast*.[44] A cast that specifies no conversion has no effect on the type or value of an expression.

Conversions that involve pointers (other than as permitted by the constraints of 6.3.16.1) shall be specified by means of an explicit cast; they have implementation-defined and undefined aspects:

A pointer may be converted to an integral type. The size of integer required and the result are implementation-defined. If the space provided is not long enough, the behavior is undefined.

An arbitrary integer may be converted to a pointer. The result is implementation-defined.[45]

A pointer to an object or incomplete type may be converted to a pointer to a different object type or a different incomplete type. The resulting pointer might not be valid if it is improperly aligned for the type pointed to. It is guaranteed, however, that a pointer to an object of a given alignment may be converted to a pointer to an object of the same

---

44 A cast does not yield an lvalue. Thus, a cast to a qualified type has the same effect as a cast to the unqualified version of the type.

45 The mapping functions for converting a pointer to an integer or an integer to a pointer are intended to be consistent with the addressing structure of the execution environment.

6.3.4   Cast operators A cast is a type–conversion operator that changes the type of an expression. It has this general form:

(new-type) expression

where *new-type* is the new type of the expression. In this example:

```
int i=10;
float j;
j = (float) i/3;
```

the cast causes **i** to be treated as a **float**, which causes the entire expression to be evaluated as a floating-point expression. The result (approximately 3.333) is then assigned to **j**.

Although you may convert pointer types, generally the results are implementation dependent or, in some cases, undefined. This is because several aspects of a pointer are tied to its base type.

alignment or a less strict alignment and back again; the result shall compare equal to the original pointer. (An object that has character type has the least strict alignment.)

A pointer to a function of one type may be converted to a pointer to a function of another type and back again; the result shall compare equal to the original pointer. If a converted pointer is used to call a function that has a type that is not compatible with the type of the called function, the behavior is undefined.

Forward references: equality operators (6.3.9), function declarators (including prototypes) (6.5.4.3), simple assignment (6.3.16.1), type names (6.5.5).

6.3.5 Multiplicative operators

Syntax

> *multiplicative-expression:*
> > *cast-expression*
> > *multiplicative-expression* * *cast-expression*
> > *multiplicative-expression* / *cast-expression*
> > *multiplicative-expression* % *cast-expression*

Constraints

Each of the operands shall have arithmetic type. The operands of the % operator shall have integral type.

Semantics

The usual arithmetic conversions are performed on the operands.

The result of the binary * operator is the product of the operands.

The result of the / operator is the quotient from the division of the first operand by the second; the result of the % operator is the remainder. In both operations, if the value of the second operand is zero, the behavior is undefined.

When integers are divided and the division is inexact, if both operands are positive the result of the / operator is the largest integer less than the algebraic quotient and the result of the % operator is positive. If either operand is negative, whether the result of the / operator is the largest integer less than or equal to the algebraic quotient or the smallest integer greater than or equal to the algebraic quotient is implementation-defined, as is the sign of the result of the % operator. If the quotient a/b is representable, the expression (a/b)*b + a%b shall equal a.

6.3.6 Additive operators

Syntax

> *additive-expression:*
> > *multiplicative-expression*
> > *additive-expression* + *multiplicative-expression*
> > *additive-expression* – *multiplicative-expression*

Constraints

For addition, either both operands shall have arithmetic type, or one operand shall be a pointer to an object type and the other shall have integral type. (Incrementing is equivalent to adding 1.)

For subtraction, one of the following shall hold:

— both operands have arithmetic type;

— both operands are pointers to qualified or unqualified versions of compatible object types; or

6.3.5 *Multiplicative operators* The *multiplicative operators* are *****, **/**, and **%**. Their operation is clear as presented in the standard, and they may only be applied to arithmetic types.

6.3.6 *Additive operators* The *additive operators* are **+** and **−**. As applied to arithmetic types, their operation is obvious. However, they may also be applied in an operation that contains a pointer and an integer, in which case their operation is less clear. The following discussion summarizes this situation.

All pointer arithmetic is performed relative to the base type of the pointer. When a pointer is incremented, it points to the next object of its base type. When it is decremented, it points to the prior object of its base type. In general, when integer n is added to pointer p with base type b, the result is a pointer that points the nth object of type b beyond the one currently pointed to by p. Consider this example:

```
float *p, f[10];
p = f; /* p points to f[0] */
p = p + 2; /* now p points to f[2] */
```

First, **p** is assigned the address of the first element in array **f**. Next, the pointer is increased by 2, which causes it to point to the third element in **f** (which is 2 beyond the first element). The same thing occurs when an integer is subtracted from a pointer, except that the result is a pointer to an object that is **n** objects before the pointer.

— the left operand is a pointer to an object type and the right operand has integral type. (Decrementing is equivalent to subtracting 1.)

Semantics

If both operands have arithmetic type, the usual arithmetic conversions are performed on them.

The result of the binary + operator is the sum of the operands.

The result of the binary − operator is the difference resulting from the subtraction of the second operand from the first.

For the purposes of these operators, a pointer to a nonarray object behaves the same as a pointer to the first element of an array of length one with the type of the object as its element type.

When an expression that has integral type is added to or subtracted from a pointer, the result has the type of the pointer operand. If the pointer operand points to an element of an array object, and the array is large enough, the result points to an element offset from the original element such that the difference of the subscripts of the resulting and original array elements equals the integral expression. In other words, if the expression **P** points to the i-th element of an array object, the expressions **(P)+N** (equivalently, **N+(P)**) and **(P)−N** (where **N** has the value n) point to, respectively, the $i+n$-th and $i−n$-th elements of the array object, provided they exist. Moreover, if the expression **P** points to the last element of an array object, the expression **(P)+1** points one past the last element of the array object, and if the expression **Q** points one past the last element of an array object, the expression **(Q)−1** points to the last element of the array object. If both the pointer operand and the result point to elements of the same array object, or one past the last element of the array object, the evaluation shall not produce an overflow; otherwise, the behavior is undefined. Unless both the pointer operand and the result point to elements of the same array object, or the pointer operand points one past the last element of an array object and the result points to an element of the same array object, the behavior is undefined if the result is used as an operand of the unary * operator.

When two pointers to elements of the same array object are subtracted, the result is the difference of the subscripts of the two array elements. The size of the result is implementation-defined, and its type (a signed integral type) is **ptrdiff_t** defined in the **<stddef.h>** header. As with any other arithmetic overflow, if the result does not fit in the space provided, the behavior is undefined. In other words, if the expressions **P** and **Q** point to, respectively, the i-th and j-th elements of an array object, the expression **(P)−(Q)** has the value $i−j$ provided the value fits in an object of type **ptrdiff_t**. Moreover, if the expression **P** points either to an element of an array object or one past the last element of an array object, and the expression **Q** points to the last element of the same array object, the expression **((Q)+1)−(P)** has the same value as **((Q)−(P))+1** and as **−((P)−((Q)+1))**, and has the value zero if the expression **P** points one past the last element of the array object, even though the expression **(Q)+1** does not point to an element of the array object. Unless both pointers point to elements of the same array object, or one past the last element of the array object, the behavior is undefined.[46]

---

46 Another way to approach pointer arithmetic is first to convert the pointer(s) to character pointer(s): In this scheme the integral expression added to or subtracted from the converted pointer is first multiplied by the size of the object originally pointed to, and the resulting pointer is converted back to the original type. For pointer subtraction, the result of the difference between the character pointers is similarly divided by the size of the object originally pointed to.

When viewed in this way, an implementation need only provide one extra byte (which may overlap another object in the program) just after the end of the object in order to satisfy the "one past the last element" requirements.

(*6.3.6 Additive operators, continued*)

Aside from addition or subtraction of an integer, the only other operation allowed on a pointer is subtraction of one pointer from another. When this occurs, the result is an integral type that represents the number of objects, of the pointers' base type, that separate the two pointers. The result is of type **ptrdiff_t**, which can hold the largest difference that two pointers can have. For example, this fragment assigns the value 3 to **i**, which is the difference, in terms of **float**s, between **p1** and **p2**:

```
float *p1, *p2, f[10];
ptrdiff_t i;

p1 = f; /* p points to f[0] */
p2 = &f[3];
i = p2 - p1; /* yields 3 */
```

Forward references: common definitions **<stddef.h>** (7.1.6).

6.3.7 Bitwise shift operators

Syntax

> *shift-expression:*
> > *additive-expression*
> > *shift-expression* **<<** *additive-expression*
> > *shift-expression* **>>** *additive-expression*

Constraints

Each of the operands shall have integral type.

Semantics

The integral promotions are performed on each of the operands. The type of the result is that of the promoted left operand. If the value of the right operand is negative or is greater than or equal to the width in bits of the promoted left operand, the behavior is undefined.

The result of **E1 << E2** is **E1** left-shifted **E2** bit positions; vacated bits are filled with zeros. If **E1** has an unsigned type, the value of the result is **E1** multiplied by the quantity, 2 raised to the power **E2**, reduced modulo **ULONG_MAX+1** if **E1** has type **unsigned long**, **UINT_MAX+1** otherwise. (The constants **ULONG_MAX** and **UINT_MAX** are defined in the header **<limits.h>**.)

The result of **E1 >> E2** is **E1** right-shifted **E2** bit positions. If **E1** has an unsigned type or if **E1** has a signed type and a nonnegative value, the value of the result is the integral part of the quotient of **E1** divided by the quantity, 2 raised to the power **E2**. If **E1** has a signed type and a negative value, the resulting value is implementation-defined.

6.3.8 Relational operators

Syntax

> *relational-expression:*
> > *shift-expression*
> > *relational-expression* **<** *shift-expression*
> > *relational-expression* **>** *shift-expression*
> > *relational-expression* **<=** *shift-expression*
> > *relational-expression* **>=** *shift-expression*

Constraints

One of the following shall hold:

— both operands have arithmetic type:

— both operands are pointers to qualified or unqualified versions of compatible object types; or

— both operands are pointers to qualified or unqualified versions of compatible incomplete types.

Semantics

If both of the operands have arithmetic type, the usual arithmetic conversions are performed.

For the purposes of these operators, a pointer to a nonarray object behaves the same as a pointer to the first element of an array of length one with the type of the object as its element type.

When two pointers are compared, the result depends on the relative locations in the address space of the objects pointed to. If the objects pointed to are members of the same aggregate object, pointers to structure members declared later compare higher than pointers to members declared earlier in the structure, and pointers to array elements with larger subscript values

6.3.7 *Bitwise shift operators* The left and right *shift operators,* **<<** and **>>**, apply only to integral types. These operators shift the bit pattern in the left operand the number of times specified by the right operand, and in the direction specified by the operator.

In essence, each left shift multiplies a number by 2, and each right shift divides the number by 2; for example:

```
int i = 1;
i = i << 2; /* i now contains 4 */
i = i >> 1; /* i now contains 2 */
```

Remember, a shift is not a rotate, so any bits shifted off an end are lost. When left-shifting, zeros are brought in on the right. When right-shifting an unsigned value or a positive value, zeros are brought in on the left. When right-shifting a negative value, generally, ones are shifted in (thus preserving the sign bit), but this is implementation dependent.

6.3.8 *Relational operators* The roles of the *relational operators* as applied to arithmetic types are self-explanatory.

When comparing pointers, if the pointers point to elements within the same array, then the pointer pointing to the element with the smaller index is less than the pointer pointing to the element with the larger index. For example, this fragment:

```
int a[10], *p1, *p2;
p1 = &a[1];
p2 = &a[3];
if(p1 < p2) printf("p1 is less than p2");
```

does, indeed, display the message "p1 is less than p2."

The standard also specifies that structure members are defined in memory from lower to higher, in the order in which they are declared. For example, this fragment:

```
struct s_type {
   int a;
   int b;
} s;
if(&s.a < &s.b) printf("less than");
```

displays "less than" because **a** is declared prior to **b** in the structure.

compare higher than pointers to elements of the same array with lower subscript values. All pointers to members of the same union object compare equal. If the objects pointed to are not members of the same aggregate or union object, the result is undefined, with the following exception. If the expression **P** points to an element of an array object and the expression **Q** points to the last element of the same array object, the pointer expression **Q+1** compares higher than **P**, even though **Q+1** does not point to an element of the array object.

If two pointers to object or incomplete types both point to the same object, or both point one past the last element of the same array object, they compare equal. If two pointers to object or incomplete types compare equal, both point to the same object, or both point one past the last element of the same array object.[47]

Each of the operators **<** (less than), **>** (greater than), **<=** (less than or equal to), and **>=** (greater than or equal to) shall yield 1 if the specified relation is true and 0 if it is false.[48] The result has type **int**.

6.3.9 Equality operators

Syntax

> *equality-expression:*
> > *relational-expression*
> > *equality-expression* **==** *relational-expression*
> > *equality-expression* **!=** *relational-expression*

Constraints

One of the following shall hold:

— both operands have arithmetic type;

— both operands are pointers to qualified or unqualified versions of compatible types;

— one operand is a pointer to an object or incomplete type and the other is a pointer to a qualified or unqualified version of **void**; or

— one operand is a pointer and the other is a null pointer constant.

Semantics

The **==** (equal to) and the **!=** (not equal to) operators are analogous to the relational operators except for their lower precedence.[49] Where the operands have types and values suitable for the relational operators, the semantics detailed in 6.3.8 apply.

If two pointers to object or incomplete types are both null pointers, they compare equal. If two pointers to object or incomplete types compare equal, they both are null pointers, or both point to the same object, or both point one past the last element of the same array object. If two pointers to function types are both null pointers or both point to the same function, they compare equal. If two pointers to function types compare equal, either both are null pointers, or both point to the same function. If one of the operands is a pointer to an object or incomplete type and the other has type pointer to a qualified or unqualified version of **void**, the pointer to an object or incomplete type is converted to the type of the other operand.

---

47 If invalid prior pointer operations, such as accesses outside array bounds, produced undefined behavior, the effect of subsequent comparisons is undefined.

48 The expression **a<b<c** is not interpreted as in ordinary mathematics. As the syntax indicates, it means **(a<b)<c**; in other words, "if **a** is less than **b** compare 1 to **c**; otherwise, compare 0 to **c**."

49 Because of the precedences, **a<b == c<d** is 1 whenever **a<b** and **c<d** have the same truth-value.

*(**6.3.8 Relational operators,** continued)*

One final important statement is made about the relational operators: The outcome of an operation is either the value 1 (when the relation is true) or the value 0 (when the relation is false). Although a true value in C is any nonzero value, the result of a relation that is true is always 1.

6.3.9   Equality operators The *equality operators* == and != are simply relational operators that have lower precedence. The same general rules for relational operators apply to the equality operators.

The standard does make one other significant statement about the equality operators, however. When two pointers compare as equal, then either they both point to the same object or they are both null. This means that any type of pointer can be compared against a null pointer.

6.3.10   Bitwise AND operator

Syntax

> *AND-expression:*
> > *equality-expression*
> > *AND-expression* **&** *equality-expression*

Constraints

Each of the operands shall have integral type.

Semantics

The usual arithmetic conversions are performed on the operands.

The result of the binary **&** operator is the bitwise AND of the operands (that is, each bit in the result is set if and only if each of the corresponding bits in the converted operands is set).

6.3.11   Bitwise exclusive OR operator

Syntax

> *exclusive-OR-expression:*
> > *AND-expression*
> > *exclusive-OR-expression* ^ *AND-expression*

Constraints

Each of the operands shall have integral type.

Semantics

The usual arithmetic conversions are performed on the operands.

The result of the ^ operator is the bitwise exclusive OR of the operands (that is, each bit in the result is set if and only if exactly one of the corresponding bits in the converted operands is set).

6.3.12   Bitwise inclusive OR operator

Syntax

> *inclusive-OR-expression:*
> > *exclusive-OR-expression*
> > *inclusive-OR-expression* | *exclusive-OR-expression*

Constraints

Each of the operands shall have integral type.

Semantics

The usual arithmetic conversions are performed on the operands.

The result of the | operator is the bitwise inclusive OR of the operands (that is, each bit in the result is set if and only if at least one of the corresponding bits in the converted operands is set).

6.3.10   Bitwise AND operator through 6.3.12   Bitwise inclusive OR operator

The bitwise operators operate upon the bits within their integral operands. That is, each operation is performed on a bit-by-bit basis. The truth table for these operators is shown here:

p	q	p & q	p | q	p ^ q
0	0	0	0	0
0	1	0	1	1
1	1	1	1	0
1	0	0	1	1

It is important to understand that these operations are performed bit by bit. Here are some examples:

```
      1 1 0 0   0 1 0 1
   &  1 1 1 1   0 0 0 0
      - - - - - - - - -
      1 1 0 0   0 0 0 0


      1 1 0 0   0 1 0 1
   |  1 1 1 1   0 0 0 0
      - - - - - - - - -
      1 1 1 1   0 1 0 1


      1 1 0 0   0 1 0 1
   ^  1 1 1 1   0 0 0 0
      - - - - - - - - -
      0 0 1 1   0 1 0 1
```

6.3.13 Logical AND operator

Syntax

> *logical-AND-expression:*
>> *inclusive-OR-expression*
>> *logical-AND-expression* **&&** *inclusive-OR-expression*

Constraints

Each of the operands shall have scalar type.

Semantics

The **&&** operator shall yield 1 if both of its operands compare unequal to 0; otherwise, it yields 0. The result has type **int**.

Unlike the bitwise binary **&** operator, the **&&** operator guarantees left-to-right evaluation; there is a sequence point after the evaluation of the first operand. If the first operand compares equal to 0, the second operand is not evaluated.

6.3.14 Logical OR operator

Syntax

> *logical-OR-expression:*
>> *logical-AND-expression*
>> *logical-OR-expression* **| |** *logical-AND-expression*

Constraints

Each of the operands shall have scalar type.

Semantics

The **| |** operator shall yield 1 if either of its operands compare unequal to 0; otherwise, it yields 0. The result has type **int**.

Unlike the bitwise **|** operator, the **| |** operator guarantees left-to-right evaluation; there is a sequence point after the evaluation of the first operand. If the first operand compares unequal to 0, the second operand is not evaluated.

6.3.15 Conditional operator

Syntax

> *conditional-expression:*
>> *logical-OR-expression*
>> *logical-OR-expression* **?** *expression* : *conditional-expression*

Constraints

The first operand shall have scalar type.

One of the following shall hold for the second and third operands:

— both operands have arithmetic type;

— both operands have compatible structure or union types;

— both operands have void type;

— both operands are pointers to qualified or unqualified versions of compatible types;

— one operand is a pointer and the other is a null pointer constant; or

— one operand is a pointer to an object or incomplete type and the other is a pointer to a qualified or unqualified version of **void.**

6.3.13 Logical AND operator, 6.3.14 Logical OR operator As discussed on this page of the standard, the logical AND and logical OR operators are straightforward. Just remember these points: Logical AND and logical OR are not applied bitwise; their two operands must be scalar types; and the result produced is either 1 (true) or 0 (false). (Remember, a scalar type is either an arithmetic type or a pointer type.)

6.3.15 Conditional operator The *conditional operator* is the **?**; it is C's only ternary operator. (A ternary operator requires three operands.) The general form of the **?** operator is

 exp1 **?** *exp2* **:** *exp3*

If *exp1* is true, then the value of the entire **?** expression is the value of *exp2*. If *exp1* is false, then the value of the entire **?** expression is *exp3*.

Semantics

The first operand is evaluated; there is a sequence point after its evaluation. The second operand is evaluated only if the first compares unequal to 0; the third operand is evaluated only if the first compares equal to 0; the value of the second or third operand (whichever is evaluated) is the result.[50]

If both the second and third operands have arithmetic type, the usual arithmetic conversions are performed to bring them to a common type and the result has that type. If both the operands have structure or union type, the result has that type. If both operands have void type, the result has void type.

If both the second and third operands are pointers or one is a null pointer constant and the other is a pointer, the result type is a pointer to a type qualified with all the type qualifiers of the types pointed-to by both operands. Furthermore, if both operands are pointers to compatible types or differently qualified versions of a compatible type, the result has the composite type; if one operand is a null pointer constant, the result has the type of the other operand; otherwise, one operand is a pointer to **void** or a qualified version of **void**, in which case the other operand is converted to type pointer to **void**, and the result has that type.

Example

The common type that results when the second and third operands are pointers is determined in two independent stages. The appropriate qualifiers, for example, do not depend on whether the two pointers have compatible types.

Given the declarations

```
const void *c_vp;
void *vp;
const int *c_ip;
volatile int *v_ip;
int *ip;
const char *c_cp;
```

the third column in the following table is the common type that is the result of a conditional expression in which the first two columns are the second and third operands (in either order):

```
c_vp  c_ip  const void *
v_ip  0     volatile int *
c_ip  v_ip  const volatile int *
vp    c_cp  const void *
ip    c_ip  const int *
vp    ip    void *
```

---

50 A conditional expression does not yield an lvalue.

*(**6.3.15 Conditional operator,** continued)*

The **?** is commonly used in place of the following type of **if** statement:

```
if(exp1) x = exp2;
else x = exp3;
```

This same statement written using the **?** looks like this:

```
x = exp1 ? exp2 : exp3;
```

It is important to understand that, based upon the value of *exp1,* either *exp2* or *exp3* is evaluated, but not both. Therefore, no side effects will be generated by the unevaluated expression.

6.3.16 Assignment operators

Syntax

> *assignment-expression:*
> > *conditional-expression*
> > *unary-expression assignment-operator assignment-expression*
>
> *assignment-operator:* one of
> > =   *=   /=   %=   +=   -=   <<=   >>=   &=   ^= |=

Constraints

An assignment operator shall have a modifiable lvalue as its left operand.

Semantics

An assignment operator stores a value in the object designated by the left operand. An assignment expression has the value of the left operand after the assignment, but is not an lvalue. The type of an assignment expression is the type of the left operand unless the left operand has qualified type, in which case it is the unqualified version of the type of the left operand. The side effect of updating the stored value of the left operand shall occur between the previous and the next sequence point.

The order of evaluation of the operands is unspecified.

6.3.16.1 Simple assignment

Constraints

One of the following shall hold:[51]

— the left operand has qualified or unqualified arithmetic type and the right has arithmetic type;

— the left operand has a qualified or unqualified version of a structure or union type compatible with the type of the right;

— both operands are pointers to qualified or unqualified versions of compatible types, and the type pointed to by the left has all the qualifiers of the type pointed to by the right;

— one operand is a pointer to an object or incomplete type and the other is a pointer to a qualified or unqualified version of **void**, and the type pointed to by the left has all the qualifiers of the type pointed to by the right; or

— the left operand is a pointer and the right is a null pointer constant.

Semantics

In *simple assignment* (=), the value of the right operand is converted to the type of the assignment expression and replaces the value stored in the object designated by the left operand.

If the value being stored in an object is accessed from another object that overlaps in any way the storage of the first object, then the overlap shall be exact and the two objects shall have qualified or unqualified versions of a compatible type; otherwise, the behavior is undefined.

---

51 The asymmetric appearance of these constraints with respect to type qualifiers is due to the conversion (specified in 6.2.2.1) that changes lvalues to "the value of the expression" which removes any type qualifiers from the type category of the expression.

6.3.16   *Assignment operators* Unlike most other computer languages, C has more than one *assignment operator*. In all cases, the value of the expression on the right is assigned to the lvalue (that is, the modifiable object) on the left. The resulting type is that of the left operand, without any qualifications. (Remember, a qualified type is either **const** or **volatile**, or both.)

6.3.16.1   *Simple assignment* The basic assignment operator is, of course, the =. Its use is both straightforward and intuitive. One point of interest, however, is that if the object on the left overlaps an object in the expression on the right, then either that overlap must be exact, or the behavior of the assignment is undefined. This means, in general terms, that to be safe you should not use the assignment operator to copy partially overlapping objects.

Example

In the program fragment

```
int f(void);
char c;
/*...*/
/*...*/ ((c = f()) == -1) /*...*/
```

the **int** value returned by the function may be truncated when stored in the **char**, and then converted back to **int** width prior to the comparison. In an implementation in which "plain" **char** has the same range of values as **unsigned char** (and **char** is narrower than **int**), the result of the conversion cannot be negative, so the operands of the comparison can never compare equal. Therefore, for full portability, the variable **c** should be declared as **int**.

6.3.16.2 Compound assignment

Constraints

For the operators **+=** and **-=** only, either the left operand shall be a pointer to an object type and the right shall have integral type, or the left operand shall have qualified or unqualified arithmetic type and the right shall have arithmetic type.

For the other operators, each operand shall have arithmetic type consistent with those allowed by the corresponding binary operator.

Semantics

A *compound assignment* of the form **E1** *op*= **E2** differs from the simple assignment expression **E1 = E1** *op* **(E2)** only in that the lvalue **E1** is evaluated only once.

6.3.17 Comma operator

Syntax

> *expression:*
> > *assignment-expression*
> > *expression , assignment-expression*

Semantics

The left operand of a comma operator is evaluated as a void expression; there is a sequence point after its evaluation. Then the right operand is evaluated; the result has its type and value.[52]

Example

As indicated by the syntax, in contexts where a comma is a punctuator (in lists of arguments to functions and lists of initializers) the comma operator as described in this subclause cannot appear. On the other hand, it can be used within a parenthesized expression or within the second expression of a conditional operator in such contexts. In the function call

```
f(a, (t=3, t+2), c)
```

the function has three arguments, the second of which has the value 5.

Forward references: initialization (6.5.7).

---

52 A comma operator does not yield an lvalue.

6.3.16.2 *Compound assignment* The compound assignment operators are

```
*=  /=  %=  +=  -=  <<=  >>=  &=  ^=  |=
```

They are, in effect, "shorthand" notation for common assignment expressions. For example, the statement **x = x + 1** can be rewritten using the **+=** assignment operator, as **x += 1**.

In general, the shorthand assignment operators convert a statement like this:

var = var op exp;

into a statement like this:

var op= exp;

Aside from saving you some keyboard effort, using the shorthand assignment operators may help a compiler to generate more efficient object code than is possible with the equivalent long form. (Frankly, compiler technology is sufficiently advanced that many compilers will do an equally good job with either form. Still, there is no reason not to give the compiler as much help as you can.)

6.3.17 *Comma operator* In English, the comma operator tells the compiler to "do this and this and this...." That is, it is used to combine two or more expressions. The value produced by the combination is the value of the rightmost expression. However, the comma's precedence is the lowest of the operators; as such, it is generally used inside parentheses. For example, consider this fragment:

```
int i=0, j=1, k;
k = i, j;
printf("%d", k);
```

which displays the value 0 because the assignment **k = i** is performed before the remainder of the comma operation. But if the fragment is rewritten as follows:

```
k = (i, j);
```

the value of **k** will now have the value 1, which is the value of **j** (the rightmost expression). Remember, the comma is a punctuator when used in a function call and in an initializer list. In these cases, you must enclose a comma expression within parentheses.

6.4 Constant expressions

Syntax

> *constant-expression:*
> > *conditional-expression*

Description

A *constant expression* can be evaluated during translation rather than runtime, and accordingly may be used in any place that a constant may be.

Constraints

Constant expressions shall not contain assignment, increment, decrement, function-call, or comma operators, except when they are contained within the operand of a **sizeof** operator.[53]

Each constant expression shall evaluate to a constant that is in the range of representable values for its type.

Semantics

An expression that evaluates to a constant is required in several contexts.[54] If a floating expression is evaluated in the translation environment, the arithmetic precision and range shall be at least as great as if the expression were being evaluated in the execution environment.

An *integral constant expression* shall have integral type and shall only have operands that are integer constants, enumeration constants, character constants, **sizeof** expressions, and floating constants that are the immediate operands of casts. Cast operators in an integral constant expression shall only convert arithmetic types to integral types, except as part of an operand to the **sizeof** operator.

More latitude is permitted for constant expressions in initializers. Such a constant expression shall evaluate to one of the following:

— an arithmetic constant expression,

— a null pointer constant,

— an address constant, or

— an address constant for an object type plus or minus an integral constant expression.

An *arithmetic constant expression* shall have arithmetic type and shall only have operands that are integer constants, floating constants, enumeration constants, character constants, and **sizeof** expressions. Cast operators in an arithmetic constant expression shall only convert arithmetic types to arithmetic types, except as part of an operand to the **sizeof** operator.

An *address constant* is a pointer to an lvalue designating an object of static storage duration, or to a function designator; it shall be created explicitly, using the unary **&** operator, or implicitly, by the use of an expression of array or function type. The array-subscript **[ ]** and member-access **.** and **->** operators, the address **&** and indirection ***** unary operators, and pointer casts may be used in the creation of an address constant, but the value of an object shall not be accessed by use of these operators.

---

53 The operand of a **sizeof** operator is not evaluated (6.3.3.4), and thus any operator in 6.3 may be used.

54 An integral constant expression must be used to specify the size of a bit-field member of a structure, the value of an enumeration constant, the size of an array, or the value of a **case** constant. Further constraints that apply to the integral constant expressions used in conditional-inclusion preprocessing directives are discussed in 6.8.1.

6.4 Constant expressions A *constant expression* is one that involves only constants. Since all constants are known at compile time, a constant expression may be evaluated during compilation. This is the typical approach taken by most compiler implementations.

This section's discussion of constant expressions is quite detailed, but is easily summarized. The standard defines two general types of constant expressions: numeric (integral and arithmetic) and address. A *numeric constant expression* evaluates to a value. An *address constant expression* evaluates to a physical machine address or to NULL. In C, constant expressions are easy and intuitive to use and generally cause little trouble.

An implementation may accept other forms of constant expressions.

The semantic rules for the evaluation of a constant expression are the same as for nonconstant expressions.[55]

Forward references: initialization (6.5.7).

---

55 Thus, in the following initialization,

```
static int i = 2 || 1 / 0;
```

the expression is a valid integral constant expression with value one.

There are no annotations for page 56.

6.5 Declarations

Syntax

> *declaration:*
>> *declaration-specifiers init-declarator-list*$_{opt}$;
>
> *declaration-specifiers:*
>> *storage-class-specifier declaration-specifiers*$_{opt}$
>> *type-specifier declaration-specifiers*$_{opt}$
>> *type-qualifier declaration-specifiers*$_{opt}$
>
> *init-declarator-list:*
>> *init-declarator*
>> *init-declarator-list , init-declarator*
>
> *init-declarator:*
>> *declarator*
>> *declarator = initializer*

Constraints

A declaration shall declare at least a declarator, a tag, or the members of an enumeration.

If an identifier has no linkage, there shall be no more than one declaration of the identifier (in a declarator or type specifier) with the same scope and in the same name space, except for tags as specified in 6.5.2.3.

All declarations in the same scope that refer to the same object or function shall specify compatible types.

Semantics

A *declaration* specifies the interpretation and attributes of a set of identifiers. A declaration that also causes storage to be reserved for an object or function named by an identifier is a *definition*.[56]

The declaration specifiers consist of a sequence of specifiers that indicate the linkage, storage duration, and part of the type of the entities that the declarators denote. The init-declarator-list is a comma-separated sequence of declarators, each of which may have additional type information, or an initializer, or both. The declarators contain the identifiers (if any) being declared.

If an identifier for an object is declared with no linkage, the type for the object shall be complete by the end of its declarator, or by the end of its init-declarator if it has an initializer.

Forward references: declarators (6.5.4), enumeration specifiers (6.5.2.2), initialization (6.5.7), tags (6.5.2.3).

---

56 Function definitions have a different syntax, described in 6.7.1.

6.5   Declarations   A *declaration* statement declares a variable, a function, structure or union or enumeration tag, or an enumeration constant name. If the statement also creates storage for the object, then the declaration statement is also a *definition*.

There is long-standing confusion about the usage of *declaration* and *definition* in C literature. As used relative to C, a declaration specifies what sort of object is being declared. This is the object's type information. A definition causes storage for an object to be created. For a variable, a declaration is also typically a definition, because storage for the variable is created when it is declared. For a function, a declaration is its prototype. A function definition is the function, itself.

The term *declarator* is used frequently in the standard. Here, the standard provides a definition. In simple language, a declarator is the name of the object being declared. For example, in this fragment:

```
int count;
```

count is a declarator.

The rest of this section examines various aspects of declarations.

6.5.1 Storage-class specifiers

Syntax

> *storage-class-specifier:*
> > **typedef**
> > **extern**
> > **static**
> > **auto**
> > **register**

Constraints

At most, one storage-class specifier may be given in the declaration specifiers in a declaration.[57]

Semantics

The **typedef** specifier is called a ''storage-class specifier'' for syntactic convenience only; it is discussed in 6.5.6. The meanings of the various linkages and storage durations were discussed in 6.1.2.2 and 6.1.2.4.

A declaration of an identifier for an object with storage-class specifier **register** suggests that access to the object be as fast as possible. The extent to which such suggestions are effective is implementation-defined.[58]

The declaration of an identifier for a function that has block scope shall have no explicit storage-class specifier other than **extern**.

Forward references: type definitions (6.5.6).

6.5.2 Type specifiers

Syntax

> *type-specifier:*
> > **void**
> > **char**
> > **short**
> > **int**
> > **long**
> > **float**
> > **double**
> > **signed**
> > **unsigned**
> > *struct-or-union-specifier*
> > *enum-specifier*
> > *typedef-name*

---

57 See ''future language directions'' (6.9.3).

58 The implementation may treat any **register** declaration simply as an **auto** declaration. However, whether or not addressable storage is actually used. the address of any part of an object declared with storage-class specifier **register** may not be computed, either explicitly (by use of the unary **&** operator as discussed in 6.3.3.2) or implicitly (by converting an array name to a pointer as discussed in 6.2.2.1). Thus the only operator that can be applied to an array declared with storage-class specifier **register** is **sizeof**.

6.5.1   Storage-class specifiers   The standard defines five *storage-class specifiers*, including **typedef**; however, **typedef** is not actually a storage-class specifier in actual usage. A storage-class specifier modifies a declaration statement by specifying how a variable will be stored. The storage-class specifier precedes all other type modifiers, and only one storage-class specifier may be applied to a declaration. For example, here is a declaration that creates a **static** integer called **count**:

```
static int count;
```

Following is a brief synopsis of the other storage-class specifiers.

A variable declared using **extern** is not a definition. Rather, it specifies the type and name of the variable and implies that a definition for this variable is found elsewhere in the program.

The specifier **static** has two uses. When applied to a local variable, it causes storage for that variable to remain in existence the entire duration of the program's execution. Typically, local variables are stored on the stack, but a **static** local variable is not. It is usually stored in the same region of memory used to hold global variables. In essence, a **static** local variable is a global variable with its scope restricted to a single function.

When **static** is applied to a global variable or function, it causes that variable or function to have file scope—that is, the global object declared as **static** is local to the file in which it is declared and is not accessible (or known) outside of it.

The **auto** specifier is redundant and seldom used. (It is used to declare a local variable, but local variables are **auto** by default.)

The **register** specifier tells the compiler to optimize (for speed) the access time to the variable being declared. Traditionally, this specifier could only be applied to integral types because it meant (as the name implies) holding the variable in a register of the CPU. However, the ANSI standard broadened this traditional definition by stating that **register** can be applied to any type of variable and that "access to the object be as fast as possible." This relaxes the requirement of actually using a CPU register. Thus, **register** can be applied to objects that are far too large to fit into a CPU register. The compiler simply optimizes access time as best it can, perhaps holding an object in cache memory, for example.

The **register** specifier is only a request to the compiler, which may be completely ignored. There are two reasons for this: First, highly optimized storage is limited and the compiler may simply run out of this resource. Second, not all objects can be optimized. For example, extremely large arrays generally must be held in the main memory of the computer because of their size.

6.5.2   Type specifiers   C contains the nine built-in *type specifiers*.

Constraints

Each list of type specifiers shall be one of the following sets (delimited by commas, when there is more than one set on a line); the type specifiers may occur in any order, possibly intermixed with the other declaration specifiers.

— **void**

— **char**

— **signed char**

— **unsigned char**

— **short**, **signed short**, **short int**, or **signed short int**

— **unsigned short**, or **unsigned short int**

— **int**, **signed**, **signed int**, or no type specifiers

— **unsigned**, or **unsigned int**

— **long**, **signed long**, **long int**, or **signed long int**

— **unsigned long**, or **unsigned long int**

— **float**

— **double**

— **long double**

— struct-or-union specifier

— enum-specifier

— typedef-name

Semantics

Specifiers for structures, unions, and enumerations are discussed in 6.5.2.1 through 6.5.2.3. Declarations of typedef names are discussed in 6.5.6. The characteristics of the other types are discussed in 6.1.2.5.

Each of the above comma-separated sets designates the same type, except that for bit-fields, the type **signed int** (or **signed**) may differ from **int** (or no type specifiers).

Forward references: enumeration specifiers (6.5.2.2), structure and union specifiers (6.5.2.1), tags (6.5.2.3), type definitions (6.5.6).

6.5.2.1 Structure and union specifiers

Syntax

>   *struct-or-union-specifier:*
>   *struct-or-union identifier*$_{opt}$ { *struct-declaration-list* }
>   *struct-or-union identifier*
>
>   *struct-or-union:*
>   **struct**
>   **union**
>
>   *struct-declaration-list:*
>   *struct-declaration*
>   *struct-declaration-list struct-declaration*

These specifiers are used to declare objects of the basic types, or to create more complex types through the use of structure or union definitions. The list of legal type-specifier combinations is shown. The meaning of these types is explained earlier in the standard.

6.5.2.1 *Structure and union specifiers* A *structure* is an aggregate data type that contains one or more members that do not overlap. A *union* is an aggregate data type that contains one or more overlapping members—that is, in a union, all members share the same memory location. Following are the general forms of a structure and a union, in more informal terms than shown in the standard:

```
struct tag {
  type member1;
  type member2;
  type member3;
  /* ... */
  type memberN;
} var-list;

union tag {
  type member1;
  type member2;
  type member3;
  /* ... */
  type memberN;
} var-list;
```

Here, *tag* is the structure or union name, and *var-list* is a comma-separated list of structure or union variables. Either the tag or the variables are optional, but not both. (Structure or union variables may be declared later in your program, as needed.)

A structure or union declaration creates a new data type (that is, it is a logical construct that has no physical representation). But storage is not actually allocated until variables of that type are defined.

Here is an example of a structure:

```
/* declare structure type */
struct sample {
  int a;
  float b;
  char s[80];
};
/* declare structure variables */
struct sample x, y, z;
```

struct-declaration:
        specifier-qualifier-list struct-declarator-list ;

specifier-qualifier-list:
        type-specifier specifier-qualifier-list$_{opt}$
        type-qualifier specifier-qualifier-list$_{opt}$

struct-declarator-list:
        struct-declarator
        struct-declarator-list , struct-declarator

struct-declarator:
        declarator
        declarator$_{opt}$: *constant-expression*

Constraints

A structure or union shall not contain a member with incomplete or function type. Hence it shall not contain an instance of itself (but may contain a pointer to an instance of itself).

The expression that specifies the width of a bit-field shall be an integral constant expression that has nonnegative value that shall not exceed the number of bits in an ordinary object of compatible type. If the value is zero, the declaration shall have no declarator.

Semantics

As discussed in 6.1.2.5, a structure is a type consisting of a sequence of named members, whose storage is allocated in an ordered sequence, and a union is a type consisting of a sequence of named members, whose storage overlap.

Structure and union specifiers have the same form.

The presence of a struct-declaration-list in a struct-or-union-specifier declares a new type, within a translation unit. The struct-declaration-list is a sequence of declarations for the members of the structure or union. If the struct-declaration-list contains no named members, the behavior is undefined. The type is incomplete until after the } that terminates the list.

A member of a structure or union may have any object type. In addition, a member may be declared to consist of a specified number of bits (including a sign bit, if any). Such a member is called a *bit-field*;[59] its width is preceded by a colon.

A bit-field shall have a type that is a qualified or unqualified version of one of **int**, **unsigned int**, or **signed int**. Whether the high-order bit position of a (possibly qualified) ''plain'' **int** bit-field is treated as a sign bit is implementation-defined. A bit-field is interpreted as an integral type consisting of the specified number of bits.

An implementation may allocate any addressable storage unit large enough to hold a bit-field. If enough space remains, a bit-field that immediately follows another bit-field in a structure shall be packed into adjacent bits of the same unit. If insufficient space remains, whether a bit-field that does not fit is put into the next unit or overlaps adjacent units is implementation-defined. The order of allocation of bit-fields within a unit (high-order to low-order or low-order to high-order) is implementation-defined. The alignment of the addressable storage unit is unspecified.

A bit-field declaration with no declarator, but only a colon and a width, indicates an unnamed bit-field.[60] As a special case of this, a bit-field structure member with a width of 0 indicates that

---

59 The unary **&** (address-of) operator may not be applied to a bit-field object; thus, there are no pointers to or arrays of bit-field objects.

60 An unnamed bit-field structure member is useful for padding to conform to externally imposed layouts.

(**6.5.2.1 Structure and union specifiers,** *continued*)

The structure **sample** is first declared. This creates the new data type; however, it does not create any variables of this type. Not until **x**, **y**, and **z** are created is storage actually allocated.

Notice that the standard specifically states that a structure or union cannot contain a function member. The use of function members—allowed in C++ (C's object-oriented extension)—is disallowed in C. Also, a structure or a union cannot contain an object of itself, though it may contain a pointer to itself. For example, the following declaration is illegal:

```
struct s_type {
  int a;
  int b;
  struct s_type s; /* illegal, can't reference self */
};
```

There is a special type of structure member called a *bit-field*, which consists of a specified number of bits. A bit-field is useful when you want to pack several Boolean values into the smallest space possible. A bit-field may be either named, or unnamed if it is only being used as a placeholder.

Here is an example of how bit-fields are declared:

```
struct bit {
  unsigned done : 1; /* 1 bit */
  unsigned EmpStatus : 4; /* 4 bits */
  int : 3; /* a 3 bit place holder */
} bt;
```

Although C's bitwise operators allow you to access the bits within a byte (or other integral type), the bit-field is valuable because it allows you to give a bit a name that you can then use to access the bit. For example, this statement assigns **done** the value 1:

```
bt.done = 1;
```

Bear in mind that despite their convenience, bit-fields may not always be the most efficient way to manipulate bits, depending upon the implementation. C's bitwise operators are the alternative.

no further bit-field is to be packed into the unit in which the previous bit-field, if any, was placed.

Each non-bit-field member of a structure or union object is aligned in an implementation-defined manner appropriate to its type.

Within a structure object, the non-bit-field members and the units in which bit-fields reside have addresses that increase in the order in which they are declared. A pointer to a structure object, suitably converted, points to its initial member (or if that member is a bit-field, then to the unit in which it resides), and vice versa. There may therefore be unnamed padding within a structure object, but not at its beginning, as necessary to achieve the appropriate alignment.

The size of a union is sufficient to contain the largest of its members. The value of at most one of the members can be stored in a union object at any time. A pointer to a union object, suitably converted, points to each of its members (or if a member is a bit-field, then to the unit in which it resides), and vice versa.

There may also be unnamed padding at the end of a structure or union, as necessary to achieve the appropriate alignment were the structure or union to be an element of an array.

Forward references: tags (6.5.2.3).

6.5.2.2 Enumeration specifiers

Syntax

> *enum-specifier:*
> > **enum** *identifier*$_{opt}$ { *enumerator-list* }
> > **enum** *identifier*
>
> *enumerator-list:*
> > *enumerator*
> > *enumerator-list , enumerator*
>
> *enumerator:*
> > *enumeration-constant*
> > *enumeration-constant* **=** *constant-expression*

Constraints

The expression that defines the value of an enumeration constant shall be an integral constant expression that has a value representable as an **int**.

Semantics

The identifiers in an enumerator list are declared as constants that have type **int** and may appear wherever such are permitted.[61] An enumerator with **=** defines its enumeration constant as the value of the constant expression. If the first enumerator has no **=**, the value of its enumeration constant is 0. Each subsequent enumerator with no **=** defines its enumeration constant as the value of the constant expression obtained by adding 1 to the value of the previous enumeration constant. (The use of enumerators with **=** may produce enumeration constants with values that duplicate other values in the same enumeration.) The enumerators of an enumeration are also known as its members.

Each enumerated type shall be compatible with an integer type; the choice of type is implementation-defined.

---

61 Thus, the identifiers of enumeration constants declared in the same scope shall all be distinct from each other and from other identifiers declared in ordinary declarators.

(*6.5.2.1 Structure and union specifiers, continued*)

Structures and unions may be padded in order to achieve a certain alignment in memory—for instance, to align a structure or union on a word or paragraph boundary. This padding must occur at the end, not at the beginning, of the object. Many computer architectures provide the most efficient access to objects that are aligned in some manner or another.

6.5.2.2 Enumeration specifiers An *enumeration* defines a set of named integer constants. It is created using the **enum** keyword, as follows:

enum *tag* { *identifier-list* } *var-list*;

Here, either the enumeration tag or the variable list (but not both) is optional. For example, here is an enumeration that defines the values **one**, **two**, and **three**:

```
enum num {one, two, three};
```

By default, the value of the first enumeration constant is 0, the second is 1, and so on, with each constant being 1 greater than the constant it follows. Therefore, in the preceding enumeration, the value of **one** is 0, **two** is 1, and **three** is 2. You can use an initializer to set an enumeration constant to a known value. For example, this modification to the preceding declaration causes the values of the constants to reflect their meaning:

```
enum num {one=1, two, three};
```

Now, **one** is 1, **two** is 2, and **three** is 3. After an initialization, subsequent constants will be greater than the initialization value.

As the standard clearly states, an enumeration type is for all intents and purposes an integer type. Therefore, you may use an enumeration variable wherever you use an integer variable.

Example

```
enum hue { chartreuse, burgundy, claret=20, winedark };
/*...*/
enum hue col, *cp;
/*...*/
col = claret;
cp = &col;
/*...*/
/*...*/ (*cp != burgundy) /*...*/
```

makes **hue** the tag of an enumeration. and then declares **col** as an object that has that type and **cp** as a pointer to an object that has that type. The enumerated values are in the set { 0. 1. 20. 21 }.

Forward references: tags (6.5.2.3).

6.5.2.3 Tags

Semantics

A type specifier of the form

struct-or-union identifier **{** *struct-declaration-list* **}**

or

enum *identifier* **{** *enumerator-list* **}**

declares the identifier to be the *tag* of the structure, union, or enumeration specified by the list. The list defines the *structure content, union content, or enumeration content*. If this declaration of the tag is visible. a subsequent declaration that uses the tag and that omits the bracketed list specifies the declared structure, union, or enumerated type. Subsequent declarations in the same scope shall omit the bracketed list.

If a type specifier of the form

struct-or-union identifier

occurs prior to the declaration that defines the content. the structure or union is an incomplete type.[62] It declares a tag that specifies a type that may be used only when the size of an object of the specified type is not needed.[63] If the type is to be completed. another declaration of the tag in the same scope (but not in an enclosed block. which declares a new type known only within that block) shall define the content. A declaration of the form

struct-or-union identifier **;**

specifies a structure or union type and declares a tag. both visible only within the scope in which the declaration occurs. It specifies a new type distinct from any type with the same tag in an enclosing scope (if any).

A type specifier of the form

---

62 A similar construction with **enum** does not exist and is not necessary as there can be no mutual dependencies between the declaration of an enumerated type and any other type.

63 It is not needed. for example. when a typedef name is declared to be a specifier for a structure or union. or when a pointer to or a function returning a structure or union is being declared. (See incomplete types in 6.1.2.5.) The specification shall be complete before such a function is called or defined.

6.5.2.3   Tags   This section spans two pages, but its principle is easy to grasp: Once you have defined a structure, union, or enumeration, you may use the tag name to declare variables. For example, consider this structure declaration:

```
struct s_type {
  int a;
  int b;
};
```

The name **s_type** is the tag of the structure, and you can use this tag to create structure variables, as shown here:

```
struct s_type s1, s2;
```

As shown, you do not redefine the structure content when declaring variables using the tag name. (If you have been programming in C for any length of time at all, you have almost certainly used this construct several times.)

You may also use the tag to forward-reference a structure or union when a mutual dependency exists, or when a structure must contain a pointer to itself. (An example of these uses is shown on the next page of the standard.)

Finally, you may define structures, unions, and enumerations that have *no* tag name. In this case, all variables must be declared in that declaration statement, because there is no way to do so later in your program. For example, in this structure:

```
struct {
  int a;
  int b;
} struct_var;
```

there is no tag name. The only variable is **struct_var**, and no others may be created later in the program. (Of course, you may add more variable names to the structure declaration.)

Generally, you will need to specify a tag name for a structure, union, or enumeration because it will be needed later in your program. Remember, in a way, a tag defines a type. (Formally, tag names are *not* type names in C.) So if you don't specify a tag while creating a structure, union, or enumeration, you have no way to refer to that new type later in your program.

> *struct-or-union* { *struct-declaration-list* }

or

> **enum** { *enumerator-list* }

specifies a new structure, union, or enumerated type, within the translation unit, that can only be referred to by the declaration of which it is a part.[64]

Examples

1. This mechanism allows declaration of a self-referential structure.

```
struct tnode {
        int count;
        struct tnode *left, *right;
};
```

specifies a structure that contains an integer and two pointers to objects of the same type. Once this declaration has been given, the declaration

```
struct tnode s, *sp;
```

declares **s** to be an object of the given type and **sp** to be a pointer to an object of the given type. With these declarations, the expression **sp->left** refers to the left **struct tnode** pointer of the object to which **sp** points; the expression **s.right->count** designates the **count** member of the right **struct tnode** pointed to from **s**.

The following alternative formulation uses the **typedef** mechanism:

```
typedef struct tnode TNODE;
struct tnode {
        int count;
        TNODE *left, *right;
};
TNODE s, *sp;
```

2. To illustrate the use of prior declaration of a tag to specify a pair of mutually referential structures, the declarations

```
struct s1 { struct s2 *s2p; /*...*/ }; /* D1 */
struct s2 { struct s1 *s1p; /*...*/ }; /* D2 */
```

specify a pair of structures that contain pointers to each other. Note, however, that if **s2** were already declared as a tag in an enclosing scope, the declaration **D1** would refer to *it*, not to the tag **s2** declared in **D2**. To eliminate this context sensitivity, the declaration

```
struct s2;
```

may be inserted ahead of **D1**. This declares a new tag **s2** in the inner scope; the declaration **D2** then completes the specification of the new type.

Forward references: type definitions (6.5.6).

---

64 Of course, when the declaration is of a typedef name, subsequent declarations can make use of the typedef name to declare objects having the specified structure, union, or enumerated type.

(*6.5.2.3 Tags, continued*)

The examples in the Tags section illustrate solutions to two common C programming problems. The first example shows how a structure may contain a pointer to itself. Remember, a structure may not contain itself, because doing so implies a recursive data structure, which C and most other languages do not support. However, the structure may contain a pointer to an object of its own type.

Notice the use of **typedef** in the first example. This sort of construct is found more and more frequently in professionally written C code.

The second example shows how two mutually dependent structures may contain pointers to each other. As the example cautions, a forward reference to **s2** may be necessary—this will prevent the wrong tag from being used if an outer scope also declares a tag with the name **s2**.

6.5.3   Type qualifiers

Syntax

> *type-qualifier:*
>> **const**
>>
>> **volatile**

Constraints

The same type qualifier shall not appear more than once in the same specifier list or qualifier list, either directly or via one or more **typedef**s.

Semantics

The properties associated with qualified types are meaningful only for expressions that are lvalues.[65]

If an attempt is made to modify an object defined with a const-qualified type through use of an lvalue with non-const-qualified type, the behavior is undefined. If an attempt is made to refer to an object defined with a volatile-qualified type through use of an lvalue with non-volatile-qualified type, the behavior is undefined.[66]

An object that has volatile-qualified type may be modified in ways unknown to the implementation or have other unknown side effects. Therefore any expression referring to such an object shall be evaluated strictly according to the rules of the abstract machine, as described in 5.1.2.3. Furthermore, at every sequence point the value last stored in the object shall agree with that prescribed by the abstract machine, except as modified by the unknown factors mentioned previously.[67] What constitutes an access to an object that has volatile-qualified type is implementation-defined.

If the specification of an array type includes any type qualifiers, the element type is so-qualified, not the array type. If the specification of a function type includes any type qualifiers, the behavior is undefined.[68]

For two qualified types to be compatible, both shall have the identically qualified version of a compatible type; the order of type qualifiers within a list of specifiers or qualifiers does not affect the specified type.

Examples

1. An object declared

   > **extern const volatile int real_time_clock;**

   may be modifiable by hardware, but cannot be assigned to, incremented, or decremented.

2. The following declarations and expressions illustrate the behavior when type qualifiers modify an aggregate type:

---

65 The implementation may place a **const** object that is not **volatile** in a read-only region of storage. Moreover, the implementation need not allocate storage for such an object if its address is never used.

66 This applies to those objects that behave as if they were defined with qualified types, even if they are never actually defined as objects in the program (such as an object at a memory-mapped input/output address).

67 A **volatile** declaration may be used to describe an object corresponding to a memory-mapped input/output port or an object accessed by an asynchronously interrupting function. Actions on objects so declared shall not be "optimized out" by an implementation or reordered except as permitted by the rules for evaluating expressions.

68 Both of these can only occur through the use of **typedef**s.

6.5.3 *Type qualifiers* Here is a summary of the information about **const** and **volatile**.

A variable declared using **const** may not be on the left side of an assignment statement. It may, however, be given an initial value when it is declared. Thus, **const** variables may not be modified through any action of your program. Consider this example:

```
const int i = 10; /* initialization valid for const */

i = 0; /* ERROR, cannot modify a const object */
```

The declaration and initialization are valid, but the attempt at assignment will produce a compile-time error message, because a **const** variable cannot be directly modified by any program statement.

Be careful, however. Depending on how **const** objects are implemented, it is possible to modify one indirectly through a pointer. For example, this next fragment may, indeed, modify the **const** variable **i**. (Many compilers display a warning about this fragment, but still accept it.)

```
const int i = 10;
int *p;

p = &i; /* obtain address of const variable */

*p = 0; /* modify a const object through p */
```

A **volatile** object may be modified in ways not specified by your program. For example, you might use **volatile** to define a variable that will be changed by some means outside your program, such as a real-time clock, another process, or (as stated in footnote 67) an interrupt routine. By specifying a variable as **volatile**, you prevent the compiler from optimizing any expression of which it is part in such a way that its value is "taken for granted" when the compiler is optimizing the object code. For instance, it is common for a compiler's optimizer to examine the value of **i** only once in this expression:

```
j = i + i;
```

However, if **i** is declared as **volatile**, it will be examined each time it is used.

```
const struct s { int mem; } cs = { 1 };
struct s ncs;    /* the object ncs is modifiable */
typedef int A[2][3];
const A a = {{4, 5, 6}, {7, 8, 9}}; /* array of array of const int */
int *pi;
const int *pci;

ncs = cs;        /* valid */
cs = ncs;        /* violates modifiable lvalue constraint for = */
pi = &ncs.mem;   /* valid */
pi = &cs.mem;    /* violates type constraints for = */
pci = &cs.mem;   /* valid */
pi = a[0];       /* invalid: a[0] has type "const int *" */
```

6.5.4 Declarators

Syntax

declarator:
  pointer$_{opt}$ *direct-declarator*

direct-declarator:
  identifier
  (*declarator*)
  direct-declarator [*constant-expression*$_{opt}$]
  direct-declarator (*parameter-type-list*)
  direct-declarator (*identifier-list*$_{opt}$)

pointer:
  * *type-qualifier-list*$_{opt}$
  * *type-qualifier-list*$_{opt}$ *pointer*

type-qualifier-list:
  type-qualifier
  type-qualifier-list type-qualifier

parameter-type-list:
  parameter-list
  parameter-list , ...

parameter-list:
  parameter-declaration
  parameter-list , *parameter-declaration*

parameter-declaration:
  declaration-specifiers declarator
  declaration-specifiers abstract-declarator$_{opt}$

identifier-list:
  identifier
  identifier-list , *identifier*

Semantics

Each declarator declares one identifier, and asserts that when an operand of the same form as the declarator appears in an expression, it designates a function or object with the scope, storage duration, and type indicated by the declaration specifiers.

In the following subclauses, consider a declaration

  T D1

6.5.4 *Declarators* A declarator is, essentially, the name of an object that is being declared. The information and constraints in this section are mostly applicable to compiler implementors.

where **T** contains the declaration specifiers that specify a type T (such as **int**) and **D1** is a declarator that contains an identifier *ident*. The type specified for the identifier *ident* in the various forms of declarator is described inductively using this notation.

If, in the declaration "**T D1**," **D1** has the form

> *identifier*

then the type specified for *ident* is T.

If, in the declaration "**T D1**," **D1** has the form

> **(D)**

then *ident* has the type specified by the declaration "**T D**." Thus, a declarator in parentheses is identical to the unparenthesized declarator, but the binding of complex declarators may be altered by parentheses.

Implementation limits

The implementation shall allow the specification of types that have at least 12 pointer, array, and function declarators (in any valid combinations) modifying an arithmetic, a structure, a union, or an incomplete type, either directly or via one or more **typedef**s.

Forward references: type definitions (6.5.6).

6.5.4.1 Pointer declarators

Semantics

If, in the declaration "**T D1**," **D1** has the form

> ***** *type-qualifier-list*$_{opt}$ **D**

and the type specified for *ident* in the declaration "**T D**" is "*derived-declarator-type-list* T," then the type specified for *ident* is "*derived-declarator-type-list type-qualifier-list* pointer to T." For each type qualifier in the list, *ident* is a so-qualified pointer.

For two pointer types to be compatible, both shall be identically qualified and both shall be pointers to compatible types.

Example

The following pair of declarations demonstrates the difference between a "variable pointer to a constant value" and a "constant pointer to a variable value."

```
const int *ptr_to_constant;
int *const constant_ptr;
```

The contents of an object pointed to by **ptr_to_constant** shall not be modified through that pointer, but **ptr_to_constant** itself may be changed to point to another object. Similarly, the contents of the **int** pointed to by **constant_ptr** may be modified, but **constant_ptr** itself shall always point to the same location.

The declaration of the constant pointer **constant_ptr** may be clarified by including a definition for the type "pointer to **int**."

```
typedef int *int_ptr;
const int_ptr constant_ptr;
```

declares **constant_ptr** as an object that has type "const-qualified pointer to **int**."

6.5.4.1 Pointer declarators This section formally states several important aspects of the C language relative to how pointers are declared. First, to declare a pointer type, precede the variable or function name with an asterisk. Second, for two pointer types to be compatible, they need to be declared with the same type qualifiers (if any), and the base types of the pointers must be compatible.

The third bit of information in this section involves the difference between *pointers to const objects* and *const pointers*. This is one of the most confusing aspects of the C language and one that even experienced professionals sometimes misunderstand. The example in the standard clearly explains this difference. For another example to aid better understanding, consider this declaration:

```
char ch;
char *const p = &ch;
```

This declaration declares a **const** pointer to the (modifiable) character **ch**. This means that **p** may not be modified, but **ch** may be.

This next example declares a pointer to a **const** object:

```
const char ch;
const char *p = &ch;
```

In this case, **p** may be changed, but the value of what it points to may not be changed (through **p**, at least).

6.5.4.2 Array declarators

Constraints

The expression delimited by [and] (which specifies the size of an array) shall be an integral constant expression that has a value greater than zero.

Semantics

If, in the declaration "**T D1**," **D1** has the form

D [*constant-expression*_{*opt*}]

and the type specified for *ident* in the declaration "**T D**" is "*derived-declarator-type-list T*," then the type specified for *ident* is "*derived-declarator-type-list* array of *T*."[69] If the size is not present, the array type is an incomplete type.

For two array types to be compatible, both shall have compatible element types, and if both size specifiers are present, they shall have the same value.

Examples

1.   ```float fa[11], *afp[17];```

declares an array of **float** numbers and an array of pointers to **float** numbers.

2.   Note the distinction between the declarations

```
extern int *x;
extern int y[];
```

The first declares **x** to be a pointer to **int**; the second declares **y** to be an array of **int** of unspecified size (an incomplete type), the storage for which is defined elsewhere.

Forward references: function definitions (6.7.1), initialization (6.5.7).

6.5.4.3 Function declarators (including prototypes)

Constraints

A function declarator shall not specify a return type that is a function type or an array type.

The only storage-class specifier that shall occur in a parameter declaration is **register**.

An identifier list in a function declarator that is not part of a function definition shall be empty.

Semantics

If, in the declaration "**T D1**," **D1** has the form

D (*parameter-type-list*)

or

D (*identifier-list*_{*opt*})

and the type specified for *ident* in the declaration "**T D**" is "*derived-declarator-type-list T*," then the type specified for *ident* is "*derived-declarator-type-list* function returning *T*."

A parameter type list specifies the types of, and may declare identifiers for, the parameters of the function. If the list terminates with an ellipsis (, . . .), no information about the number or types of the parameters after the comma is supplied.[70] The special case of **void** as the only

---

69 When several "array of" specifications are adjacent, a multidimensional array is declared.

70 The macros defined in the **<stdarg.h>** header (7.8) may be used to access arguments that correspond to the ellipsis.

6.5.4.2 *Array declarators* As you probably know, arrays are declared by enclosing each dimension of the array between square brackets. For example, the following lines declare a 10-element, one-dimensional array of integers and a 4-by-5, two-dimensional array of **float**s:

```
int int_array[10];
float float_array[4][5];
```

An array declared without a dimension size being specified is an *unsized array,* which is an incomplete type. Unsized arrays are often used in conjunction with initializations. For example, in this fragment:

```
char s[] = "this is a test";
int i[] = {1, 2, 3};
```

the compiler uses the number of the initializers to automatically compute the size of the array. This use of an unsized array can simplify your programming because it removes the requirement that you manually count the number of initializers.

The examples shown in the standard clarify several aspects of array declarations. Here is an additional point regarding Example 2: It is possible to change what object **x** points to, because it is a pointer. You cannot, however, change the object "pointed to" by **y**, because it describes an array.

6.5.4.3 *Function declarators (including prototypes)* This section begins with two important restrictions relating to function return types: A function cannot return either a function or an array. A function cannot be returned for rather obvious reasons (pointers to functions *can* be returned, however). The reasons for not allowing arrays to be returned are both historical and practical. Historically, the C language has never allowed arrays to be returned. Practically speaking, values are returned in registers when size permits or occasionally on the stack. Thus, the overhead of returning an array could be enormous. It is far more efficient to simply return a pointer to an array, when one is needed as a return value. Arrays as return values have little practical value.

A parameter to a function may not be specified as **extern**, **static**, or **auto**. It may be specified as **register**, however. (The use of **register** parameters is quite common in C programs.)

When a function has a variable number of parameters, this is denoted in the function's declaration (or prototype) by the ellipsis. To access a variable number of arguments, use the standard macros **va_arg()**, **va_start()**, and **va_end()**, which are described in Section 7.8 of this standard.

item in the list specifies that the function has no parameters.

In a parameter declaration, a single typedef name in parentheses is taken to be an abstract declarator that specifies a function with a single parameter, not as redundant parentheses around the identifier for a declarator.

The storage-class specifier in the declaration specifiers for a parameter declaration, if present, is ignored unless the declared parameter is one of the members of the parameter type list for a function definition.

An identifier list declares only the identifiers of the parameters of the function. An empty list in a function declarator that is part of a function definition specifies that the function has no parameters. The empty list in a function declarator that is not part of a function definition specifies that no information about the number or types of the parameters is supplied.[71]

For two function types to be compatible, both shall specify compatible return types.[72] Moreover, the parameter type lists, if both are present, shall agree in the number of parameters and in use of the ellipsis terminator; corresponding parameters shall have compatible types. If one type has a parameter type list and the other type is specified by a function declarator that is not part of a function definition and that contains an empty identifier list, the parameter list shall not have an ellipsis terminator and the type of each parameter shall be compatible with the type that results from the application of the default argument promotions. If one type has a parameter type list and the other type is specified by a function definition that contains a (possibly empty) identifier list, both shall agree in the number of parameters, and the type of each prototype parameter shall be compatible with the type that results from the application of the default argument promotions to the type of the corresponding identifier. (For each parameter declared with function or array type, its type for these comparisons is the one that results from conversion to a pointer type, as in 6.7.1. For each parameter declared with qualified type, its type for these comparisons is the unqualified version of its declared type.)

Examples

1.   The declaration

```
int f(void), *fip(), (*pfi)();
```

declares a function **f** with no parameters returning an **int**, a function **fip** with no parameter specification returning a pointer to an **int**, and a pointer **pfi** to a function with no parameter specification returning an **int**. It is especially useful to compare the last two. The binding of ***fip()** is ***(fip())**, so that the declaration suggests, and the same construction in an expression requires, the calling of a function **fip**, and then using indirection through the pointer result to yield an **int**. In the declarator **(*pfi)()**, the extra parentheses are necessary to indicate that indirection through a pointer to a function yields a function designator, which is then used to call the function: it returns an **int**.

If the declaration occurs outside of any function, the identifiers have file scope and external linkage. If the declaration occurs inside a function, the identifiers of the functions **f** and **fip** have block scope and either internal or external linkage (depending on what file scope declarations for these identifiers are visible), and the identifier of the pointer **pfi** has block scope and no linkage.

2.   The declaration

---

71 See "future language directions" (6.9.4).

72 If both function types are "old style," parameter types are not compared.

*(**6.5.4.3 Function declarators,** continued)*

Much of the language on this page is highly technical, difficult to follow, and related mostly to compiler implementors. What follows is a summary of the important points of general interest.

When the parameter list in a function prototype contains the word **void**, it means that the function has no parameters. If the parameter list in a function declaration is empty, it makes no statement whatsoever about the parameters. In C, the following two statements are not equivalent:

```
int f(void); /* no parameters */
int f(); /* no information about parameters */
```

The reason for these two different declarations is for compatibility with older C code. Remember, prototypes were added to C by the ANSI standard. Prior to prototypes, only the return type of a function could be declared in advance; parameters could not. Thus, before the addition of prototypes, it was not possible to declare the type and number of parameters to a function prior to that function's definition. To allow compatibility with older C code, an empty parameter list in a declaration simply means that no statement at all is made about the parameters.

The examples on this and the following page of the standard illustrate several points about declaring function pointers.

```
int (*apfi[3])(int *x, int *y);
```

declares an array **apfi** of three pointers to functions returning **int**. Each of these functions has two parameters that are pointers to **int**. The identifiers **x** and **y** are declared for descriptive purposes only and go out of scope at the end of the declaration of **apfi**.

3. The declaration

```
int (*fpfi(int (*)(long), int))(int, ...);
```

declares a function **fpfi** that returns a pointer to a function returning an **int**. The function **fpfi** has two parameters: a pointer to a function returning an **int** (with one parameter of type **long**), and an **int**. The pointer returned by **fpfi** points to a function that has one **int** parameter and accepts zero or more additional arguments of any type.

Forward references: function definitions (6.7.1), type names (6.5.5).

6.5.5 Type names

Syntax

> *type-name:*
>   *specifier-qualifier-list abstract-declarator$_{opt}$*
>
> *abstract-declarator:*
>   *pointer*
>   *pointer$_{opt}$ direct-abstract-declarator*
>
> *direct-abstract-declarator:*
>   (*abstract-declarator*)
>   *direct-abstract-declarator$_{opt}$* [*constant-expression$_{opt}$*]
>   *direct-abstract-declarator$_{opt}$* (*parameter-type-list$_{opt}$*)

Semantics

In several contexts, it is desired to specify a type. This is accomplished using a *type name*, which is syntactically a declaration for a function or an object of that type that omits the identifier.[73]

Example

The constructions

    (a)   `int`
    (b)   `int *`
    (c)   `int *[3]`
    (d)   `int (*)[3]`
    (e)   `int *()`
    (f)   `int (*)(void)`
    (g)   `int (*const [])(unsigned int, ...)`

name respectively the types (a) **int**, (b) pointer to **int**, (c) array of three pointers to **int**, (d) pointer to an array of three **int**s, (e) function with no parameter specification returning a pointer to **int**, (f) pointer to function with no parameters returning an **int**, and (g) array of an unspecified number of constant pointers to functions, each with one parameter that has type **unsigned int** and an unspecified number of other parameters, returning an **int**.

---

73 As indicated by the syntax, empty parentheses in a type name are interpreted as ''function with no parameter specification,'' rather than redundant parentheses around the omitted identifier.

6.5.5 Type names As the standard states, a type name is simply a name for a data type without any attendant identifier. Type names are often used in function prototypes, in which case no actual parameter names are technically required. For example, the following is a perfectly valid function prototype:

```
int f(int, float, char *);
```

Using parameter names in a function prototype helps the compiler generate more meaningful error messages (by allowing a mismatched parameter to be specified by its name), but is otherwise irrelevant.

You may want to pay special attention to the examples in this section, especially Examples (c) and (d). These show the difference between declaring an array of pointers and a pointer to an array type.

6.5.6   Type definitions

Syntax

> *typedef-name:*
>> *identifier*

Semantics

In a declaration whose storage-class specifier is **typedef**. each declarator defines an identifier to be a typedef name that specifies the type specified for the identifier in the way described in 6.5.4. A **typedef** declaration does not introduce a new type, only a synonym for the type so specified. That is, in the following declarations:

```
typedef T type_ident;
type_ident D;
```

type_ident is defined as a typedef name with the type specified by the declaration specifiers in **T** (known as *T*), and the identifier in **D** has the type "*der'... ...clarator-type-list T*" where the *derived-declarator-type-list* is specified by the declarators of **D**. A typedef name shares the same name space as other identifiers declared in ordinary declarators. If the identifier is redeclared in an inner scope or is declared as a member of a structure or union in the same or an inner scope, the type specifiers shall not be omitted in the inner declaration.

Examples

1.   After

```
typedef int MILES, KLICKSP();
typedef struct { double re, im; } complex;
```

the constructions

```
MILES distance;
extern KLICKSP *metricp;
complex x;
complex z, *zp;
```

are all valid declarations. The type of **distance** is **int**, that of **metricp** is "pointer to function with no parameter specification returning **int**," and that of **x** and **z** is the specified structure; **zp** is a pointer to such a structure. The object **distance** has a type compatible with any other **int** object.

2.   After the declarations

```
typedef struct s1 { int x; } t1, *tp1;
typedef struct s2 { int x; } t2, *tp2;
```

type **t1** and the type pointed to by **tp1** are compatible. Type **t1** is also compatible with type **struct s1**, but not compatible with the types **struct s2**, **t2**, the type pointed to by **tp2**, and **int**.

3.   The following obscure constructions

```
typedef signed int t;
typedef int plain;
struct tag {
        unsigned t:4;
        const t:5;
        plain r:5;
};
```

declare a typedef name **t** with type **signed int**, a typedef name **plain** with type **int**, and a structure with three bit-field members, one named **t** that contains values in the range

6.5.6 Type definitions The key to understanding **typedef** is that it does not create a new type. It simply creates a new name for an existing type. The explanation and examples in this section explain and illustrate typical uses of **typedef**. From a different perspective, consider that **typedef**s are useful for two main reasons: convenience and portability. Let's examine each.

First, convenience: One of the most convenient uses of **typedef** is to create a single-token structure type. The following declaration illustrates why this is useful:

```
struct s_type {
  int a;
  int b;
};
```

To declare a variable of type **s_type**, you must use this declaration:

```
struct s_type s_var;
```

There is certainly nothing whatsoever wrong with this declaration, but it does require two tokens, *struct* and *s_type*. If you apply **typedef** to the declaration of **s_type**, however, as shown here:

```
typedef struct _s_type {
  int a;
  int b;
} s_type; /* this is now the new type name */
```

then you can declare variables of this structure using the following declaration:

```
s_type var1, var2;
```

The point is that a **typedef** can sometimes simplify a complex declaration.

The second use for **typedef** is to support the creation of portable code. For example, if you create a program that is dependent upon the physical size of a data type, you might want to **typedef** that data type; that way, if it is ever recompiled for a different CPU or environment, only the **typedef** statement need be changed if the size of the type differs.

To understand this process, assume that you are creating a portable program that requires unsigned integers to be 2 bytes long. You know that an unsigned integer in your development environment is 2 bytes long, but it may be as long as 4 bytes in other situations. So you use a **typedef** to create a new type name for unsigned integers, as shown here:

```
typedef unsigned int WORD;
```

[0,15], an unnamed const-qualified bit-field which (if it could be accessed) would contain values in at least the range [−15,+15], and one named **r** that contains values in the range [0,31] or values in at least the range [−15,+15]. (The choice of range is implementation-defined.) The first two bit-field declarations differ in that **unsigned** is a type specifier (which forces **t** to be the name of a structure member), while **const** is a type qualifier (which modifies **t** which is still visible as a typedef name). If these declarations are followed in an inner scope by

```
t f(t (t));
long t;
```

then a function **f** is declared with type "function returning **signed int** with one unnamed parameter with type pointer to function returning **signed int** with one unnamed parameter with type **signed int**," and an identifier **t** with type **long**.

4. On the other hand, typedef names can be used to improve code readability. All three of the following declarations of the **signal** function specify exactly the same type, the first without making use of any typedef names.

```
typedef void fv(int), (*pfv)(int);

void (*signal(int, void (*)(int)))(int);
fv *signal(int, fv *);
pfv signal(int, pfv);
```

Forward references: the **signal** function (7.7.1.1).

6.5.7 Initialization

Syntax

> *initializer:*
>> *assignment-expression*
>> { *initializer-list* }
>> { *initializer-list* , }
>
> *initializer-list:*
>> *initializer*
>> *initializer-list* , *initializer*

Constraints

There shall be no more initializers in an initializer list than there are objects to be initialized.

The type of the entity to be initialized shall be an object type or an array of unknown size.

All the expressions in an initializer for an object that has static storage duration or in an initializer list for an object that has aggregate or union type shall be constant expressions.

If the declaration of an identifier has block scope, and the identifier has external or internal linkage, the declaration shall have no initializer for the identifier.

Semantics

An initializer specifies the initial value stored in an object.

All unnamed structure or union members are ignored during initialization.

If an object that has automatic storage duration is not initialized explicitly, its value is indeterminate.[74] If an object that has static storage duration is not initialized explicitly, it is

(*6.5.6 Type definitions,* continued)

Now, if **WORD** is used whenever you need an unsigned integer, when the program is ported to an environment only the **typedef** statement need be changed; all other references will be automatically corrected.

6.5.7 Initialization An *initialization* is the statement that gives an initial value to a variable when it is declared. The general form of an initialization is

   type var = initializer;

The type of the initializer must be compatible with that of the variable being declared. For example:

```
int i = 10;

double f = 1123.2387;
```

   The standard makes two significant statements about what occurs when an initialization is *not* present. First, an uninitialized local (that is, automatic) variable contains an unknown value. (Many compilers will set an uninitialized local variable to zero, but you must *never* assume this!) A global variable or a local variable that is declared as **static** will automatically be set to zero if no explicit initialization is present.

initialized implicitly as if every member that has arithmetic type were assigned 0 and every member that has pointer type were assigned a null pointer constant.

The initializer for a scalar shall be a single expression, optionally enclosed in braces. The initial value of the object is that of the expression; the same type constraints and conversions as for simple assignment apply, taking the type of the scalar to be the unqualified version of its declared type.

A brace-enclosed initializer for a union object initializes the member that appears first in the declaration list of the union type.

The initializer for a structure or union object that has automatic storage duration either shall be an initializer list as described below, or shall be a single expression that has compatible structure or union type. In the latter case, the initial value of the object is that of the expression.

The rest of this subclause deals with initializers for objects that have aggregate or union type.

An array of character type may be initialized by a character string literal, optionally enclosed in braces. Successive characters of the character string literal (including the terminating null character if there is room or if the array is of unknown size) initialize the elements of the array.

An array with element type compatible with **wchar_t** may be initialized by a wide string literal, optionally enclosed in braces. Successive codes of the wide string literal (including the terminating zero-valued code if there is room or if the array is of unknown size) initialize the elements of the array.

Otherwise, the initializer for an object that has aggregate type shall be a brace-enclosed list of initializers for the members of the aggregate, written in increasing subscript or member order; and the initializer for an object that has union type shall be a brace-enclosed initializer for the first member of the union.

If the aggregate contains members that are aggregates or unions, or if the first member of a union is an aggregate or union, the rules apply recursively to the subaggregates or contained unions. If the initializer of a subaggregate or contained union begins with a left brace, the initializers enclosed by that brace and its matching right brace initialize the members of the subaggregate or the first member of the contained union. Otherwise, only enough initializers from the list are taken to account for the members of the subaggregate or the first member of the contained union; any remaining initializers are left to initialize the next member of the aggregate of which the current subaggregate or contained union is a part.

If there are fewer initializers in a brace-enclosed list than there are members of an aggregate, the remainder of the aggregate shall be initialized implicitly the same as objects that have static storage duration.

If an array of unknown size is initialized, its size is determined by the number of initializers provided for its elements. At the end of its initializer list, the array no longer has incomplete type.

Examples

1. The declaration

        int x[] = { 1, 3, 5 };

    defines and initializes **x** as a one-dimensional array object that has three elements, as no size was specified and there are three initializers.

---

74 Unlike in the base document, any automatic duration object may be initialized.

(*6.5.7 Initialization,* continued)

The standard is quite clear and thorough in its treatment of initializations. However, here are less formal explanations of some of the more common initializations.

Arrays are initialized by specifying the initializers using a comma-separated list enclosed between curly braces. For example, this initializes the array **count** with the values 1 through 10:

```
int count[10] = {1, 2, 3, 4, 5, 6, 7, 8, 9, 10};
```

Multidimensional arrays are initialized in the same fashion, with the initializers being assigned in storage order. For example, this fragment displays the numbers 1 through 10:

```
int i, j;
int count[2][5] = {1, 2, 3, 4, 5, 6, 7, 8, 9, 10};

for(i=0; i<2; i++)
  for(j=0; j<5; j++) printf("%d ", count[i][j]);
```

If you don't specify sufficient initializers to fill an array, the remaining elements are filled with zeros.

Although the preceding initialization form for a multidimensional array is perfectly valid (and commonly used), you may also bracket each row in the array (called a *subaggregate* by the standard). Doing so makes the initialization look like this:

```
int count[2][5] = {
  {1, 2, 3, 4, 5},
  {6, 7, 8, 9, 10}
};
```

When using subaggregate groupings, if you don't supply enough initializers in a subgroup, the remaining members of that group are initialized to zero. For example:

```
int count[2][5] = {
  {1, 2, 3},
  {6, 7, 8, 9, 10}
};
```

Here, elements **count[0][3]** and **count[0][4]** are initialized to 0.

2. The declaration

```
float y[4][3] = {
        { 1, 3, 5 },
        { 2, 4, 6 },
        { 3, 5, 7 },
};
```

is a definition with a fully bracketed initialization: 1, 3, and 5 initialize the first row of **y** (the array object **y[0]**), namely **y[0][0]**, **y[0][1]**, and **y[0][2]**. Likewise the next two lines initialize **y[1]** and **y[2]**. The initializer ends early, so **y[3]** is initialized with zeros. Precisely the same effect could have been achieved by

```
float y[4][3] = {
        1, 3, 5, 2, 4, 6, 3, 5, 7
};
```

The initializer for **y[0]** does not begin with a left brace, so three items from the list are used. Likewise the next three are taken successively for **y[1]** and **y[2]**.

3. The declaration

```
float z[4][3] = {
        { 1 }, { 2 }, { 3 }, { 4 }
};
```

initializes the first column of **z** as specified and initializes the rest with zeros.

4. The declaration

```
struct { int a[3], b; } w[] = { { 1 }, 2 };
```

is a definition with an inconsistently bracketed initialization. It defines an array with two element structures: **w[0].a[0]** is 1 and **w[1].a[0]** is 2; all the other elements are zero.

5. The declaration

```
short q[4][3][2] = {
        { 1 },
        { 2, 3 },
        { 4, 5, 6 }
};
```

contains an incompletely but consistently bracketed initialization. It defines a three-dimensional array object: **q[0][0][0]** is 1, **q[1][0][0]** is 2, **q[1][0][1]** is 3, and 4, 5, and 6 initialize **q[2][0][0]**, **q[2][0][1]**, and **q[2][1][0]**, respectively; all the rest are zero. The initializer for **q[0][0]** does not begin with a left brace, so up to six items from the current list may be used. There is only one, so the values for the remaining five elements are initialized with zero. Likewise, the initializers for **q[1][0]** and **q[2][0]** do not begin with a left brace, so each uses up to six items, initializing their respective two-dimensional subaggregates. If there had been more than six items in any of the lists, a diagnostic message would have been issued. The same initialization result could have been achieved by:

```
short q[4][3][2] = {
        1, 0, 0, 0, 0, 0,
        2, 3, 0, 0, 0, 0,
        4, 5, 6
};
```

or by:

(*6.5.7 Initialization,* continued)

You don't have to specify the size of an array when it is initialized. For example, the following creates a ten-element integer array initialized to the values 1 through 10:

```
int count[] = {1, 2, 3, 4, 5, 6, 7, 8, 9, 10};
```

You may use a string literal to initialize a character array. In this case, the string may be enclosed between double quotation marks. This example shows two ways to initialize an array with the string "Hi":

```
char s1[] = {'H', 'i', '\0'};
char s2[] = "Hi";
```

Both of these declarations declare arrays that contain a null-terminated string. In the first case, the null must be included manually. In the second, it is automatically added by the compiler.

Global variables and **static** local variables must be initialized using only constants. It is common to initialize local nonstatic variables using constants, but you may use any identifier in the scope of the declaration, including a function call. For example, this is a valid fragment:

```
void f()
{
   int i = atoi("9673");
```

Because **i** is a nonstatic local variable, it may call the standard library function **atoi()** (which returns the integer equivalent of its string argument) to provide an initial value.

```
short q[4][3][2] = {
        {
                { 1 },
        },
        {
                { 2, 3 },
        },
        {
                { 4, 5 },
                { 6 },
        }
};
```

in a fully bracketed form.

Note that the fully bracketed and minimally bracketed forms of initialization are, in general, less likely to cause confusion.

6. One form of initialization that completes array types involves typedef names. Given the declaration

```
typedef int A[];
```

the declaration

```
A a = {1, 2}, b = {3, 4, 5};
```

is identical to

```
int a[] = {1, 2}, b[] = {3, 4, 5};
```

due to the rules for incomplete types.

7. The declaration

```
char s[] = "abc", t[3] = "abc";
```

defines "plain" **char** array objects **s** and **t** whose elements are initialized with character string literals. This declaration is identical to

```
char s[] = { 'a', 'b', 'c', '\0' },
     t[] = { 'a', 'b', 'c' };
```

The contents of the arrays are modifiable. On the other hand, the declaration

```
char *p = "abc";
```

defines **p** with type "pointer to **char**" that is initialized to point to an object with type "array of **char**" with length 4 whose elements are initialized with a character string literal. If an attempt is made to use **p** to modify the contents of the array, the behavior is undefined.

Forward references: common definitions **<stddef.h>** (7.1.5).

There are no annotations for page 74.

6.6 Statements

Syntax

> *statement:*
>> *labeled-statement*
>> *compound-statement*
>> *expression-statement*
>> *selection-statement*
>> *iteration-statement*
>> *jump-statement*

Semantics

A *statement* specifies an action to be performed. Except as indicated, statements are executed in sequence.

A *full expression* is an expression that is not part of another expression. Each of the following is a full expression: an initializer; the expression in an expression statement; the controlling expression of a selection statement (**if** or **switch**); the controlling expression of a **while** or **do** statement; each of the three (optional) expressions of a **for** statement; the (optional) expression in a **return** statement. The end of a full expression is a sequence point.

Forward references: expression and null statements (6.6.3), selection statements (6.6.4), iteration statements (6.6.5), the **return** statement (6.6.6.4).

6.6.1 Labeled statements

Syntax

> *labeled-statement:*
>> *identifier* : *statement*
>> **case** *constant-expression* : *statement*
>> **default** : *statement*

Constraints

A **case** or **default** label shall appear only in a **switch** statement. Further constraints on such labels are discussed under the **switch** statement.

Semantics

Any statement may be preceded by a prefix that declares an identifier as a label name. Labels in themselves do not alter the flow of control, which continues unimpeded across them.

Forward references: the **goto** statement (6.6.6.1), the **switch** statement (6.6.4.2).

6.6.2 Compound statement, or block

Syntax

> *compound-statement:*
>> { *declaration-list*$_{opt}$ *statement-list*$_{opt}$ }
>
> *declaration-list:*
>> *declaration*
>> *declaration-list declaration*
>
> *statement-list:*
>> *statement*
>> *statement-list statement*

6.6 Statements Aside from preprocessor directives, a C program contains two general categories of instructions: statements and declarations. The preceding section described declarations. This section discusses C's statements. As the standard says, a *statement* performs an *action*. The standard defines six types of statements: labeled, compound, expression, selection, iteration, and jump. In the C syntax, a statement may also be null.

Many of the C statements rely upon the concept of true and false. (Remember, in C, true is any nonzero value, and false is zero.)

6.6.1 Labeled statements A labeled statement is either a **case** or **default** statement within a **switch** statement, or a label, which may be the target of the **goto**. A label is an identifier followed by a colon. For example, here are some labels:

done: skip: sig1:

6.6.2 Compound statement, or block A compound statement is what most C programmers commonly call a *block*. A block creates a logical unit and defines a scope. Variables defined within a block are local variables that are created when that block is entered, and destroyed upon exit. Variables defined within a block are known only within the scope of that block and not outside of it.

A block may be the target of another statement or may simply exist on its own. The following program illustrates the use of a stand-alone block:

```
#include <stdio.h>

main(void)
{
  int i; /* this is in the main block */

  i = 10;
  { /* begin a block */
    int i; /* this is local to block */
    /* these statements refer to i in inner block */
    i = 1000;
    printf("i in inner block: %d\n", i);
  }
  /* this uses i in main block */
  printf("i in outer block: %d\n", i);
  return 0;
}
```

Semantics

A *compound statement* (also called a *block*) allows a set of statements to be grouped into one syntactic unit, which may have its own set of declarations and initializations (as discussed in 6.1.2.4). The initializers of objects that have automatic storage duration are evaluated and the values are stored in the objects in the order their declarators appear in the translation unit.

6.6.3 Expression and null statements

Syntax

> *expression-statement:*
> > *expression*$_{opt}$;

Semantics

The expression in an expression statement is evaluated as a void expression for its side effects.[75]

A *null statement* (consisting of just a semicolon) performs no operations.

Examples

1. If a function call is evaluated as an expression statement for its side effects only, the discarding of its value may be made explicit by converting the expression to a void expression by means of a cast:

    ```
    int p(int);
    /*...*/
    (void)p(0);
    ```

2. In the program fragment

    ```
    char *s;
    /*...*/
    while (*s++ != '\0')
        ;
    ```

    a null statement is used to supply an empty loop body to the iteration statement.

3. A null statement may also be used to carry a label just before the closing } of a compound statement.

    ```
    while (loop1) {
        /*...*/
        while (loop2) {
            /*...*/
            if (want_out)
                goto end_loop1;
            /*...*/
        }
        /*...*/
    end_loop1: ;
    }
    ```

Forward references: iteration statements (6.6.5).

---

75 Such as assignments, and function calls which have side effects.

(*6.6.2 Compound statement, or block,* continued)

This program displays the following:

i in inner block: 1000

i in outer block: 10

As you can see, **i** in the inner block is separate from the **i** in the outer block.

6.6.3   *Expression and null statements*   In simple terms, an *expression statement* is a stand-alone expression that is evaluated. The most common form of an expression statement is the function call. For example, the following three lines are expression statements:

```
printf("Enter a string: ");
gets(s);
strcpy(p, s);
```

Each expression is evaluated so that the functions involved are executed. Remember, the standard uses the term *side effect* for actions performed by functions. In this context, side effect does not have a negative connotation.

Statements may be empty. For example, the following is a common way to create a time-delay loop:

```
for(x=0; x<10000; x++) ; /* do nothing */
```

In this case, a null statement is the target of the **for** loop.

6.6.4 Selection statements

Syntax

> *selection-statement:*
>> **if** **(** *expression* **)** *statement*
>> **if** **(** *expression* **)** *statement* **else** *statement*
>> **switch** **(** *expression* **)** *statement*

Semantics

A selection statement selects among a set of statements depending on the value of a controlling expression.

6.6.4.1 The **if** statement

Constraints

The controlling expression of an **if** statement shall have scalar type.

Semantics

In both forms, the first substatement is executed if the expression compares unequal to 0. In the **else** form, the second substatement is executed if the expression compares equal to 0. If the first substatement is reached via a label, the second substatement is not executed.

An **else** is associated with the lexically immediately preceding **else**-less **if** that is in the same block (but not in an enclosed block).

6.6.4.2 The **switch** statement

Constraints

The controlling expression of a **switch** statement shall have integral type. The expression of each **case** label shall be an integral constant expression. No two of the **case** constant expressions in the same **switch** statement shall have the same value after conversion. There may be at most one **default** label in a **switch** statement. (Any enclosed **switch** statement may have a **default** label or **case** constant expressions with values that duplicate **case** constant expressions in the enclosing **switch** statement.)

Semantics

A **switch** statement causes control to jump to, into, or past the statement that is the *switch body*, depending on the value of a controlling expression, and on the presence of a **default** label and the values of any **case** labels on or in the switch body. A **case** or **default** label is accessible only within the closest enclosing **switch** statement.

The integral promotions are performed on the controlling expression. The constant expression in each **case** label is converted to the promoted type of the controlling expression. If a converted value matches that of the promoted controlling expression, control jumps to the statement following the matched **case** label. Otherwise, if there is a **default** label, control jumps to the labeled statement. If no converted **case** constant expression matches and there is no **default** label, no part of the switch body is executed.

Implementation limits

As discussed previously (5.2.4.1), the implementation may limit the number of **case** values in a **switch** statement.

Example

In the artificial program fragment

6.6.4   *Selection statements*   What the standard calls *selection statements* are also commonly called *conditional statements*. A selection statement chooses alternative execution paths based upon the outcome of some condition. The selection statements are the **if** and the **switch**.

6.6.4.1   *The if statement*   The general form of the **if** statement is

> if(*exp*) *statement1*;
> else *statement2*;

The value of the expression *exp* determines whether *statement1* or *statement2* is executed. If *exp* is nonzero (true), then *statement1* executes. If *exp* is zero (false), then *statement2* executes. In no circumstance do both statements execute during a single execution of the **if**.

The targets of either or both the **if** and the **else** may also be blocks. Further, the **else** statement is optional. If the **else** is not present and the value of *exp* is false, no action takes place and execution begins with the next line of code following the **if**. In the case of nested **if**s, an **else** always associates with the closest **if** within the same block that does not already have an **else** associated with it. For example, in this case:

```
if(exp1)
   if(exp2) printf("2nd if");
   else printf("alternative to 2nd if");
```

the indentation illustrates the **if** to which the **else** is linked.

6.6.4.2   *The switch statement*   A **switch** statement selects between two or more different execution paths. The general form of the **switch** is

> switch(*exp*) {
>   case const1: *statement sequence*
>   break;
>   case const2: *statement sequence*
>   break;
>   ...
>   case constN: *statement sequence*
>   break;
>   default: *statement sequence*
> }

```
switch (expr)
{
        int i = 4;
        f(i);
case 0:
        i = 17;    /* falls through into default code */
default:
        printf("%d\n", i);
}
```

the object whose identifier is **i** exists with automatic storage duration (within the block) but is never initialized, and thus if the controlling expression has a nonzero value, the call to the **printf** function will access an indeterminate value. Similarly, the call to the function **f** cannot be reached.

6.6.5 Iteration statements

Syntax

iteration-statement:
        while (*expression*) *statement*
        do *statement* **while** (*expression*) ;
        for (*expression*$_{opt}$; *expression*$_{opt}$; *expression*$_{opt}$) *statement*

Constraints

The controlling expression of an iteration statement shall have scalar type.

Semantics

An iteration statement causes a statement called the *loop body* to be executed repeatedly until the controlling expression compares equal to 0.

6.6.5.1 The while statement

The evaluation of the controlling expression takes place before each execution of the loop body.

6.6.5.2 The do statement

The evaluation of the controlling expression takes place after each execution of the loop body.

6.6.5.3 The for statement

Except for the behavior of a **continue** statement in the loop body, the statement

    for (*expression-1* ; *expression-2* ; *expression-3*) *statement*

and the sequence of statements

    expression-1 ;
    while (*expression-2*) {
        statement
        expression-3 ;
    }

are equivalent.[76]

---

76 Thus, *expression-1* specifies initialization for the loop; *expression-2*, the controlling expression, specifies an evaluation made before each iteration, such that execution of the loop continues until the expression compares equal to 0; *expression-3* specifies an operation (such as incrementing) that is performed after each iteration.

(*6.6.4.2 The switch statement,* continued)

The execution path is chosen when a match occurs between the value of *exp* and one of the constants in a **case** statement. If no match occurs, then the **default** case is executed. However, the **default** statement is optional; if it does not exist (and no constant is matched), no action takes place. The **break** statements are also optional, and if they're not present, execution simply continues into the next **case** or into the **default** statement. The type of *exp* and the **case** constants must be integral.

One additional point: The statements associated with a **case** do not form a block. Instead, they are simply sequences of related statements.

The following fragment illustrates the **switch** statement:

```
int i=2;
switch(i) {
  case 1: printf("case 1\n");
    break;
  case 2: printf("case 2 with no break, plus\n");
  case 3: printf("case 3\n");
    break;
  default: printf("default case\n");
}
```

Since **i** is 2, **case** 2 is matched and this fragment is displayed:

```
case 2 with no break, plus
case 3
```

Because there is no **break** statement ending **case** 2's statement sequence, **case** 2 falls through into **case** 3.

6.6.5 Iteration statements The C *iteration* (loop) statements are **for**, **while**, and **do-while**. Loops are controlled by scalar expressions. (A scalar is either an arithmetic or pointer type.) Loops continue to execute as long as the controlling expression is true (nonzero). Also, remember that an expression includes such things as function calls and can be as simple as a single variable or constant.

6.6.5.1 The while statement through 6.6.5.3 The for statement The standard gives the general form of the **while**, **do**, and **for** statements. Of course, the target of these loops may also be blocks. Because these loops are well known to even beginning C programmers, only the following points of interest are presented here.

The **do-while** is the only C loop that will always execute at least once, because its conditional expression is checked at the bottom of the loop. (The other loops test the condition at the top.)

Both *expression-1* and *expression-3* may be omitted. Each is evaluated as a void expression. An omitted *expression-2* is replaced by a nonzero constant.

Forward references: the `continue` statement (6.6.6.2).

6.6.6 Jump statements

Syntax

> *jump-statement:*
>> `goto` *identifier* `;`
>> `continue` `;`
>> `break` `;`
>> `return` *expression*$_{opt}$ `;`

Semantics

A jump statement causes an unconditional jump to another place.

6.6.6.1 The `goto` statement

Constraints

The identifier in a `goto` statement shall name a label located somewhere in the enclosing function.

Semantics

A `goto` statement causes an unconditional jump to the statement prefixed by the named label in the enclosing function.

Example

It is sometimes convenient to jump into the middle of a complicated set of statements. The following outline presents one possible approach to a problem based on these three assumptions:

1. The general initialization code accesses objects only visible to the current function.

2. The general initialization code is too large to warrant duplication.

3. The code to determine the next operation must be at the head of the loop. (To allow it to be reached by `continue` statements, for example.)

```
/*...*/
goto first_time;
for (;;) {
        /* determine next operation */
        /*...*/
        if (need to reinitialize) {
                /* reinitialize-only code */
                /*...*/
        first_time:
                /* general initialization code */
                /*...*/
                continue;
        }
        /* handle other operations */
        /*...*/

}
```

(*6.6.5.1 through 6.6.5.3,* continued)

The expressions in a **for** loop are optional. When the second expression (the conditional expression) is missing, the loop will run forever. The most common way to create an intentional infinite loop is shown here:

```
for( ; ; ) /* ... */ ;
```

6.6.6 *Jump statements* Most C programmers think of the **goto** as being C's only jump statement, but the standard defines three additional jump statements: **continue**, **break**, and **return**. One reason for categorizing these as jump statements is that each one causes execution to unconditionally transfer to another place (although calling **return** a *jump* statement is a bit artificial).

6.6.6.1 *The goto statement* The **goto** is C's unconditional jump. It jumps to the specified label, bypassing any intervening code. Jumps may occur in a forward or backward direction. Here is **goto**'s general form:

```
goto label;
/* ... */
label:
```

where *label* is the label that is **goto**'s target.

Keep in mind that a **goto** statement will only transfer execution to another location within the same function in which the **goto** statement occurs; it is not possible to jump to another function. (It *is* possible to execute an interfunction jump by using **setjmp()** and **longjmp()**. However, this is a specialized action.)

Though use of the **goto** is discouraged (or not even supported) by other languages, it is occasionally employed in C programs to jump out of (or into) deeply nested routines—often when a catastrophic error occurs. For example, here the **goto** exits a set of nested loops if an error occurs:

```
while(x) {
  do {
    for(i=0; i<100; i++) {
      /* ... */
      if(error) goto done; /* jump on error */
    }
  } while(!over);
}
done: /* continue after error ... */
```

6.6.6.2 The `continue` statement

Constraints

A `continue` statement shall appear only in or as a loop body.

Semantics

A `continue` statement causes a jump to the loop-continuation portion of the smallest enclosing iteration statement; that is, to the end of the loop body. More precisely, in each of the statements

```
while (/*...*/) {          do {                      for (/*...*/) {
   /*...*/                    /*...*/                    /*...*/
   continue;                 continue;                 continue;
   /*...*/                    /*...*/                   /*...*/
contin: ;                  contin: ;                 contin: ;
}                          } while (/*...*/);        }
```

unless the `continue` statement shown is in an enclosed iteration statement (in which case it is interpreted within that statement), it is equivalent to **goto contin;** .[77]

6.6.6.3 The `break` statement

Constraints

A `break` statement shall appear only in or as a switch body or loop body.

Semantics

A `break` statement terminates execution of the smallest enclosing **switch** or iteration statement.

6.6.6.4 The `return` statement

Constraints

A `return` statement with an expression shall not appear in a function whose return type is **void**.

Semantics

A `return` statement terminates execution of the current function and returns control to its caller. A function may have any number of **return** statements, with and without expressions.

If a `return` statement with an expression is executed, the value of the expression is returned to the caller as the value of the function call expression. If the expression has a type different from that of the function in which it appears, it is converted as if it were assigned to an object of that type.

If a `return` statement without an expression is executed, and the value of the function call is used by the caller, the behavior is undefined. Reaching the **}** that terminates a function is equivalent to executing a **return** statement without an expression.

---

77 Following the `contin:` label is a null statement.

6.6.6.2 The continue statement The **continue** statement causes the next iteration of the enclosing loop to take place. In the case of the **while** or **do-while**, execution jumps to the conditional expression. In the **for**, execution jumps to the increment expression and then to the conditional expression. For example, the following code prints the numbers 0 through 9:

```
for(i=0; i<10; i++) {
  printf("%d", i);
  continue;
}
```

The **continue** statement may only be used within a loop.

6.6.6.3 The break statement The **break** statement has two uses. In a **switch** statement, it causes the termination of a statement sequence, thus terminating the **switch** (see Section 6.6.4.2). When used in a loop, **break** causes the immediate termination of the loop. For example, this fragment prints only the numbers 1 through 5:

```
for(i=0; i<10; i++) {
  printf("%d", i);
  if(i==5) break; /* stop the loop at 5 */
}
```

6.6.6.4 The return statement The **return** statement causes a function to immediately return to the routine that called it. The **return** statement has these two forms:

```
return ; /* return no value */
return exp; /* return a value */
```

If the function has a return type other than **void**, then the second form of the **return** statement is used to return the value of *exp* to the calling routine. If the function is declared as returning **void**, then the first form of **return** causes the function to terminate but does not pass any value back to the caller. Technically, even if the function has a non-**void** return type, the function need not actually return a value. However, the caller will then receive an indeterminate value.

Unlike many other computer languages, in C a single function may have two or more **return** statements. The use of multiple **return** statements can greatly simplify certain algorithms.

Note that the standard formally states that reaching the closing curly brace of a function is the equivalent of executing a **return** statement without a value. Thus, functions do not have to include a **return** statement if one is not needed.

6.7 External definitions

Syntax

> *translation-unit:*
> > *external-declaration*
> > *translation-unit external-declaration*
>
> *external-declaration:*
> > *function-definition*
> > *declaration*

Constraints

The storage-class specifiers **auto** and **register** shall not appear in the declaration specifiers in an external declaration.

There shall be no more than one external definition for each identifier declared with internal linkage in a translation unit. Moreover, if an identifier declared with internal linkage is used in an expression (other than as a part of the operand of a **sizeof** operator), there shall be exactly one external definition for the identifier in the translation unit.

Semantics

As discussed in 5.1.1.1, the unit of program text after preprocessing is a translation unit, which consists of a sequence of external declarations. These are described as "external" because they appear outside any function (and hence have file scope). As discussed in 6.5, a declaration that also causes storage to be reserved for an object or a function named by the identifier is a definition.

An *external definition* is an external declaration that is also a definition of a function or an object. If an identifier declared with external linkage is used in an expression (other than as part of the operand of a **sizeof** operator), somewhere in the entire program there shall be exactly one external definition for the identifier; otherwise, there shall be no more than one.[78]

6.7.1 Function definitions

Syntax

> *function-definition:*
> > *declaration-specifiers*$_{opt}$ *declarator declaration-list*$_{opt}$ *compound-statement*

Constraints

The identifier declared in a function definition (which is the name of the function) shall have a function type, as specified by the declarator portion of the function definition.[79]

---

78 Thus, if an identifier declared with external linkage is not used in an expression, there need be no external definition for it.

79 The intent is that the type category in a function definition cannot be inherited from a typedef:

```
typedef int F(void);          /* type F is "function of no arguments returning int" */
F f, g;                       /* f and g both have type compatible with F */
F f { /*...*/ }               /* WRONG: syntax/constraint error */
F g() { /*...*/ }             /* WRONG: declares that g returns a function */
int f(void) { /*...*/ }       /* RIGHT: f has type compatible with F */
int g() { /*...*/ }           /* RIGHT: g has type compatible with F */
F *e(void) { /*...*/ }        /* e returns a pointer to a function */
F *((e))(void) { /*...*/ }    /* same: parentheses irrelevant */
int (*fp)(void);              /* fp points to a function that has type F */
F *Fp;                        /* Fp points to a function that has type F */
```

6.7 External definitions An *external definition* refers to something that has file scope. It is something that is defined outside of a function. Thus, an external definition is either a function or a global variable definition.

The language of this section is a bit obscure, so here are its main points: First, the specifiers **auto** and **register** cannot be used on global variables. Second, each global variable or function can be defined only once within a program. (See sections 6.7.1 and 6.7.2.)

6.7.1 Function definitions C defines two types of *function definition* styles: the old form and the modern form. The general form of a modern function definition is shown here:

```
type func-name(param-list)
{
  /* body of function */
}
```

where *type* is the return type of the function, *func-name* is the name of the function, and *param-list* specifies a comma-separated list of the parameters to the function. Each parameter must include its own type specifier. The parameter list may also be declared as **void** when no parameters are required. If the return type of the function is not specified, it is automatically defaulted to **int**.

The return type of a function shall be **void** or an object type other than array.

The storage-class specifier, if any, in the declaration specifiers shall be either **extern** or **static**.

If the declarator includes a parameter type list, the declaration of each parameter shall include an identifier (except for the special case of a parameter list consisting of a single parameter of type **void**, in which there shall not be an identifier). No declaration list shall follow.

If the declarator includes an identifier list, each declaration in the declaration list shall have at least one declarator, and those declarators shall declare only identifiers from the identifier list. An identifier declared as a typedef name shall not be redeclared as a parameter. The declarations in the declaration list shall contain no storage-class specifier other than **register** and no initializations.

Semantics

The declarator in a function definition specifies the name of the function being defined and the identifiers of its parameters. If the declarator includes a parameter type list, the list also specifies the types of all the parameters; such a declarator also serves as a function prototype for later calls to the same function in the same translation unit. If the declarator includes an identifier list,[80] the types of the parameters may be declared in a following declaration list. Any parameter that is not declared has type **int**.

If a function that accepts a variable number of arguments is defined without a parameter type list that ends with the ellipsis notation, the behavior is undefined.

On entry to the function the value of each argument expression shall be converted to the type of its corresponding parameter, as if by assignment to the parameter. Array expressions and function designators as arguments are converted to pointers before the call. A declaration of a parameter as ''array of *type*'' shall be adjusted to ''pointer to *type*,'' and a declaration of a parameter as ''function returning *type*'' shall be adjusted to ''pointer to function returning *type*,'' as in 6.2.2.1. The resulting parameter type shall be an object type.

Each parameter has automatic storage duration. Its identifier is an lvalue.[81] The layout of the storage for parameters is unspecified.

Examples

1. In the following:

    ```
    extern int max(int a, int b)
    {
            return a > b ? a : b;
    }
    ```

    extern is the storage-class specifier and **int** is the type specifier (each of which may be omitted as those are the defaults); **max(int a, int b)** is the function declarator; and

    ```
    { return a > b ? a : b; }
    ```

    is the function body. The following similar definition uses the identifier-list form for the parameter declarations:

---

80 See ''future language directions'' (6.9.5).

81 A parameter is in effect declared at the head of the compound statement that constitutes the function body, and therefore may not be redeclared in the function body (except in an enclosed block).

(**6.7.1 Function definitions,** *continued*)

The old form of a function definition looks like this:

type func-name(identifier-list)
parameter-declarations
{
* /* body of function */*
}

In this case, only the parameter names are specified in the identifier list. The parameters are actually declared in the *parameter-declaration*. This old form of a function definition is currently accepted for compatibility with older C code. It should not be used for new programs.

To understand the difference between the modern and old forms, here is the same function defined using both forms:

```
/* Modern function definition. */
float f(int a, char c)
{
    /* ... */
}


/* Old-form function definition. */
float f(a, c)
int a;
char c;
{
    /* ... */
}
```

One important point about the old-form function definition is that it does not serve as a prototype for the function. Thus, using the old form allows a function to be called with the incorrect number or type of parameters, without any error messages being issued by the compiler.

Because the old-form function declaration is supported by the standard for compatibility with older programs, its use is not recommended for new programs. Also, it is possible that future revisions to the C standard will drop support for the old form altogether.

```
extern int max(a, b)
int a, b;
{
        return a > b ? a : b;
}
```

Here **int a, b;** is the declaration list for the parameters, which may be omitted because those are the defaults. The difference between these two definitions is that the first form acts as a prototype declaration that forces conversion of the arguments of subsequent calls to the function, whereas the second form may not.

2. To pass one function to another, one might say

```
int f(void);
/*...*/
g(f);
```

Note that **f** must be declared explicitly in the calling function, as its appearance in the expression **g(f)** was not followed by **(**. Then the definition of **g** might read

```
g(int (*funcp)(void))
{
        /*...*/ (*funcp)() /* or funcp() ... */
}
```

or, equivalently,

```
g(int func(void))
{
        /*...*/ func() /* or (*func)() ... */
}
```

6.7.2 External object definitions

Semantics

If the declaration of an identifier for an object has file scope and an initializer, the declaration is an external definition for the identifier.

A declaration of an identifier for an object that has file scope without an initializer, and without a storage-class specifier or with the storage-class specifier **static**, constitutes a *tentative definition*. If a translation unit contains one or more tentative definitions for an identifier, and the translation unit contains no external definition for that identifier, then the behavior is exactly as if the translation unit contains a file scope declaration of that identifier, with the composite type as of the end of the translation unit, with an initializer equal to 0.

If the declaration of an identifier for an object is a tentative definition and has internal linkage, the declared type shall not be an incomplete type.

Example

```
int i1 = 1;             /* definition, external linkage */
static int i2 = 2;      /* definition, internal linkage */
extern int i3 = 3;      /* definition, external linkage */
int i4;                 /* tentative definition, external linkage */
static int i5;          /* tentative definition, internal linkage */
```

(*6.7.1 Function definitions, continued*)

Although discussed by the standard earlier (see Section 6.3.2.2), it is again formally stated here that a function cannot return an array. You can, however, return a pointer, which may alleviate this restriction in some cases.

To declare a function that takes a variable number of parameters, end its parameter list with an ellipsis. To access variable length arguments, you must utilize the standard library macros **va_arg()**, **va_start()**, and **va_end()**.

6.7.2 External object definitions   Though the C language allows a global variable to be *declared* more than once (in different files, perhaps), it does not allow a global variable to be *defined* more than once. (Remember, a declaration specifies the type of variable. A definition allocates storage for the variable.)

The standard states that when a global variable declaration contains an initializer, then this statement is also a definition of the variable, and storage is allocated for it. When a global variable declaration does *not* include an initializer, it temporarily becomes a *tentative definition*. If, by the end of the file (translation unit), no other definition is specified, then the tentative definition becomes the actual definition and the variable is given the default initial value 0.

It is important to understand that even when a global variable is declared using the **extern** storage-class specifier, if that declaration includes an initialization, it then becomes a definition for that variable. For example, this fragment is wrong because it attempts to define **count** twice:

```
/* this is wrong */
extern int count = 10;
int count = 10;
```

In this case, both declarations of **count** are also definitions, and this is not allowed. However, this is perfectly legal:

```
/* this is OK */
extern int count;
int count = 10;
```

Here the **extern** declaration is not a definition, because no initializer is present.

```
int i1;              /* valid tentative definition, refers to previous */
int i2;              /* 6.1.2.2 renders undefined, linkage disagreement */
int i3;              /* valid tentative definition, refers to previous */
int i4;              /* valid tentative definition, refers to previous */
int i5;              /* 6.1.2.2 renders undefined, linkage disagreement */

extern int i1;       /* refers to previous, whose linkage is external */
extern int i2;       /* refers to previous, whose linkage is internal */
extern int i3;       /* refers to previous, whose linkage is external */
extern int i4;       /* refers to previous, whose linkage is external */
extern int i5;       /* refers to previous, whose linkage is internal */
```

There are no annotations for page 84.

6.8 Preprocessing directives

Syntax

preprocessing-file:
> *group*_{opt}

group:
> *group-part*
> *group group-part*

group-part:
> *pp-tokens*_{opt} *new-line*
> *if-section*
> *control-line*

if-section:
> *if-group elif-groups*_{opt} *else-group*_{opt} *endif-line*

if-group:
> **# if**   *constant-expression new-line group*_{opt}
> **# ifdef**   *identifier new-line group*_{opt}
> **# ifndef** *identifier new-line group*_{opt}

elif-groups:
> *elif-group*
> *elif-groups elif-group*

elif-group:
> **# elif**   *constant-expression new-line group*_{opt}

else-group:
> **# else**   *new-line group*_{opt}

endif-line:
> **# endif**   *new-line*

control-line:
> **# include** *pp-tokens new-line*
> **# define**   *identifier replacement-list new-line*
> **# define**   *identifier lparen identifier-list*_{opt}) *replacement-list new-line*
> **# undef**   *identifier new-line*
> **# line**   *pp-tokens new-line*
> **# error**   *pp-tokens*_{opt} *new-line*
> **# pragma** *pp-tokens*_{opt} *new-line*
> **#**   *new-line*

lparen:
> the left-parenthesis character without preceding white-space

replacement-list:
> *pp-tokens*_{opt}

pp-tokens:
> *preprocessing-token*
> *pp-tokens preprocessing-token*

new-line:
> the new-line character

6.8   *Preprocessing directives*   This section of the standard discusses the preprocessor and its directives. The C preprocessor is the part of the compiler that performs initial text substitutions, manipulations, conditional inclusion, and various other activities that occur prior to the translation of your source code into object code.

The preprocessor directives are *not* C keywords. They *are*, however, an integral part of most C programs and substantially expand the programming environment. Unlike most other computer languages, C relies heavily on the preprocessor to accomplish several fundamental programming goals, including

◆ Portability (through directives such as **#define**, **#if**, and **#ifdef**)

◆ Source code control and maintenance (using **#include** and **#pragma**)

◆ Debugging (using **#error**, **#line**, and conditional compilation)

◆ Implementation-specific instructions (through **#pragma**)

◆ In-line expansion of code, rather than function calls (using function-like **#define**s)

In addition to the preprocessing directives, the C preprocessor also contains three preprocessing operators: **defined, #**, and **##**.

Description

A preprocessing directive consists of a sequence of preprocessing tokens that begins with a **#** preprocessing token that is either the first character in the source file (optionally after white space containing no new-line characters) or that follows white space containing at least one new-line character, and is ended by the next new-line character.[82]

Constraints

The only white-space characters that shall appear between preprocessing tokens within a preprocessing directive (from just after the introducing **#** preprocessing token through just before the terminating new-line character) are space and horizontal-tab (including spaces that have replaced comments or possibly other white-space characters in translation phase 3).

Semantics

The implementation can process and skip sections of source files conditionally, include other source files, and replace macros. These capabilities are called *preprocessing*, because conceptually they occur before translation of the resulting translation unit.

The preprocessing tokens within a preprocessing directive are not subject to macro expansion unless otherwise stated.

6.8.1 Conditional inclusion

Constraints

The expression that controls conditional inclusion shall be an integral constant expression except that: it shall not contain a cast; identifiers (including those lexically identical to keywords) are interpreted as described below;[83] and it may contain unary operator expressions of the form

> **defined** *identifier*

or

> **defined** (*identifier*)

which evaluate to 1 if the identifier is currently defined as a macro name (that is, if it is predefined or if it has been the subject of a **#define** preprocessing directive without an intervening **#undef** directive with the same subject identifier), 0 if it is not.

Each preprocessing token that remains after all macro replacements have occurred shall be in the lexical form of a token.

Semantics

Preprocessing directives of the forms

> **# if**   *constant-expression new-line group*$_{opt}$
> **# elif** *constant-expression new-line group*$_{opt}$

check whether the controlling constant expression evaluates to nonzero.

Prior to evaluation, macro invocations in the list of preprocessing tokens that will become the controlling constant expression are replaced (except for those macro names modified by the **defined** unary operator), just as in normal text. If the token **defined** is generated as a result of this replacement process or use of the **defined** unary operator does not match one of the two

---

82 Thus, preprocessing directives are commonly called "lines." These "lines" have no other syntactic significance, as all white space is equivalent except in certain situations during preprocessing (see the **#** character string literal creation operator in 6.8.3.2, for example).

83 Because the controlling constant expression is evaluated during translation phase 4, all identifiers either are or are not macro names — there simply are no keywords, enumeration constants, etc.

(*6.8 Preprocessing directives,* continued)

A preprocessing directive must be the first token on a line, and the directive ends at the end of its line (when the new-line character is encountered). The directive may be preceded with white space, but not by any other C construct. For example:

```
/* these directives are legal */
#define one
    #define two

/* these directives are illegal */
int i; #include <stdio.h>
main() #define COUNT 21
```

Preprocessing directives are limited to one line; that is, a preprocessor directive cannot span two or more lines in the way that a C-language statement can. However, you may span two or more lines with a directive by using the \ at the end of each line to be continued (see the examples in Section 6.8.3.5).

6.8.1   Conditional inclusion   The term *conditional inclusion* may be unfamiliar to you. The standard uses it to describe what most C programmers call *conditional compilation.* The preprocessing directives that control conditional inclusion are **#if**, **#elif**, **#else**, **#endif**, **#ifdef**, and **#ifndef**. The standard's description of these directives is somewhat formal and difficult to follow, so here is a summary of the operation of these directives.

The conditional compilation directives operate in pairs. A conditional compilation statement sequence is begun using either **#if**, **#ifdef**, or **#ifndef**. The sequence is terminated by **#endif** (or, in the case of **#if**, an alternative statement sequence may be begun using **#elif**). Here are the general forms of these directives:

#if *constant-exp*	#ifdef *identifier*	#ifndef *identifier*
statement sequence	*statement sequence*	*statement sequence*
#elif *constant-exp*	#else	#else
statement sequence	*statement sequence*	*statement sequence*
#else	#endif	#endif
statement sequence		
#endif		

Both the **#elif** and **#else** directives and their related statement sequences are optional. Technically, the **#elif** can be used with **#ifdef** and **#ifndef**, but seldom is.

specified forms prior to macro replacement, the behavior is undefined. After all replacements due to macro expansion and the **defined** unary operator have been performed, all remaining identifiers are replaced with the pp-number 0, and then each preprocessing token is converted into a token. The resulting tokens comprise the controlling constant expression which is evaluated according to the rules of 6.4 using arithmetic that has at least the ranges specified in 5.2.4.2, except that **int** and **unsigned int** act as if they have the same representation as, respectively, **long** and **unsigned long**. This includes interpreting character constants, which may involve converting escape sequences into execution character set members. Whether the numeric value for these character constants matches the value obtained when an identical character constant occurs in an expression (other than within a **#if** or **#elif** directive) is implementation-defined.[84] Also, whether a single-character character constant may have a negative value is implementation-defined.

Preprocessing directives of the forms

> **# ifdef**   *identifier new-line group*$_{opt}$
> **# ifndef** *identifier new-line group*$_{opt}$

check whether the identifier is or is not currently defined as a macro name. Their conditions are equivalent to **#if defined** *identifier* and **#if !defined** *identifier* respectively.

Each directive's condition is checked in order. If it evaluates to false (zero), the group that it controls is skipped: directives are processed only through the name that determines the directive in order to keep track of the level of nested conditionals; the rest of the directives' preprocessing tokens are ignored, as are the other preprocessing tokens in the group. Only the first group whose control condition evaluates to true (nonzero) is processed. If none of the conditions evaluates to true, and there is a **#else** directive, the group controlled by the **#else** is processed; lacking a **#else** directive, all the groups until the **#endif** are skipped.[85]

Forward references: macro replacement (6.8.3), source file inclusion (6.8.2).

6.8.2 Source file inclusion

Constraints

A **#include** directive shall identify a header or source file that can be processed by the implementation.

Semantics

A preprocessing directive of the form

> **# include** *<h-char-sequence> new-line*

searches a sequence of implementation-defined places for a header identified uniquely by the specified sequence between the **<** and **>** delimiters, and causes the replacement of that directive by the entire contents of the header. How the places are specified or the header identified is implementation-defined.

---

84 Thus, the constant expression in the following **#if** directive and **if** statement is not guaranteed to evaluate to the same value in these two contexts.

> **#if 'z' - 'a' == 25**
> **if ('z' - 'a' == 25)**

85 As indicated by the syntax, a preprocessing token shall not follow a **#else** or **#endif** directive before the terminating new-line character. However, comments may appear anywhere in a source file, including within a preprocessing directive.

*(**6.8.1 Conditional inclusion,** continued)*

The expression associated with the **#if** must either be a constant expression, or use the preprocessing operator **defined**. If the expression is true, the statement sequence is compiled. If it is false and there is an **#elif**, that expression is checked. If it is true, its statement sequence is compiled. If it is false (or if the **#elif** does not exist), the **#else** statement sequence (if present) is compiled.

The statement sequence within an **#ifdef** section is compiled only if the identifier associated with the **#ifdef** is currently defined (as anything). If it is not, and there is an **#else** directive, that statement sequence is compiled instead.

When the identifier associated with an **#ifndef** is *not* defined, its code section is compiled. If it is defined, then if there is an **#else** directive, that code section is compiled.

Here is an example that illustrates several of the conditional compilation directives:

```
#include <stdio.h>

#define OK
#define DEBUGLEVEL 2
main(void)
{
#ifdef OK
  printf("This will be compiled when OK is defined.\n");
#endif
  printf("This is always compiled.\n");
#if DEBUGLEVEL == 2
  printf("Debug level 2 is on.\n");
#elif DEBUGLEVEL == 1
  printf("Debug level 1 is on.\n");
#else
  printf("No debugging.\n");
#endif
  /* ... */
}
```

The foregoing program displays these lines:

```
This will be compiled when OK is defined.
This is always compiled.
Debug level 2 is on.
```

6.8.2   Source file inclusion   The **#include** directive is used to include another source file in the program currently being compiled. As you know, the **#include** directive appears in nearly every C program because it is used to include the standard header files that contain the prototypes, macros, and **typedefs** required by the standard library functions. Of course, it can be used to include header files that you create or any other type of source file.

A preprocessing directive of the form

> **# include** *"q-char-sequence"* *new-line*

causes the replacement of that directive by the entire contents of the source file identified by the specified sequence between the " delimiters. The named source file is searched for in an implementation-defined manner. If this search is not supported, or if the search fails, the directive is reprocessed as if it read

> **# include** <*h-char-sequence*> *new-line*

with the identical contained sequence (including **>** characters, if any) from the original directive.

A preprocessing directive of the form

> **# include** *pp-tokens* *new-line*

(that does not match one of the two previous forms) is permitted. The preprocessing tokens after **include** in the directive are processed just as in normal text. (Each identifier currently defined as a macro name is replaced by its replacement list of preprocessing tokens.) The directive resulting after all replacements shall match one of the two previous forms.[86] The method by which a sequence of preprocessing tokens between a **<** and a **>** preprocessing token pair or a pair of **"** characters is combined into a single header name preprocessing token is implementation-defined.

There shall be an implementation-defined mapping between the delimited sequence and the external source file name. The implementation shall provide unique mappings for sequences consisting of one or more letters (as defined in 5.2.1) followed by a period (.) and a single letter. The implementation may ignore the distinctions of alphabetical case and restrict the mapping to six significant characters before the period.

A **#include** preprocessing directive may appear in a source file that has been read because of a **#include** directive in another file, up to an implementation-defined nesting limit (see 5.2.4.1).

Examples

1. The most common uses of **#include** preprocessing directives are as in the following:

```
#include <stdio.h>
#include "myprog.h"
```

2. This illustrates macro-replaced **#include** directives:

```
#if VERSION == 1
        #define INCFILE   "vers1.h"
#elif VERSION == 2
        #define INCFILE   "vers2.h"    /* and so on */
#else
        #define INCFILE   "versN.h"
#endif
#include INCFILE
```

Forward references: macro replacement (6.8.3).

---

86 Note that adjacent string literals are not concatenated into a single string literal (see the translation phases in 5.1.1.2); thus, an expansion that results in two string literals is an invalid directive.

(**6.8.2 Source file inclusion,** *continued*)

The **#include** statement has these two forms:

#include <*filename*>

#include "*filename*"

Both these statement forms cause a source file to be included; the difference is how the search for that file (that is, where and how the compiler looks for the specified file) is conducted. The standard allows great flexibility on this account. In simplified terms, here is the difference between the two **#include** forms:

◆   When the file name is enclosed between angle brackets, the compiler searches for the file in an implementation-defined manner. Typically, this means the compiler searches the standard include directory or directories. If it cannot find the file using this method, the search fails and a compile-time error occurs.

◆   When the file name is enclosed between double quotation marks, the compiler first searches for the file in some implementation-defined manner—which is (almost always) different from that used when the file name is enclosed between angle brackets. If this search fails, the search is retried using the method associated with the angle bracket version. If this search also fails, a compile-time error is reported. Typically, enclosing a file name between double quotation marks causes the compiler to first check the current directory before trying the standard include directory.

The standard permits a file that has been included using an **#include** statement to include files of its own, using **#include**. Indeed, this is a common occurrence in C programming. But be careful; in some situations, indirectly including the same file two or more times may cause difficulties.

6.8.3 Macro replacement

Constraints

Two replacement lists are identical if and only if the preprocessing tokens in both have the same number, ordering, spelling, and white-space separation, where all white-space separations are considered identical.

An identifier currently defined as a macro without use of lparen (an *object-like* macro) may be redefined by another **#define** preprocessing directive provided that the second definition is an object-like macro definition and the two replacement lists are identical.

An identifier currently defined as a macro using lparen (a *function-like* macro) may be redefined by another **#define** preprocessing directive provided that the second definition is a function-like macro definition that has the same number and spelling of parameters, and the two replacement lists are identical.

The number of arguments in an invocation of a function-like macro shall agree with the number of parameters in the macro definition, and there shall exist a **)** preprocessing token that terminates the invocation.

A parameter identifier in a function-like macro shall be uniquely declared within its scope.

Semantics

The identifier immediately following the **define** is called the *macro name*. There is one name space for macro names. Any white-space characters preceding or following the replacement list of preprocessing tokens are not considered part of the replacement list for either form of macro.

If a **#** preprocessing token, followed by an identifier, occurs lexically at the point at which a preprocessing directive could begin, the identifier is not subject to macro replacement.

A preprocessing directive of the form

> **# define** *identifier replacement-list new-line*

defines an object-like macro that causes each subsequent instance of the macro name[87] to be replaced by the replacement list of preprocessing tokens that constitute the remainder of the directive. The replacement list is then rescanned for more macro names as specified below.

A preprocessing directive of the form

> **# define** *identifier lparen identifier-list*$_{opt}$ **)** *replacement-list new-line*

defines a function-like macro with arguments, similar syntactically to a function call. The parameters are specified by the optional list of identifiers, whose scope extends from their declaration in the identifier list until the new-line character that terminates the **#define** preprocessing directive. Each subsequent instance of the function-like macro name followed by a **(** as the next preprocessing token introduces the sequence of preprocessing tokens that is replaced by the replacement list in the definition (an invocation of the macro). The replaced sequence of preprocessing tokens is terminated by the matching **)** preprocessing token, skipping intervening matched pairs of left and right parenthesis preprocessing tokens. Within the sequence of preprocessing tokens making up an invocation of a function-like macro, new-line is considered a normal white-space character.

---

[87] Since, by macro-replacement time, all character constants and string literals are preprocessing tokens, not sequences possibly containing identifier-like subsequences (see 5.1.1.2, translation phases), they are never scanned for macro names or parameters.

6.8.3 Macro replacement A *macro replacement* is essentially a string substitution in which a character sequence (called a *replacement list* by the standard) is substituted for a macro name. This substitution is done by the preprocessor. A macro name is defined using the **#define** preprocessor directive. There are two general types of macros: *object-like* and *function-like*.

An object-like macro defines an identifier, and a replacement list that is substituted for the identifier each time it is encountered in the source file. For example, given this fragment:

```
#define ONE 1
printf("%d", ONE);
```

after macro substitution the **printf()** line becomes: **printf("%d",   1);**

In this case, the macro name **ONE** is replaced by the digit 1 by the preprocessor, because that is how **ONE** is defined in the **#define** directive.

A function-like macro is syntactically similar to a function. Because the function-like macro may have parameters, it involves a more sophisticated text substitution than an object-like macro. The purpose of function-like macros is to provide a convenient, in-line alternative to short functions, bypassing the overhead of an actual call/return. Here is a short example that uses a function-like macro:

```
#include <stdio.h>
#define ABS(a) ((a) < 0 ? -(a) : a)
main(void)
{
  int i=-10;
  printf("%d ", ABS(-20));
  printf("%d ", ABS(20));
  printf("%d ", ABS(i));
  printf("%d ", ABS(i+11));
  return 0;
}
```

The foregoing program displays **20 20 10 1**. Each time **ABS** is encountered, its argument is automatically substituted for **a** in its replacement list. Therefore, the first **printf()** statement will look like this after substitution:

```
printf("%d ", ABS(((-20) < 0 ? -(-20) : (-20))));
```

The parentheses surrounding **a** in the **#define** statement are necessary to ensure the correct outcome for all possible expressions that can be used as arguments. For example, the following statement would display –30 instead of 10 if **a** were not properly parenthesized:

```
printf("%d", ABS(10-20));
```

The sequence of preprocessing tokens bounded by the outside-most matching parentheses forms the list of arguments for the function-like macro. The individual arguments within the list are separated by comma preprocessing tokens, but comma preprocessing tokens between matching inner parentheses do not separate arguments. If (before argument substitution) any argument consists of no preprocessing tokens, the behavior is undefined. If there are sequences of preprocessing tokens within the list of arguments that would otherwise act as preprocessing directives, the behavior is undefined.

6.8.3.1 Argument substitution

After the arguments for the invocation of a function-like macro have been identified, argument substitution takes place. A parameter in the replacement list, unless preceded by a **#** or **##** preprocessing token or followed by a **##** preprocessing token (see below), is replaced by the corresponding argument after all macros contained therein have been expanded. Before being substituted, each argument's preprocessing tokens are completely macro replaced as if they formed the rest of the translation unit; no other preprocessing tokens are available.

6.8.3.2 The # operator

Constraints

Each **#** preprocessing token in the replacement list for a function-like macro shall be followed by a parameter as the next preprocessing token in the replacement list.

Semantics

If, in the replacement list, a parameter is immediately preceded by a **#** preprocessing token, both are replaced by a single character string literal preprocessing token that contains the spelling of the preprocessing token sequence for the corresponding argument. Each occurrence of white space between the argument's preprocessing tokens becomes a single space character in the character string literal. White space before the first preprocessing token and after the last preprocessing token comprising the argument is deleted. Otherwise, the original spelling of each preprocessing token in the argument is retained in the character string literal, except for special handling for producing the spelling of string literals and character constants: a \ character is inserted before each " and \ character of a character constant or string literal (including the delimiting " characters). If the replacement that results is not a valid character string literal, the behavior is undefined. The order of evaluation of **#** and **##** operators is unspecified.

6.8.3.3 The ## operator

Constraints

A **##** preprocessing token shall not occur at the beginning or at the end of a replacement list for either form of macro definition.

Semantics

If, in the replacement list, a parameter is immediately preceded or followed by a **##** preprocessing token, the parameter is replaced by the corresponding argument's preprocessing token sequence.

For both object-like and function-like macro invocations, before the replacement list is reexamined for more macro names to replace, each instance of a **##** preprocessing token in the replacement list (not from an argument) is deleted and the preceding preprocessing token is concatenated with the following preprocessing token. If the result is not a valid preprocessing token, the behavior is undefined. The resulting token is available for further macro replacement. The order of evaluation of **##** operators is unspecified.

6.8.3.1 *Argument substitution* This section states that when an argument to a function-like macro is, itself, a macro, then all macro substitutions take place on that argument before it is substituted into the function-like macro. For example, given this fragment:

```
#define SUM -10+100
#define ABS(a) ((a) < 0 ? -(a) : a)
/* ... */
printf("%d", ABS(SUM));
```

the value 90 will be displayed. The substitutions inside the call to **printf()** occur like this: First, **−10+100** is substituted for **SUM**. Next, this expression is substituted for **a** in the **ABS** macro.

6.8.3.2 *The # operator* The **#** preprocessing operator is sometimes called the *stringize* operator because it transforms the parameter in a function-like macro that it precedes into a quoted string. This example:

```
#define makestring(str) # str
printf(" %s ", makestring(one));
printf(makestring(two));
```

displays **one two** because **makestring()** transforms the symbols **one** and **two** into quoted strings that may be used by **printf()**. That is, after macro replacements have taken place, the first **printf()** call looks like this:

```
printf(" %s ", "one");
```

The **#** applies only to function-like macros. Additional examples of the **#** operator are shown in Section 6.8.3.5 of the standard.

6.8.3.3 *The ## operator* The **##** operator is commonly called the *pasting* operator because it concatenates two preprocessing tokens into one single token. For example, **one##two** becomes the token **onetwo**. Here is a more practical example:

6.8.3.4 Rescanning and further replacement

After all parameters in the replacement list have been substituted, the resulting preprocessing token sequence is rescanned with all subsequent preprocessing tokens of the source file for more macro names to replace.

If the name of the macro being replaced is found during this scan of the replacement list (not including the rest of the source file's preprocessing tokens), it is not replaced. Further, if any nested replacements encounter the name of the macro being replaced, it is not replaced. These nonreplaced macro name preprocessing tokens are no longer available for further replacement even if they are later (re)examined in contexts in which that macro name preprocessing token would otherwise have been replaced.

The resulting completely macro-replaced preprocessing token sequence is not processed as a preprocessing directive even if it resembles one.

6.8.3.5 Scope of macro definitions

A macro definition lasts (independent of block structure) until a corresponding **#undef** directive is encountered or (if none is encountered) until the end of the translation unit.

A preprocessing directive of the form

**undef** *identifier new-line*

causes the specified identifier no longer to be defined as a macro name. It is ignored if the specified identifier is not currently defined as a macro name.

Examples

1. The simplest use of this facility is to define a "manifest constant," as in

```
#define TABSIZE 100

int table[TABSIZE];
```

2. The following defines a function-like macro whose value is the maximum of its arguments. It has the advantages of working for any compatible types of the arguments and of generating in-line code without the overhead of function calling. It has the disadvantages of evaluating one or the other of its arguments a second time (including side effects) and generating more code than a function if invoked several times. It also cannot have its address taken, as it has none.

```
#define max(a, b)  ((a) > (b) ? (a) : (b))
```

The parentheses ensure that the arguments and the resulting expression are bound properly.

3. To illustrate the rules for redefinition and reexamination, the sequence

```
#define x       3
#define f(a)    f(x * (a))
#undef  x
#define x       2
#define g       f
#define z       z[0]
#define h       g(~
#define m(a)    a(w)
#define w       0,1
#define t(a)    a

f(y+1) + f(f(z)) % t(t(g)(0) + t)(1);
g(x+(3,4)-w) | h 5) & m
        (f)^m(m);
```

(*6.8.3.3 The ## operator,* continued)

```
#include <stdio.h>

#define concat(a, b) a ## b

void main(void)
{
  int count1 = 10;
  int count2 = 20;

  printf("%d ", concat(count, 1));
  printf("%d ", concat(count, 2));
}
```

The foregoing program displays **10 20** because **concat()** pastes together its two arguments. For example, the first **printf()** call will look like this after macro substitution:

```
printf("%d ", count1);
```

The **##** operator can be used with both function-like and object-like macros. Additional examples are shown in Section 6.8.3.5 of the standard.

6.8.3.4 *Rescanning and further replacement* In essence, this section states that macro substitutions will occur until no more can be made. However, in no case will a macro substitution be applied recursively.

6.8.3.5 *Scope of macro definitions* A macro definition created using a **#define** has, essentially, file scope—whether its definition occurs within or outside of a block. Once defined, the macro remains defined until the end of the file, or until it is explicitly undefined using the **#undef** preprocessing directive. For example:

```
#define COUNT 10
/* ... COUNT is defined here ... */
#undef COUNT
/* COUNT is now undefined */
```

On the remainder of page 91 and continuing on page 92, numerous examples of the C preprocessor are shown; these are worth the effort of working through on your own.

results in

```
f(2 * (y+1)) + f(2 * (f(2 * (z[0])))) % f(2 * (0)) + t(1);
f(2 * (2+(3,4)-0,1)) | f(2 * (~ 5)) & f(2 * (0,1))^m(0,1);
```

4. To illustrate the rules for creating character string literals and concatenating tokens, the sequence

```
#define str(s)      # s
#define xstr(s)     str(s)
#define debug(s, t) printf("x" # s "= %d, x" # t "= %s", \
                       x ## s, x ## t)
#define INCFILE(n)  vers ## n   /* from previous #include example */
#define glue(a, b)  a ## b
#define xglue(a, b) glue(a, b)
#define HIGHLOW     "hello"
#define LOW         LOW ", world"

debug(1, 2);
fputs(str(strncmp("abc\0d", "abc", '\4')  /* this goes away */
    == 0) str(: @\n), s);
#include xstr(INCFILE(2).h)
glue(HIGH, LOW);
xglue(HIGH, LOW)
```

results in

```
printf("x" "1" "= %d, x" "2" "= %s", x1, x2);
fputs("strncmp(\"abc\\0d\", \"abc\", '\\4') == 0" ": @\n", s);
#include "vers2.h"    (after macro replacement, before file access)
"hello";
"hello" ", world"
```

or, after concatenation of the character string literals,

```
printf("x1= %d, x2= %s", x1, x2);
fputs("strncmp(\"abc\\0d\", \"abc\", '\\4') == 0: @\n", s);
#include "vers2.h"    (after macro replacement, before file access)
"hello";
"hello, world"
```

Space around the # and ## tokens in the macro definition is optional.

5. And finally, to demonstrate the redefinition rules, the following sequence is valid.

```
#define OBJ_LIKE       (1-1)
#define OBJ_LIKE       /* white space */ (1-1) /* other */
#define FTN_LIKE(a)    ( a )
#define FTN_LIKE( a )(       /* note the white space */ \
                        a /* other stuff on this line
                          */ )
```

But the following redefinitions are invalid:

```
#define OBJ_LIKE       (0)      /* different token sequence */
#define OBJ_LIKE       (1 - 1)  /* different white space */
#define FTN_LIKE(b)    ( a )    /* different parameter usage */
#define FTN_LIKE(b)    ( b )    /* different parameter spelling */
```

There are no annotations for page 92.

6.8.4 Line control

Constraints

The string literal of a **#line** directive, if present, shall be a character string literal.

Semantics

The *line number* of the current source line is one greater than the number of new-line characters read or introduced in translation phase 1 (5.1.1.2) while processing the source file to the current token.

A preprocessing directive of the form

> **# line** *digit-sequence new-line*

causes the implementation to behave as if the following sequence of source lines begins with a source line that has a line number as specified by the digit sequence (interpreted as a decimal integer). The digit sequence shall not specify zero, nor a number greater than 32767.

A preprocessing directive of the form

> **# line** *digit-sequence "s-char-sequence$_{opt}$" new-line*

sets the line number similarly and changes the presumed name of the source file to be the contents of the character string literal.

A preprocessing directive of the form

> **# line** *pp-tokens new-line*

(that does not match one of the two previous forms) is permitted. The preprocessing tokens after **line** on the directive are processed just as in normal text (each identifier currently defined as a macro name is replaced by its replacement list of preprocessing tokens). The directive resulting after all replacements shall match one of the two previous forms and is then processed as appropriate.

6.8.5 Error directive

Semantics

A preprocessing directive of the form

> **# error** *pp-tokens$_{opt}$ new-line*

causes the implementation to produce a diagnostic message that includes the specified sequence of preprocessing tokens.

6.8.6 Pragma directive

Semantics

A preprocessing directive of the form

> **# pragma** *pp-tokens$_{opt}$ new-line*

causes the implementation to behave in an implementation-defined manner. Any pragma that is not recognized by the implementation is ignored.

6.8.4   *Line control*   The **#line** directive is used mostly for source code control. It is used to change the line number of a line of source code, and/or the file name of the file being compiled. (These items are stored in the built-in macros __**LINE**__ and __**FILE**__. See Section 6.8.8.) Remember, neither the source line number nor the file name affects the outcome of a compilation, but are used to report error messages and the like.

The **#line** directive has this general form:

#line *line-num* "*filename*"

where *line-num* is a decimal number that becomes the new line number of the line that follows the **#line** directive. The string containing the *filename* is optional; when present, it becomes the name of the file being compiled. For example:

```
#include <stdio.h>

void main(void)
{
  printf("%d %s\n", __LINE__, __FILE__);
#line 100 "MYFILE"
  printf("%d %s\n", __LINE__, __FILE__);
}
```

Here the two **printf()** calls produce different results, with the second displaying this output: **100 MYFILE**.

6.8.5   *Error directive*   The **#error** preprocessing directive is used for debugging. It causes compilation to stop and displays an implementation-defined message. It will also display any tokens that you include. A common form of the message displayed by **#error** is shown here:

Error *filename* *line-num* *message*

where *filename* is the name of the file, *line-num* is the number of the line that contains the **#error** directive, and *message* contains the tokens that follow **#error** (if any) that you included.

6.8.6   *Pragma directive*   The **#pragma** directive is used to pass implementation-specific instructions to a compiler. The reason for its inclusion as a preprocessing directive is to allow a portable way to embed a compiler-specific instruction, while still allowing the program to be compiled by a different implementation that does not recognize that instruction. If the compiler does not recognize the tokens that follow **#pragma**, it simply ignores the statement.

6.8.7 Null directive

Semantics

A preprocessing directive of the form

> **#** *new-line*

has no effect.

6.8.8 Predefined macro names

The following macro names shall be defined by the implementation:

__LINE__   The line number of the current source line (a decimal constant).

__FILE__   The presumed name of the source file (a character string literal).

__DATE__   The date of translation of the source file (a character string literal of the form
"**Mmm dd yyyy**", where the names of the months are the same as those generated
by the **asctime** function, and the first character of **dd** is a space character if the
value is less than 10). If the date of translation is not available, an
implementation-defined valid date shall be supplied.

__TIME__   The time of translation of the source file (a character string literal of the form
"**hh:mm:ss**" as in the time generated by the **asctime** function). If the time of
translation is not available, an implementation-defined valid time shall be supplied.

__STDC__   The decimal constant 1, intended to indicate a conforming implementation.

The values of the predefined macros (except for **__LINE__** and **__FILE__**) remain
constant throughout the translation unit.

None of these macro names, nor the identifier **defined**, shall be the subject of a **#define**
or a **#undef** preprocessing directive. All predefined macro names shall begin with a leading
underscore followed by an uppercase letter or a second underscore.

Forward references: the **asctime** function (7.12.3.1).

(*6.8.6 Pragma directive,* continued)

For example, a compiler designed for the 8086 family of processors might use the following **#pragma** as a request to compile for the large memory model:

```
#pragma large
```

If a program containing this **#pragma** is compiled using another compiler that does not recognize *large* as a valid pragma, the statement is simply ignored.

6.8.7 Null directive A **#** on a line by itself is called a *null directive* and performs no function whatsoever.

6.8.8 Predefined macro names The standard defines five built-in macro names that may be used in any C program. You do not have to include any special header file in order to have access to these macro names. However, **__STDC__** is only defined when a standard implementation is used.

The following program shows how the contents of each macro can be displayed:

```
#include <stdio.h>

void main(void)
{
  printf("Filename: %s\n", __FILE__);
  printf("Compiled on %s ", __DATE__);
  printf("at %s\n", __TIME__);
  printf("Current line: %d\n", __LINE__);

  #ifdef __STDC__
    printf("Standard C");
  #else
    printf("Not Standard");
  #endif
}
```

Be aware that virtually all commercial compilers support several additional implementation-specific, built-in macros. Additional built-in macros are often used to determine various settings and the operation of certain subsystems.

6.9 Future language directions

6.9.1 External names

Restriction of the significance of an external name to fewer than 31 characters or to only one case is an obsolescent feature that is a concession to existing implementations.

6.9.2 Character escape sequences

Lowercase letters as escape sequences are reserved for future standardization. Other characters may be used in extensions.

6.9.3 Storage-class specifiers

The placement of a storage-class specifier other than at the beginning of the declaration specifiers in a declaration is an obsolescent feature.

6.9.4 Function declarators

The use of function declarators with empty parentheses (not prototype-format parameter type declarators) is an obsolescent feature.

6.9.5 Function definitions

The use of function definitions with separate parameter identifier and declaration lists (not prototype-format parameter type and identifier declarators) is an obsolescent feature.

6.9.6 Array parameters

The use of two parameters declared with an array type (prior to their adjustment to pointer type) in separate lvalues to designate the same object is an obsolescent feature.

6.9 *Future language directions* Pay attention to the items in this section, which indicate what might change in a revision to the standard. Any feature flagged as obsolete should be avoided when writing new programs, because there is a good chance that support for that feature will be removed from later versions of the standard. Most importantly, use prototypes for all functions, and use the modern (not the old form) function definition syntax. (Remember, the old form separates the parameter names from their type specifications. Refer to Section 6.7.1.)

7 Library

7.1 Introduction

7.1.1 Definitions of terms

A *string* is a contiguous sequence of characters terminated by and including the first null character. A "pointer to" a string is a pointer to its initial (lowest addressed) character. The "length" of a string is the number of characters preceding the null character and its "value" is the sequence of the values of the contained characters, in order.

A *letter* is a printing character in the execution character set corresponding to any of the 52 required lowercase and uppercase letters in the source character set, listed in 5.2.1.

The *decimal-point character* is the character used by functions that convert floating-point numbers to or from character sequences to denote the beginning of the fractional part of such character sequences.[88] It is represented in the text and examples by a period, but may be changed by the **setlocale** function.

Forward references: character handling (7.3), the **setlocale** function (7.4.1.1).

7.1.2 Standard headers

Each library function is declared in a *header*,[89] whose contents are made available by the **#include** preprocessing directive. The header declares a set of related functions, plus any necessary types and additional macros needed to facilitate their use.

The standard headers are

<assert.h>	**<locale.h>**	**<stddef.h>**
<ctype.h>	**<math.h>**	**<stdio.h>**
<errno.h>	**<setjmp.h>**	**<stdlib.h>**
<float.h>	**<signal.h>**	**<string.h>**
<limits.h>	**<stdarg.h>**	**<time.h>**

If a file with the same name as one of the above < and > delimited sequences, not provided as part of the implementation, is placed in any of the standard places for a source file to be included, the behavior is undefined.

Headers may be included in any order; each may be included more than once in a given scope, with no effect different from being included only once, except that the effect of including **<assert.h>** depends on the definition of **NDEBUG**. If used, a header shall be included outside of any external declaration or definition, and it shall first be included before the first reference to any of the functions or objects it declares, or to any of the types or macros it defines. However, if the identifier is declared or defined in more than one header, the second and subsequent associated headers may be included after the initial reference to the identifier. The program shall not have any macros with names lexically identical to keywords currently defined prior to the inclusion.

Forward references: diagnostics (7.2).

---

[88] The functions that make use of the decimal-point character are **localeconv**, **fprintf**, **fscanf**, **printf**, **scanf**, **sprintf**, **sscanf**, **vfprintf**, **vprintf**, **vsprintf**, **atof**, and **strtod**.

[89] A header is not necessarily a source file, nor are the < and > delimited sequences in header names necessarily valid source file names.

Part 7   Library

7.1.1   *Definitions of terms*   The terms in this section are clearly defined, but you will want to take note of two small points: First, the length of a string does not include its null terminator. Second, the character used for the decimal point may be set to something other than a period. This is to accommodate the conventions used in various nonEnglish-speaking countries. You must keep this fact in mind if you create a function (perhaps some sort of conversion routine) that relies upon a character that is used as a decimal point.

7.1.2   *Standard headers*   A *header file* contains the prototypes, macros, and types that are required to support one (or more) of the standard library subsystems supplied with a conforming compiler. Rather than using one large header file, the standard defines 15 *standard header files*, each associated with a particular library subsystem. The reason for these separate files is easy to understand: Header files must be compiled, and compilation takes time. Thus, by using separate files, your program need only include (and thus compile) the header information related to the functions that you actually use, instead of having to compile information about all functions in the standard library.

Because header files contain information that the compiler must have prior to the first use in your program of a function declared by the header, it is common practice to place the **#include** statements for the standard headers near the top of each file in your program. (Indeed, this is a generally accepted C programming practice.)

The vast majority of the Library section (Part 7) of the standard is devoted to a description of the standard library functions. All conforming C compilers will supply all of the functions described here.

7.1.3 Reserved identifiers

Each header declares or defines all identifiers listed in its associated subclause, and optionally declares or defines identifiers listed in its associated future library directions subclause and identifiers which are always reserved either for any use or for use as file scope identifiers.

— All identifiers that begin with an underscore and either an uppercase letter or another underscore are always reserved for any use.

— All identifiers that begin with an underscore are always reserved for use as identifiers with file scope in both the ordinary identifier and tag name spaces.

— Each macro name listed in any of the following subclauses (including the future library directions) is reserved for any use if any of its associated headers is included.

— All identifiers with external linkage in any of the following subclauses (including the future library directions) are always reserved for use as identifiers with external linkage.[90]

— Each identifier with file scope listed in any of the following subclauses (including the future library directions) is reserved for use as an identifier with file scope in the same name space if any of its associated headers is included.

No other identifiers are reserved. If the program declares or defines an identifier with the same name as an identifier reserved in that context (other than as allowed by 7.1.7), the behavior is undefined.[91]

7.1.4 Errors <errno.h>

The header **<errno.h>** defines several macros, all relating to the reporting of error conditions.

The macros are

>   **EDOM**
>   **ERANGE**

which expand to integral constant expressions with distinct nonzero values, suitable for use in **#if** preprocessing directives; and

>   **errno**

which expands to a modifiable lvalue[92] that has type **int**, the value of which is set to a positive error number by several library functions. It is unspecified whether **errno** is a macro or an identifier declared with external linkage. If a macro definition is suppressed in order to access an actual object, or a program defines an identifier with the name **errno**, the behavior is undefined.

The value of **errno** is zero at program startup, but is never set to zero by any library function.[93] The value of **errno** may be set to nonzero by a library function call whether or not there is an error, provided the use of **errno** is not documented in the description of the function in this International Standard.

---

90 The list of reserved identifiers with external linkage includes **errno**, **setjmp**, and **va_end**.

91 Since macro names are replaced whenever found, independent of scope and name space, macro names matching any of the reserved identifier names must not be defined if an associated header, if any, is included.

92 The macro **errno** need not be the identifier of an object. It might expand to a modifiable lvalue resulting from a function call (for example, ***errno()**).

93 Thus, a program that uses **errno** for error checking should set it to zero before a library function call, then inspect it before a subsequent library function call. Of course, a library function can save the value of **errno** on entry and then set it to zero, as long as the original value is restored if **errno**'s value is still zero just before the return.

7.1.3   *Reserved identifiers* The standard makes some very important statements about reserved identifiers that are often either overlooked or ignored by many programmers. For example, identifiers that begin with an underscore followed by an uppercase letter or another underscore are reserved for possible use. For instance, this means you should not create the following identifiers in any C program:

```
__OK  _ONE_  __TWO__  __DONE__
```

Frankly, many C programmers are not aware of the rules described in this section. The trouble caused by using a reserved identifier is that your program may compile correctly in one environment, when you write it, but may fail to compile correctly at a future time or with another compiler.

7.1.4   *Errors <errno.h>* The C standard library supports a small error-reporting subsystem that requires the use of the **errno.h** header file. This file defines the two macros **EDOM** and **ERANGE** which, as you will see later in this section, stand for *domain error* and *range error*. The header also defines **errno**, which is a global lvalue (usually a global variable); it can be set by various library functions to some value that indicates an error has occurred and, possibly, the nature of that error. Your program can then check this value to determine a response to the problem. If **errno** is zero, then no error has been detected.

The following statement displays the current contents of **errno**:

```
printf("errno: %d\n", errno);
```

Remember, to have access to **errno**, you must include **errno.h** in your program.

Additional macro definitions, beginning with **E** and a digit or **E** and an uppercase letter.[94] may also be specified by the implementation.

7.1.5 Limits <float.h> and <limits.h>

The headers **<float.h>** and **<limits.h>** define several macros that expand to various limits and parameters.

The macros, their meanings, and the constraints (or restrictions) on their values are listed in 5.2.4.2.

7.1.6 Common definitions <stddef.h>

The following types and macros are defined in the standard header **<stddef.h>**. Some are also defined in other headers, as noted in their respective subclauses.

The types are

>   **ptrdiff_t**

which is the signed integral type of the result of subtracting two pointers;

>   **size_t**

which is the unsigned integral type of the result of the **sizeof** operator; and

>   **wchar_t**

which is an integral type whose range of values can represent distinct codes for all members of the largest extended character set specified among the supported locales; the null character shall have the code value zero and each member of the basic character set defined in 5.2.1 shall have a code value equal to its value when used as the lone character in an integer character constant.

The macros are

>   **NULL**

which expands to an implementation-defined null pointer constant; and

>   **offsetof**(*type*, *member-designator*)

which expands to an integral constant expression that has type **size_t**, the value of which is the offset in bytes, to the structure member (designated by *member-designator*), from the beginning of its structure (designated by *type*). The *member-designator* shall be such that given

>   **static** *type* **t;**

then the expression **&(t.**member-designator**)** evaluates to an address constant. (If the specified member is a bit-field, the behavior is undefined.)

Forward references: localization (7.4).

---

94 See "future library directions" (7.13.1).

7.1.5 Limits <float.h> and <limits.h> The header files **float.h** and **limits.h** define macros to the various limits imposed by the implementation. The following program uses these headers to display various limits:

```
#include <stdio.h>
#include <limits.h>
#include <float.h>

void main(void)
{
  printf("SCHAR_MIN: %d\n", SCHAR_MIN);
  printf("SCHAR_MAX: %d\n", SCHAR_MAX);

  printf("INT_MIN: %d\n", INT_MIN);
  printf("INT_MAX: %d\n", INT_MAX);

  printf("FLT_MIN_EXP: %d\n", FLT_MIN_EXP);
  printf("FLT_MAX_EXP: %d\n", FLT_MAX_EXP);
}
```

7.1.6 Common definitions <stddef.h> The macros and types defined in the **stddef.h** header are generally applicable to all programs. However, many of the items defined in this header are also defined in other headers, so it is common for this header to be omitted from a program.

Most of this section is easy to understand—except perhaps the macro **offsetof()**. In essence, it returns the number of bytes from the start of a structure at which the specified member is found. For example, consider this program:

```
#include <stdio.h>
#include <stddef.h>

struct s_type {
  int a, b;
} ob;

void main(void)
{
  printf("%d %d", offsetof(struct s_type, a),
         offsetof(struct s_type, b));
}
```

7.1.7 Use of library functions

Each of the following statements applies unless explicitly stated otherwise in the detailed descriptions that follow. If an argument to a function has an invalid value (such as a value outside the domain of the function, or a pointer outside the address space of the program, or a null pointer), the behavior is undefined. If a function argument is described as being an array, the pointer actually passed to the function shall have a value such that all address computations and accesses to objects (that would be valid if the pointer did point to the first element of such an array) are in fact valid. Any function declared in a header may be additionally implemented as a macro defined in the header, so a library function should not be declared explicitly if its header is included. Any macro definition of a function can be suppressed locally by enclosing the name of the function in parentheses, because the name is then not followed by the left parenthesis that indicates expansion of a macro function name. For the same syntactic reason, it is permitted to take the address of a library function even if it is also defined as a macro.[95] The use of **#undef** to remove any macro definition will also ensure that an actual function is referred to. Any invocation of a library function that is implemented as a macro shall expand to code that evaluates each of its arguments exactly once, fully protected by parentheses where necessary, so it is generally safe to use arbitrary expressions as arguments. Likewise, those function-like macros described in the following subclauses may be invoked in an expression anywhere a function with a compatible return type could be called.[96] All object-like macros listed as expanding to integral constant expressions shall additionally be suitable for use in **#if** preprocessing directives.

Provided that a library function can be declared without reference to any type defined in a header, it is also permissible to declare the function, either explicitly or implicitly, and use it without including its associated header. If a function that accepts a variable number of arguments is not declared (explicitly or by including its associated header), the behavior is undefined.

Example

The function **atoi** may be used in any of several ways:

— by use of its associated header (possibly generating a macro expansion)

```
#include <stdlib.h>
const char *str;
/*...*/
i = atoi(str);
```

---

95 This means that an implementation must provide an actual function for each library function, even if it also provides a macro for that function.

96 Because external identifiers and some macro names beginning with an underscore are reserved, implementations may provide special semantics for such names. For example, the identifier _BUILTIN_abs could be used to indicate generation of in-line code for the **abs** function. Thus, the appropriate header could specify

```
#define abs(x) _BUILTIN_abs(x)
```

for a compiler whose code generator will accept it.

In this manner, a user desiring to guarantee that a given library function such as **abs** will be a genuine function may write

```
#undef abs
```

whether the implementation's header provides a macro implementation of **abs** or a built-in implementation. The prototype for the function, which precedes and is hidden by any macro definition, is thereby revealed also.

*(**7.1.6   Common definitions <stddef.h>,** continued)*

Assuming integers are two bytes long, this program displays **0 2** because member **a** is at the beginning of the structure **s_type**, and member **b** is found two bytes into the structure.

Notice the syntax used by **offsetof()** in this program. This syntax is generalizable to any structure. Simply substitute the proper structure and member names.

7.1.7   Use of library functions   The most salient point of this section is that standard library functions, in some cases, may also be implemented as function-like macros. When this is (or might be) the case, there are two ways for your program to ensure that the actual function, rather than the macro, is called.

One way is to enclose the function name within parentheses. For example, the following statement ensures that the "call" to **abs()** will indeed result in a function call and not, possibly, in a function-like macro expansion:

```
x - (abs)(i/j);
```

The other way you can force the compiler to call the actual library function and bypass any function-like macro is to **#undef** the function name. Thus, (as footnote 96 shows), this next statement also causes **abs()** to be called, rather than expanded in-line:

```
#undef abs
```

Keep in mind that **abs()** is used here as an example. In your compiler, it may not be defined as a function-like macro to begin with.

This section also states that you need not actually include the standard header files when using library functions that don't rely upon any type or types defined in the headers. You are free to manually create within your program a prototype for a standard function. It is generally easier, however, to simply include the appropriate header files, and this is the approach taken by most C programmers.

— by use of its associated header (assuredly generating a true function reference)

```
#include <stdlib.h>
#undef atoi
const char *str;
/*...*/
i = atoi(str);
```

or

```
#include <stdlib.h>
const char *str;
/*...*/
i = (atoi)(str);
```

— by explicit declaration

```
extern int atoi(const char *);
const char *str;
/*...*/
i = atoi(str);
```

— by implicit declaration

```
const char *str;
/*...*/
i = atoi(str);
```

There are no annotations for page 100.

7.2 Diagnostics `<assert.h>`

The header `<assert.h>` defines the **assert** macro and refers to another macro,

    NDEBUG

which is *not* defined by `<assert.h>`. If **NDEBUG** is defined as a macro name at the point in the source file where `<assert.h>` is included, the **assert** macro is defined simply as

    #define assert(ignore) ((void)0)

The **assert** macro shall be implemented as a macro, not as an actual function. If the macro definition is suppressed in order to access an actual function, the behavior is undefined.

7.2.1 Program diagnostics

7.2.1.1 The assert macro

Synopsis

    #include <assert.h>
    void assert(int expression);

Description

The **assert** macro puts diagnostics into programs. When it is executed, if **expression** is false (that is, compares equal to 0), the **assert** macro writes information about the particular call that failed (including the text of the argument, the name of the source file, and the source line number — the latter are respectively the values of the preprocessing macros __**FILE**__ and __**LINE**__) on the standard error file in an implementation-defined format.[97] It then calls the **abort** function.

Returns

The **assert** macro returns no value.

Forward references: the **abort** function (7.10.4.1).

---

97 The message written might be of the form

    Assertion failed: *expression*, file *xyz*, line *nnn*

7.2 Diagnostics <assert.h> The **assert()** macro is used to embed debugging statements into your program. When its controlling expression is false, it causes the
expression, the source file name, and line number to be displayed. You can use
assert() to monitor expressions that will be true if your program is operating
correctly, and that become false if an error occurs. The **assert()** macro can be
deactivated by defining **NDEBUG** before the inclusion of **assert.h** in your program.
In this case, the **assert()** macro is defined as a non-operation.

Here is one way in which **assert()** might be used. Assume, for the sake of this
example, that a variable called **count** must never exceed 100 within a loop. You
might code the loop like this:

```
do {
  /* ... */
  assert(count <= 100); /* count must never exceed 100 */
} while(!done);
```

In this fragment, if **count** ever exceeds 100, a message is displayed and execution
stops.

7.3 Character handling <ctype.h>

The header **<ctype.h>** declares several functions useful for testing and mapping characters.[98] In all cases the argument is an **int**. the value of which shall be representable as an **unsigned char** or shall equal the value of the macro **EOF**. If the argument has any other value, the behavior is undefined.

The behavior of these functions is affected by the current locale. Those functions that have implementation-defined aspects only when not in the **"C"** locale are noted below.

The term *printing character* refers to a member of an implementation-defined set of characters. each of which occupies one printing position on a display device; the term *control character* refers to a member of an implementation-defined set of characters that are not printing characters.[99]

Forward references: **EOF** (7.9.1). localization (7.4).

7.3.1 Character testing functions

The functions in this subclause return nonzero (true) if and only if the value of the argument **c** conforms to that in the description of the function.

7.3.1.1 The isalnum function

Synopsis

```
#include <ctype.h>
int isalnum(int c);
```

Description

The **isalnum** function tests for any character for which **isalpha** or **isdigit** is true.

7.3.1.2 The isalpha function

Synopsis

```
#include <ctype.h>
int isalpha(int c);
```

Description

The **isalpha** function tests for any character for which **isupper** or **islower** is true, or any character that is one of an implementation-defined set of characters for which none of **iscntrl**. **isdigit**. **ispunct**. or **isspace** is true. In the **"C"** locale, **isalpha** returns true only for the characters for which **isupper** or **islower** is true.

7.3.1.3 The iscntrl function

Synopsis

```
#include <ctype.h>
int iscntrl(int c);
```

---

98 See "future library directions" (7.13.2).

99 In an implementation that uses the seven-bit ASCII character set. the printing characters are those whose values lie from 0x20 (space) through 0x7E (tilde); the control characters are those whose values lie from 0 (NUL) through 0x1F (US). and the character 0x7F (DEL).

7.3   Character handling <ctype.h>   Although the standard states that all character-handling functions define their arguments as type **int**, it is perfectly valid (indeed, it is the common practice) to call these functions with character values. Also, functions that return a character do so using a return type of **int**. However, the low-order byte contains the character. Thus this return value may be assigned to a variable of type **char** without any problems. Remember, C's automatic type conversions handle the conversion of a character into an integer (and vice versa) smoothly.

7.3.1   Character-testing functions   The 11 character-testing functions are used to determine what category a character is part of. The standard defines these (possibly overlapping) groups:

alphabetic	alphanumeric
punctuation	control
visible	printable
digit	lowercase
white space	uppercase
hexadecimal digit	

The character-testing functions are particularly useful when you're performing common programming tasks, such as dissecting a string into its individual tokens, or parsing a file name.

7.3.1.1 through 7.3.1.11   The standard clearly describes the actions of the character testing functions so no further commentary is required here. The following program illustrates their use:

```
#include <stdio.h>
#include <ctype.h>

void main(void)
{
  char c[7] = {'1', 'a', '.', ' ', 'x', '\t', 'A'};
  int i;

  for(i=0; i<7; i++) {
    if(isalnum(c[i])) printf("%c is alphanumeric\n", c[i]);
    if(isalpha(c[i])) printf("%c is alphabetic\n", c[i]);
```

Description

The **iscntrl** function tests for any control character.

7.3.1.4 The **isdigit** function

Synopsis

```
#include <ctype.h>
int isdigit(int c);
```

Description

The **isdigit** function tests for any decimal-digit character (as defined in 5.2.1).

7.3.1.5 The **isgraph** function

Synopsis

```
#include <ctype.h>
int isgraph(int c);
```

Description

The **isgraph** function tests for any printing character except space (' ').

7.3.1.6 The **islower** function

Synopsis

```
#include <ctype.h>
int islower(int c);
```

Description

The **islower** function tests for any character that is a lowercase letter or is one of an implementation-defined set of characters for which none of **iscntrl**, **isdigit**, **ispunct**, or **isspace** is true. In the "C" locale, **islower** returns true only for the characters defined as lowercase letters (as defined in 5.2.1).

7.3.1.7 The **isprint** function

Synopsis

```
#include <ctype.h>
int isprint(int c);
```

Description

The **isprint** function tests for any printing character including space (' ').

7.3.1.8 The **ispunct** function

Synopsis

```
#include <ctype.h>
int ispunct(int c);
```

Description

The **ispunct** function tests for any printing character that is neither space (' ') nor a character for which **isalnum** is true.

*(**7.3.1.1 through 7.3.1.11,** continued)*

```
        if(iscntrl(c[i])) printf("%d is control\n", c[i]);
        if(isdigit(c[i])) printf("%c is digit\n", c[i]);
        if(isgraph(c[i])) printf("%c is visible\n", c[i]);
        if(isprint(c[i])) printf("%c is printable\n", c[i]);
        if(islower(c[i])) printf("%c is lowercase\n", c[i]);
        if(isupper(c[i])) printf("%c is uppercase\n", c[i]);
        if(ispunct(c[i])) printf("%c is punctuation\n", c[i]);
        if(isspace(c[i])) printf("%c is whitespace\n", c[i]);
        if(isxdigit(c[i])) printf("%c is hexadecimal digit\n", c[i]);
    }
}
```

This program displays the following output:

```
1 is alphanumeric
1 is digit
1 is visible
1 is printable
1 is hexadecimal digit
a is alphanumeric
a is alphabetic
a is visible
a is printable
a is lowercase
a is hexadecimal digit
. is visible
. is printable
. is puntuation
  is printable
  is whitespace
x is alphanumeric
x is alphabetic
x is visible
x is printable
x is lowercase
9 is control
      is whitespace
A is alphanumeric
A is alphabetic
A is visible
A is printable
A is uppercase
A is hexadecimal digit
```

7.3.1.9 The `isspace` function

Synopsis

```
#include <ctype.h>
int isspace(int c);
```

Description

The `isspace` function tests for any character that is a standard white-space character or is one of an implementation-defined set of characters for which `isalnum` is false. The standard white-space characters are the following: space (`' '`), form feed (`'\f'`), new-line (`'\n'`), carriage return (`'\r'`), horizontal tab (`'\t'`), and vertical tab (`'\v'`). In the "C" locale, `isspace` returns true only for the standard white-space characters.

7.3.1.10 The `isupper` function

Synopsis

```
#include <ctype.h>
int isupper(int c);
```

Description

The `isupper` function tests for any character that is an uppercase letter or is one of an implementation-defined set of characters for which none of `iscntrl`, `isdigit`, `ispunct`, or `isspace` is true. In the "C" locale, `isupper` returns true only for the characters defined as uppercase letters (as defined in 5.2.1).

7.3.1.11 The `isxdigit` function

Synopsis

```
#include <ctype.h>
int isxdigit(int c);
```

Description

The `isxdigit` function tests for any hexadecimal-digit character (as defined in 6.1.3.2).

7.3.2 Character case mapping functions

7.3.2.1 The `tolower` function

Synopsis

```
#include <ctype.h>
int tolower(int c);
```

Description

The `tolower` function converts an uppercase letter to the corresponding lowercase letter.

Returns

If the argument is a character for which `isupper` is true and there is a corresponding character for which `islower` is true, the `tolower` function returns the corresponding character; otherwise, the argument is returned unchanged.

7.3.2.2 The `toupper` function

Synopsis

```
#include <ctype.h>
int toupper(int c);
```

7.3.2   *Character case mapping functions*   The functions **tolower()** and **toupper()** return the lower- or uppercase equivalent of their arguments, respectively. If either of these functions is called with a character that is not a letter or with the character already in the desired case, no change is made to the character and it is returned as is. For example, consider the following:

```
#include <stdio.h>
#include <ctype.h>

void main(void)
{
  printf("%c", tolower('A'));
  printf("%c", tolower('1'));
  printf("%c", toupper('x'));
  printf("%c", toupper('5'));
}
```

This program displays **a1X5**. Notice that each function returns unaltered an argument that is not a letter.

Description

The **toupper** function converts a lowercase letter to the corresponding uppercase letter.

Returns

If the argument is a character for which **islower** is true and there is a corresponding character for which **isupper** is true, the **toupper** function returns the corresponding character; otherwise, the argument is returned unchanged.

There are no annotations for page 105.

7.4 Localization <code><locale.h></code>

The header <code><locale.h></code> declares two functions, one type, and defines several macros.

The type is

    <code>struct lconv</code>

which contains members related to the formatting of numeric values. The structure shall contain at least the following members, in any order. The semantics of the members and their normal ranges is explained in 7.4.2.1. In the <code>"C"</code> locale, the members shall have the values specified in the comments.

```
char *decimal_point;        /* "." */
char *thousands_sep;        /* "" */
char *grouping;             /* "" */
char *int_curr_symbol;      /* "" */
char *currency_symbol;      /* "" */
char *mon_decimal_point;    /* "" */
char *mon_thousands_sep;    /* "" */
char *mon_grouping;         /* "" */
char *positive_sign;        /* "" */
char *negative_sign;        /* "" */
char int_frac_digits;       /* CHAR_MAX */
char frac_digits;           /* CHAR_MAX */
char p_cs_precedes;         /* CHAR_MAX */
char p_sep_by_space;        /* CHAR_MAX */
char n_cs_precedes;         /* CHAR_MAX */
char n_sep_by_space;        /* CHAR_MAX */
char p_sign_posn;           /* CHAR_MAX */
char n_sign_posn;           /* CHAR_MAX */
```

The macros defined are **NULL** (described in 7.1.6); and

```
LC_ALL
LC_COLLATE
LC_CTYPE
LC_MONETARY
LC_NUMERIC
LC_TIME
```

which expand to integral constant expressions with distinct values, suitable for use as the first argument to the **setlocale** function. Additional macro definitions, beginning with the characters **LC_** and an uppercase letter,[100] may also be specified by the implementation.

---

100 See ''future library directions'' (7.13.3).

7.4 *Localization <locale.h>* If you live in an English-speaking country and write programs that will be used only by English-speaking people, then *localization* is not important to you. More and more often, however, programmers are called upon to write programs that can be easily translated into other languages. To aid in the translation process, C defines several language-specific attributes. These are specified within the **lconv** structure, as shown in the standard. By using the information in this structure, it is possible to write programs that (to a large extent) automatically adjust for particular language environments.

7.4.1 Locale control

7.4.1.1 The `setlocale` function

Synopsis

```
#include <locale.h>
char *setlocale(int category, const char *locale);
```

Description

The **setlocale** function selects the appropriate portion of the program's locale as specified by the **category** and **locale** arguments. The **setlocale** function may be used to change or query the program's entire current locale or portions thereof. The value **LC_ALL** for **category** names the program's entire locale; the other values for **category** name only a portion of the program's locale. **LC_COLLATE** affects the behavior of the **strcoll** and **strxfrm** functions. **LC_CTYPE** affects the behavior of the character handling functions[101] and the multibyte functions. **LC_MONETARY** affects the monetary formatting information returned by the **localeconv** function. **LC_NUMERIC** affects the decimal-point character for the formatted input/output functions and the string conversion functions, as well as the nonmonetary formatting information returned by the **localeconv** function. **LC_TIME** affects the behavior of the **strftime** function.

A value of "C" for **locale** specifies the minimal environment for C translation; a value of "" for **locale** specifies the implementation-defined native environment. Other implementation-defined strings may be passed as the second argument to **setlocale**.

At program startup, the equivalent of

```
setlocale(LC_ALL, "C");
```

is executed.

The implementation shall behave as if no library function calls the **setlocale** function.

Returns

If a pointer to a string is given for **locale** and the selection can be honored, the **setlocale** function returns a pointer to the string associated with the specified **category** for the new locale. If the selection cannot be honored, the **setlocale** function returns a null pointer and the program's locale is not changed.

A null pointer for **locale** causes the **setlocale** function to return a pointer to the string associated with the **category** for the program's current locale; the program's locale is not changed.[102]

The pointer to string returned by the **setlocale** function is such that a subsequent call with that string value and its associated category will restore that part of the program's locale. The string pointed to shall not be modified by the program, but may be overwritten by a subsequent call to the **setlocale** function.

Forward references: formatted input/output functions (7.9.6), the multibyte character functions (7.10.7), the multibyte string functions (7.10.8), string conversion functions (7.10.1), the **strcoll** function (7.11.4.3), the **strftime** function (7.12.3.5), the **strxfrm** function (7.11.4.5).

---

101 The only functions in 7.3 whose behavior is not affected by the current locale are **isdigit** and **isxdigit**.

102 The implementation must arrange to encode in a string the various categories due to a heterogeneous locale when **category** has the value **LC_ALL**.

7.4.1.1   The setlocale function   The **setlocale()** function sets all or a specified portion of those items described in the **lconv** structure, so that they are compatible with the locale pointed to by the *locale* parameter. The value of *category* must be one of the **LC_** macros defined by **locale.h**. If *category* is **LC_ALL**, then all locale-specific items are adjusted. Otherwise, only the specified subgroup is changed.

Remember, a **locale** is, essentially, a language or a region. When the locale is set, the various locale-specific information is adjusted to be in accordance with the specified locale.

All C compilers support the "C" locale. You will need to check your compiler manuals for other locales that may be supported.

7.4.2 Numeric formatting convention inquiry

7.4.2.1 The `localeconv` function

Synopsis

```
#include <locale.h>
struct lconv *localeconv(void);
```

Description

The `localeconv` function sets the components of an object with type **struct lconv** with values appropriate for the formatting of numeric quantities (monetary and otherwise) according to the rules of the current locale.

The members of the structure with type **char *** are pointers to strings, any of which (except **decimal_point**) can point to "", to indicate that the value is not available in the current locale or is of zero length. The members with type **char** are nonnegative numbers, any of which can be **CHAR_MAX** to indicate that the value is not available in the current locale. The members include the following:

char *decimal_point
> The decimal-point character used to format nonmonetary quantities.

char *thousands_sep
> The character used to separate groups of digits before the decimal-point character in formatted nonmonetary quantities.

char *grouping
> A string whose elements indicate the size of each group of digits in formatted nonmonetary quantities.

char *int_curr_symbol
> The international currency symbol applicable to the current locale. The first three characters contain the alphabetic international currency symbol in accordance with those specified in ISO 4217:1987. The fourth character (immediately preceding the null character) is the character used to separate the international currency symbol from the monetary quantity.

char *currency_symbol
> The local currency symbol applicable to the current locale.

char *mon_decimal_point
> The decimal-point used to format monetary quantities.

char *mon_thousands_sep
> The separator for groups of digits before the decimal-point in formatted monetary quantities.

char *mon_grouping
> A string whose elements indicate the size of each group of digits in formatted monetary quantities.

char *positive_sign
> The string used to indicate a nonnegative-valued formatted monetary quantity.

char *negative_sign
> The string used to indicate a negative-valued formatted monetary quantity.

char int_frac_digits
> The number of fractional digits (those after the decimal-point) to be displayed in a internationally formatted monetary quantity.

7.4.2.1   *The localeconv function* The **localeconv()** function returns a pointer to a **lconv** structure that contains the current locale settings. This structure is statically allocated and may be overwritten by other events, such as a call to **setlocale()**. You must not alter this structure, but your program is free to use the information contained in the structure to add international support to your programs.

The standard is straightforward in its descriptions of the members of the **lconv** structure. On page 110, examples illustrate some of the differences in numeric and monetary representations among languages.

char frac_digits

> The number of fractional digits (those after the decimal-point) to be displayed in a formatted monetary quantity.

char p_cs_precedes

> Set to 1 or 0 if the **currency_symbol** respectively precedes or succeeds the value for a nonnegative formatted monetary quantity.

char p_sep_by_space

> Set to 1 or 0 if the **currency_symbol** respectively is or is not separated by a space from the value for a nonnegative formatted monetary quantity.

char n_cs_precedes

> Set to 1 or 0 if the **currency_symbol** respectively precedes or succeeds the value for a negative formatted monetary quantity.

char n_sep_by_space

> Set to 1 or 0 if the **currency_symbol** respectively is or is not separated by a space from the value for a negative formatted monetary quantity.

char p_sign_posn

> Set to a value indicating the positioning of the **positive_sign** for a nonnegative formatted monetary quantity.

char n_sign_posn

> Set to a value indicating the positioning of the **negative_sign** for a negative formatted monetary quantity.

The elements of **grouping** and **mon_grouping** are interpreted according to the following:

CHAR_MAX No further grouping is to be performed.

0 The previous element is to be repeatedly used for the remainder of the digits.

other The integer value is the number of digits that comprise the current group. The next element is examined to determine the size of the next group of digits before the current group.

The value of **p_sign_posn** and **n_sign_posn** is interpreted according to the following:

0 Parentheses surround the quantity and **currency_symbol**.

1 The sign string precedes the quantity and **currency_symbol**.

2 The sign string succeeds the quantity and **currency_symbol**.

3 The sign string immediately precedes the **currency_symbol**.

4 The sign string immediately succeeds the **currency_symbol**.

The implementation shall behave as if no library function calls the **localeconv** function.

Returns

The **localeconv** function returns a pointer to the filled-in object. The structure pointed to by the return value shall not be modified by the program, but may be overwritten by a subsequent call to the **localeconv** function. In addition, calls to the **setlocale** function with categories **LC_ALL**, **LC_MONETARY**, or **LC_NUMERIC** may overwrite the contents of the structure.

Example

The following table illustrates the rules which may well be used by four countries to format monetary quantities.

There are no annotations for page 109.

Country	Positive format	Negative format	International format
Italy	L.1.234	-L.1.234	ITL.1.234
Netherlands	F 1.234,56	F -1.234,56	NLG 1.234,56
Norway	kr1.234,56	kr1.234,56-	NOK 1.234,56
Switzerland	SFrs.1,234.56	SFrs.1,234.56C	CHF 1,234.56

For these four countries, the respective values for the monetary members of the structure returned by **localeconv** are:

	Italy	Netherlands	Norway	Switzerland
int_curr_symbol	"ITL."	"NLG "	"NOK "	"CHF "
currency_symbol	"L."	"F"	"kr"	"SFrs."
mon_decimal_point	""	","	","	"."
mon_thousands_sep	"."	"."	"."	","
mon_grouping	"\3"	"\3"	"\3"	"\3"
positive_sign	""	""	""	""
negative_sign	"-"	"-"	"-"	"C"
int_frac_digits	0	2	2	2
frac_digits	0	2	2	2
p_cs_precedes	1	1	1	1
p_sep_by_space	0	1	0	0
n_cs_precedes	1	1	1	1
n_sep_by_space	0	1	0	0
p_sign_posn	1	1	1	1
n_sign_posn	1	4	2	2

There are no annotations for page 110.

7.5 Mathematics <math.h>

The header **<math.h>** declares several mathematical functions and defines one macro. The functions take **double** arguments and return **double** values.[103] Integer arithmetic functions and conversion functions are discussed later.

The macro defined is

    HUGE_VAL

which expands to a positive **double** expression, not necessarily representable as a **float**.[104]

Forward references: integer arithmetic functions (7.10.6), the **atof** function (7.10.1.1), the **strtod** function (7.10.1.4).

7.5.1 Treatment of error conditions

The behavior of each of these functions is defined for all representable values of its input arguments. Each function shall execute as if it were a single operation, without generating any externally visible exceptions.

For all functions, a *domain error* occurs if an input argument is outside the domain over which the mathematical function is defined. The description of each function lists any required domain errors; an implementation may define additional domain errors, provided that such errors are consistent with the mathematical definition of the function.[105] On a domain error, the function returns an implementation-defined value; the value of the macro **EDOM** is stored in **errno**.

Similarly, a *range error* occurs if the result of the function cannot be represented as a **double** value. If the result overflows (the magnitude of the result is so large that it cannot be represented in an object of the specified type), the function returns the value of the macro **HUGE_VAL**, with the same sign (except for the **tan** function) as the correct value of the function; the value of the macro **ERANGE** is stored in **errno**. If the result underflows (the magnitude of the result is so small that it cannot be represented in an object of the specified type), the function returns zero; whether the integer expression **errno** acquires the value of the macro **ERANGE** is implementation-defined.

7.5.2 Trigonometric functions

7.5.2.1 The acos function

Synopsis

    #include <math.h>
    double acos(double x);

Description

The **acos** function computes the principal value of the arc cosine of **x**. A domain error occurs for arguments not in the range [−1, +1].

---

103 See "future library directions" (7.13.4).

104 **HUGE_VAL** can be positive infinity in an implementation that supports infinities.

105 In an implementation that supports infinities, this allows infinity as an argument to be a domain error if the mathematical domain of the function does not include infinity.

7.5 Mathematics \<math.h> When using the mathematical functions, remember one important point: You must include **math.h**. Since these functions accept **double** arguments and return **double** values, the prototypes contained in **math.h** are crucial to the correct operation of your program.

Note that to use most of the functions described in this section, you need to have an understanding of trigonometry, logarithms, and various other mathematical transformations. If you understand these operations, you will have no trouble applying these functions.

7.5.1 Treatment of error conditions Error handling is very important in most mathematical applications. Though this section of the standard is quite clear, the following discussion restates the material from a different point of view.

The standard states that there are two types of errors that may occur in a program using the mathematical functions: *domain* errors and *range* errors.

A domain error occurs when the argument used to call the function is not within the domain over which that function is designed to operate. For example, attempting to take the square root of a negative generates a domain error because the square root of a negative number is undefined. When a domain error occurs, the global error variable **errno** is set to the macro-defined value **EDOM**, and the return value of the function is meaningless. Therefore, if you are using a function in such a way that domain errors are possible, you must monitor the value of **errno** carefully.

A range error occurs when the value returned by a mathematical function cannot be represented by a **double** value. This can happen when the return value is either too large *or* too small. If the value is too large, the macro-defined value **HUGE_VAL** is returned and **errno** is set to **ERANGE**. If the value is too small, 0 is returned and **errno** *may be* set to **ERANGE**, depending upon your implementation.

The key point to understand about watching for errors when you are using the mathematical functions is that in some situations you will need to monitor both the return value of the function and the value of **errno**. This extra error-checking may seem tedious, but it is the only way you can ensure that all errors are trapped.

7.5.2 Trigonometric functions The descriptions of the *trigonometric functions* are straightforward, and the programs on the following page illustrate the use of several of these functions. One point to notice: Angles are specified and returned in radians, not degrees.

Returns

The **acos** function returns the arc cosine in the range [0, π] radians.

7.5.2.2 The **asin** function

Synopsis

```
#include <math.h>
double asin(double x);
```

Description

The **asin** function computes the principal value of the arc sine of **x**. A domain error occurs for arguments not in the range [−1, +1].

Returns

The **asin** function returns the arc sine in the range [−π/2, +π/2] radians.

7.5.2.3 The **atan** function

Synopsis

```
#include <math.h>
double atan(double x);
```

Description

The **atan** function computes the principal value of the arc tangent of **x**.

Returns

The **atan** function returns the arc tangent in the range [−π/2, +π/2] radians.

7.5.2.4 The **atan2** function

Synopsis

```
#include <math.h>
double atan2(double y, double x);
```

Description

The **atan2** function computes the principal value of the arc tangent of **y/x**, using the signs of both arguments to determine the quadrant of the return value. A domain error may occur if both arguments are zero.

Returns

The **atan2** function returns the arc tangent of **y/x**, in the range [−π, +π] radians.

7.5.2.5 The **cos** function

Synopsis

```
#include <math.h>
double cos(double x);
```

Description

The **cos** function computes the cosine of **x** (measured in radians).

Returns

The **cos** function returns the cosine value.

7.5.2.2 through 7.5.2.7 This short program demonstrates the **sin()**, **cos()**, and **tan()** functions:

```
#include <stdio.h>
#include <math.h>

void main(void)
{
  printf("Sine of 0.5: %lf\n", sin(0.5));
  printf("Cosine of 0.5: %lf\n", cos(0.5));
  printf("Tangent of 0.5: %lf\n", tan(0.5));
}
```

This next program rotates a point in two-dimensional space through an angle of 1 radian:

```
/* This program rotates a point in 2-dimensional space. */
#include <stdio.h>
#include <math.h>

#define THETA 1

void main(void)
{
  double x = 1.0, y = 1.0;
  double newx, newy;

  newx = x * cos(THETA) + y * sin(THETA);
  newy = -x * sin(THETA) + y * cos(THETA);

  printf("%lf, %lf rotated through 1 radian is: ", x, y);
  printf("%lf, %lf\n", newx, newy);
}
```

Note that the foregoing examples do not perform any error checking because each function is known to be called with values within the domain of the function. However, you should check for errors when appropriate in your own applications.

7.5.2.6 The `sin` function

Synopsis

```
#include <math.h>
double sin(double x);
```

Description

The `sin` function computes the sine of **x** (measured in radians).

Returns

The `sin` function returns the sine value.

7.5.2.7 The `tan` function

Synopsis

```
#include <math.h>
double tan(double x);
```

Description

The `tan` function returns the tangent of **x** (measured in radians).

Returns

The `tan` function returns the tangent value.

7.5.3 Hyperbolic functions

7.5.3.1 The `cosh` function

Synopsis

```
#include <math.h>
double cosh(double x);
```

Description

The `cosh` function computes the hyperbolic cosine of **x**. A range error occurs if the magnitude of **x** is too large.

Returns

The `cosh` function returns the hyperbolic cosine value.

7.5.3.2 The `sinh` function

Synopsis

```
#include <math.h>
double sinh(double x);
```

Description

The `sinh` function computes the hyperbolic sine of **x**. A range error occurs if the magnitude of **x** is too large.

Returns

The `sinh` function returns the hyperbolic sine value.

7.5.3   *Hyperbolic functions*   The descriptions of the *hyperbolic functions* are straightforward and need no further comment.

7.5.3.3 The `tanh` function

Synopsis

```
#include <math.h>
double tanh(double x);
```

Description

The **tanh** function computes the hyperbolic tangent of **x**.

Returns

The **tanh** function returns the hyperbolic tangent value.

7.5.4 Exponential and logarithmic functions

7.5.4.1 The `exp` function

Synopsis

```
#include <math.h>
double exp(double x);
```

Description

The **exp** function computes the exponential function of **x**. A range error occurs if the magnitude of **x** is too large.

Returns

The **exp** function returns the exponential value.

7.5.4.2 The `frexp` function

Synopsis

```
#include <math.h>
double frexp(double value, int *exp);
```

Description

The **frexp** function breaks a floating-point number into a normalized fraction and an integral power of 2. It stores the integer in the **int** object pointed to by **exp**.

Returns

The **frexp** function returns the value **x**, such that **x** is a **double** with magnitude in the interval [1/2, 1) or zero, and **value** equals **x** times 2 raised to the power ***exp**. If **value** is zero, both parts of the result are zero.

7.5.4.3 The `ldexp` function

Synopsis

```
#include <math.h>
double ldexp(double x, int exp);
```

Description

The **ldexp** function multiplies a floating-point number by an integral power of 2. A range error may occur.

Returns

The **ldexp** function returns the value of **x** times 2 raised to the power **exp**.

7.5.4 *Exponential and logarithmic functions* This section clearly describes the operation of the *logarithmic* and *exponential functions*.

One interesting function that you may find useful outside the realm of numerical programming is **modf()**, which breaks down a floating-point value into its integral and fractional parts. The following program demonstrates **modf()**:

```
/* This program demonstrates modf(). */
#include <stdio.h>
#include <math.h>

void main(void)
{
  double x = 123.987;
  double integral;
  double frac;

  frac = modf(x, &integral); /* break down x */

  printf("Integral part: %lf, fractional part: %lf",
         integral, frac);
}
```

Here is the output from this program:

```
Integral part: 123.000000, fractional part: 0.987000
```

7.5.4.4 The log function

Synopsis

```
#include <math.h>
double log(double x);
```

Description

The **log** function computes the natural logarithm of **x**. A domain error occurs if the argument is negative. A range error may occur if the argument is zero.

Returns

The **log** function returns the natural logarithm.

7.5.4.5 The log10 function

Synopsis

```
#include <math.h>
double log10(double x);
```

Description

The **log10** function computes the base-ten logarithm of **x**. A domain error occurs if the argument is negative. A range error may occur if the argument is zero.

Returns

The **log10** function returns the base-ten logarithm.

7.5.4.6 The modf function

Synopsis

```
#include <math.h>
double modf(double value, double *iptr);
```

Description

The **modf** function breaks the argument **value** into integral and fractional parts, each of which has the same sign as the argument. It stores the integral part as a **double** in the object pointed to by **iptr**.

Returns

The **modf** function returns the signed fractional part of **value**.

7.5.5 Power functions

7.5.5.1 The pow function

Synopsis

```
#include <math.h>
double pow(double x, double y);
```

Description

The **pow** function computes **x** raised to the power **y**. A domain error occurs if **x** is negative and **y** is not an integral value. A domain error occurs if the result cannot be represented when **x** is zero and **y** is less than or equal to zero. A range error may occur.

Returns

The **pow** function returns the value of **x** raised to the power **y**.

There are no annotations for page 115.

7.5.5.2 The sqrt function

Synopsis

```
#include <math.h>
double sqrt(double x);
```

Description

The **sqrt** function computes the nonnegative square root of **x**. A domain error occurs if the argument is negative.

Returns

The **sqrt** function returns the value of the square root.

7.5.6 Nearest integer, absolute value, and remainder functions

7.5.6.1 The ceil function

Synopsis

```
#include <math.h>
double ceil(double x);
```

Description

The **ceil** function computes the smallest integral value not less than **x**.

Returns

The **ceil** function returns the smallest integral value not less than **x**, expressed as a double.

7.5.6.2 The fabs function

Synopsis

```
#include <math.h>
double fabs(double x);
```

Description

The **fabs** function computes the absolute value of a floating-point number **x**.

Returns

The **fabs** function returns the absolute value of **x**.

7.5.6.3 The floor function

Synopsis

```
#include <math.h>
double floor(double x);
```

Description

The **floor** function computes the largest integral value not greater than **x**.

Returns

The **floor** function returns the largest integral value not greater than **x**, expressed as a double.

7.5.6 Nearest integer, absolute value, and remainder functions The operation of these functions is clearly described in the standard, and demonstrated in the following program:

```
#include <stdio.h>
#include <math.h>

void main(void)
{
  double x = 123.987;

  printf("The remainder of 10.0/3/0 is %lf\n", fmod(10.0, 3.0));
  printf("Ceiling of %lf is %lf\n", x, ceil(x));
  printf("Floor of %lf is %lf\n", x, floor(x));
  printf("Absolute value of -123.23 is %lf\n", fabs(-123.23));
}
```

Here is the output from the foregoing program:

```
The remainder of 10.0/3.0 is 1.000000
Ceiling of 123.987000 is 124.000000
Floor of 123.987000 is 123.000000
Absolute value of -123.23 is 123.230000
```

7.5.6.4 The **fmod** function

Synopsis

```
#include <math.h>
double fmod(double x, double y);
```

Description

The **fmod** function computes the floating-point remainder of **x/y**.

Returns

The **fmod** function returns the value $x - i * y$, for some integer i such that, if **y** is nonzero, the result has the same sign as **x** and magnitude less than the magnitude of **y**. If **y** is zero, whether a domain error occurs or the **fmod** function returns zero is implementation-defined.

There are no annotations for page 117.

7.6 Nonlocal jumps <setjmp.h>

The header **<setjmp.h>** defines the macro **setjmp**, and declares one function and one type, for bypassing the normal function call and return discipline.[106]

The type declared is

    jmp_buf

which is an array type suitable for holding the information needed to restore a calling environment.

It is unspecified whether **setjmp** is a macro or an identifier declared with external linkage. If a macro definition is suppressed in order to access an actual function, or a program defines an external identifier with the name **setjmp**, the behavior is undefined.

7.6.1 Save calling environment

7.6.1.1 The setjmp macro

Synopsis

```
#include <setjmp.h>
int setjmp(jmp_buf env);
```

Description

The **setjmp** macro saves its calling environment in its **jmp_buf** argument for later use by the **longjmp** function.

Returns

If the return is from a direct invocation, the **setjmp** macro returns the value zero. If the return is from a call to the **longjmp** function, the **setjmp** macro returns a nonzero value.

Environmental constraint

An invocation of the **setjmp** macro shall appear only in one of the following contexts:

— the entire controlling expression of a selection or iteration statement;

— one operand of a relational or equality operator with the other operand an integral constant expression, with the resulting expression being the entire controlling expression of a selection or iteration statement;

— the operand of a unary ! operator with the resulting expression being the entire controlling expression of a selection or iteration statement; or

— the entire expression of an expression statement (possibly cast to **void**).

---

106 These functions are useful for dealing with unusual conditions encountered in a low-level function of a program.

7.6 Nonlocal jumps <setjmp.h> As you probably know, generally the only way to transfer control from one function to another is for the first function to call the second one. For example, using **goto** it is impossible to jump from one function to another, bypassing the normal call mechanism. However, the two library functions **setjump()** and **longjmp()** allow a C program to execute an *interfunction jump*—that is, one function can branch directly into the middle of another.

Keep in mind that interfunction jumps are intended to be applied carefully and sparingly. They are included in standard C to handle a variety of unique and unusual circumstances. They are *not* intended to bypass the normal function call and return mechanism used for the vast majority of programming situations.

One good use for an interfunction jump is when a catastrophic error occurs in a deeply nested function, and when the best response to that error is returning to a "safe point" outside that function and executing what is, in effect, a program reset.

The functions **setjmp()** and **longjmp()** work together; **setjmp()** establishes the point in one function to which **longjmp()** will branch. The **setjmp()** function does this by saving the current state of the stack and of the CPU registers in a buffer of type **jmp_buf** (**jmp_buf** is defined in the header file **setjmp.h**). Once this is done, when your program wants to jump back to the point at which **setjmp()** was called, it executes a **longjmp()**, which uses the contents of the jump buffer to reset the machine to its previous settings. Execution then resumes immediately after the point at which **setjmp()** was called. In effect, your program will think that execution is continuing after a call to **setjmp()**, though in reality an interfunction jump has just been accomplished.

The **setjmp()** function returns 0 when it is actually called, during which the jump buffer is initialized. (Remember, when **setjmp()** is actually called, it is saving the current state of the machine.) When **setjmp()** "returns" after you execute a call to **longjmp()**, its return value will be that specified by the *val* parameter to **longjmp()**, which must be nonzero.

To understand the relationship between **setjmp()** and **longjmp()**, study this short program:

```
/* This program demonstrates setjmp() and longjmp(). */
#include <stdio.h>
#include <setjmp.h>

jmp_buf jumpbuf; /* long jump buffer */

void f(void);
```

7.6.2 Restore calling environment

7.6.2.1 The `longjmp` function

Synopsis

```
#include <setjmp.h>
void longjmp(jmp_buf env, int val);
```

Description

The `longjmp` function restores the environment saved by the most recent invocation of the `setjmp` macro in the same invocation of the program, with the corresponding `jmp_buf` argument. If there has been no such invocation, or if the function containing the invocation of the `setjmp` macro has terminated execution[107] in the interim, the behavior is undefined.

All accessible objects have values as of the time `longjmp` was called, except that the values of objects of automatic storage duration that are local to the function containing the invocation of the corresponding `setjmp` macro that do not have volatile-qualified type and have been changed between the `setjmp` invocation and `longjmp` call are indeterminate.

As it bypasses the usual function call and return mechanisms, the `longjmp` function shall execute correctly in contexts of interrupts, signals and any of their associated functions. However, if the `longjmp` function is invoked from a nested signal handler (that is, from a function invoked as a result of a signal raised during the handling of another signal), the behavior is undefined.

Returns

After `longjmp` is completed, program execution continues as if the corresponding invocation of the `setjmp` macro had just returned the value specified by `val`. The `longjmp` function cannot cause the `setjmp` macro to return the value 0; if `val` is 0, the `setjmp` macro returns the value 1.

---

107 For example, by executing a **return** statement or because another `longjmp` call has caused a transfer to a `setjmp` invocation in a function earlier in the set of nested calls.

(*7.6   Nonlocal jumps <setjmp.h>, continued*)

```c
void main(void)
{
  int result;

  printf("This is first printf() call in main().");

  result = setjmp(jumpbuf); /* save environment */
  printf("\nThis is printf() after the setjmp() statement.\n");

  /* execute only when setjmp() called the first time. */
  if(!result) {
    printf("Executing call to f().\n");
    f();
  }

  if(result==1)
    printf("Interfunction branch has been executed.\n");
}

void f(void)
{
  int i;

  for(i=0; i<10; i++) {
    if(i==5) longjmp(jumpbuf, 1); /* branch out of f() */
    printf("%d ", i);
  }
}
```

Here is the output displayed by the foregoing program:

```
This is first printf() call in main().
This is printf() after the setjmp() statement.
Executing call to f().
0 1 2 3 4
This is printf() after the setjmp() statement.
Interfunction branch has been executed.
```

It is important to understand that not all aspects of your program will be reset by performing a **longjmp()**. For example, global variables that have been changed after the call to **setjmp()** will remain altered after a call to **longjmp()**.

7.7 Signal handling `<signal.h>`

The header `<signal.h>` declares a type and two functions and defines several macros, for handling various *signals* (conditions that may be reported during program execution).

The type defined is

> `sig_atomic_t`

which is the integral type of an object that can be accessed as an atomic entity, even in the presence of asynchronous interrupts.

The macros defined are

> `SIG_DFL`
> `SIG_ERR`
> `SIG_IGN`

which expand to constant expressions with distinct values that have type compatible with the second argument to and the return value of the `signal` function, and whose value compares unequal to the address of any declarable function; and the following, each of which expands to a positive integral constant expression that is the signal number corresponding to the specified condition:

`SIGABRT`   abnormal termination, such as is initiated by the **abort** function

`SIGFPE`   an erroneous arithmetic operation, such as zero divide or an operation resulting in overflow

`SIGILL`   detection of an invalid function image, such as an illegal instruction

`SIGINT`   receipt of an interactive attention signal

`SIGSEGV`   an invalid access to storage

`SIGTERM`   a termination request sent to the program

An implementation need not generate any of these signals, except as a result of explicit calls to the **raise** function. Additional signals and pointers to undeclarable functions, with macro definitions beginning, respectively, with the letters `SIG` and an uppercase letter or with `SIG_` and an uppercase letter,[108] may also be specified by the implementation. The complete set of signals, their semantics, and their default handling is implementation-defined; all signal numbers shall be positive.

7.7.1 Specify signal handling

7.7.1.1 The `signal` function

Synopsis

```
#include <signal.h>
void (*signal(int sig, void (*func)(int)))(int);
```

Description

The **signal** function chooses one of three ways in which receipt of the signal number **sig** is to be subsequently handled. If the value of **func** is **SIG_DFL**, default handling for that signal will occur. If the value of **func** is **SIG_IGN**, the signal will be ignored. Otherwise,

---

108 See "future library directions" (7.13.5). The names of the signal numbers reflect the following terms (respectively): abort, floating-point exception, illegal instruction, interrupt, segmentation violation, and termination.

7.7 Signal handling <signal.h> There are two *signal-handling functions* supported by standard C: **signal()** and **raise()**. These functions may work together or be used independently.

The purpose of **signal()** is to allow a C program to respond to various events generated by the underlying environment. Typically, these events are interrupts occurring due to some sort of error condition to which your program may wish to respond. The **signal()** function is used to route a specific interrupt (that is, a signal) to its own signal-handling function. The purpose of **raise()** is to send a signal (possibly by generating a software interrupt). If you have defined a function to handle this signal using **signal()**, then this function will automatically respond to it.

Not every C program will need to handle signals. For the majority of programs, the default operation of the C run-time package and of the operating system is sufficient. However, in cases where you want your program to take as much control as it can over the execution environment, signal processing will be important.

There are at least six signals that can be generated, and these are described in the standard (your environment may support others). For instance, if the program is about to be aborted, the signal **SIGABRT** is sent to your program. If you have a signal handler in place for **SIGABRT**, then you can take appropriate actions—such as closing disk files or notifying the user—prior to full program termination.

In many implementations, signal handlers are treated as interrupt functions. As such, several restrictions may apply. Be sure to check your compiler's library manual carefully on this issue.

7.7.1 Specify signal handling The **signal()** function designates how a specific signal will be handled when it is received. This function's first parameter, *sig,* specifies the signal that the handler will respond to; the signal must be one of the standard signals or an implementation-specific signal. The second parameter is a pointer to a function that is the signal handler. Signal handlers must have this prototype:

    void *sighandler*(int *sig*);

where *sighandler* is the name of the handler. The parameter *sig* receives the signal when the handler is executed.

func shall point to a function to be called when that signal occurs. Such a function is called a *signal handler*.

When a signal occurs, if **func** points to a function, first the equivalent of **signal(sig, SIG_DFL);** is executed or an implementation-defined blocking of the signal is performed. (If the value of **sig** is **SIGILL**, whether the reset to **SIG_DFL** occurs is implementation-defined.) Next the equivalent of **(*func)(sig);** is executed. The function **func** may terminate by executing a **return** statement or by calling the **abort**, **exit**, or **longjmp** function. If **func** executes a **return** statement and the value of **sig** was **SIGFPE** or any other implementation-defined value corresponding to a computational exception, the behavior is undefined. Otherwise, the program will resume execution at the point it was interrupted.

If the signal occurs other than as the result of calling the **abort** or **raise** function, the behavior is undefined if the signal handler calls any function in the standard library other than the **signal** function itself (with a first argument of the signal number corresponding to the signal that caused the invocation of the handler) or refers to any object with static storage duration other than by assigning a value to a static storage duration variable of type **volatile sig_atomic_t**. Furthermore, if such a call to the **signal** function results in a **SIG_ERR** return, the value of **errno** is indeterminate.[109]

At program startup, the equivalent of

        signal(sig, SIG_IGN);

may be executed for some signals selected in an implementation-defined manner; the equivalent of

        signal(sig, SIG_DFL);

is executed for all other signals defined by the implementation.

The implementation shall behave as if no library function calls the **signal** function.

Returns

If the request can be honored, the **signal** function returns the value of **func** for the most recent call to **signal** for the specified signal **sig**. Otherwise, a value of **SIG_ERR** is returned and a positive value is stored in **errno**.

Forward references: the **abort** function (7.10.4.1), the **exit** function (7.10.4.3).

7.7.2 Send signal

7.7.2.1 The **raise** function

Synopsis

        ```
        #include <signal.h>
        int raise(int sig);
        ```

Description

The **raise** function sends the signal **sig** to the executing program.

Returns

The **raise** function returns zero if successful, nonzero if unsuccessful.

---

109 If any signal is generated by an asynchronous signal handler, the behavior is undefined.

7.7.1.1   *The signal function* You may optionally use the predefined macros **SIG_DFL** and **SIG_IGN** for the second parameter to **signal()**, instead of passing the address of a signal handler function. If you use **SIG_DFL**, the default processing for the specified signal is used. Default processing occurs automatically when a signal is generated. Therefore, the only reason to specify default signal-processing is to cancel a previously specified signal handler and allow default processing to once again resume. If you specify **SIG_IGN**, the signal is simply ignored. Use **SIG_IGN** carefully, because most signals indicate that some condition fundamental to your program may be missing.

7.7.2   *Send signal* The **raise()** function allows your program to manually send a signal to a signal handler. This program demonstrates the operation of **signal()** and **raise()**:

```
/* This program demonstrates raise() and signal(). */
#include <stdio.h>
#include <stdlib.h>
#include <signal.h>

void mysig(int sig);
void donothing(void);

void main(void)
{
  signal(SIGTERM, mysig);

  donothing();
  printf("This will not be displayed.\n");
}

void mysig(int sig)
{
  printf("\n\aTermination signal %d received.\n", sig);
  exit(0);
}

void donothing(void)
{
  int i;

  for(i=1; i<1000; i++) {
    printf("%4d ", i);
    if(!(i%10)) printf("\n");
    if(i == 100) raise(SIGTERM); /* signal termination */
  }
}
```

7.8 Variable arguments <stdarg.h>

The header **<stdarg.h>** declares a type and defines three macros, for advancing through a list of arguments whose number and types are not known to the called function when it is translated.

A function may be called with a variable number of arguments of varying types. As described in 6.7.1, its parameter list contains one or more parameters. The rightmost parameter plays a special role in the access mechanism, and will be designated *parmN* in this description.

The type declared is

    va_list

which is a type suitable for holding information needed by the macros **va_start**, **va_arg**, and **va_end**. If access to the varying arguments is desired, the called function shall declare an object (referred to as **ap** in this subclause) having type **va_list**. The object **ap** may be passed as an argument to another function; if that function invokes the **va_arg** macro with parameter **ap**, the value of **ap** in the calling function is indeterminate and shall be passed to the **va_end** macro prior to any further reference to **ap**.

7.8.1 Variable argument list access macros

The **va_start** and **va_arg** macros described in this subclause shall be implemented as macros, not as actual functions. It is unspecified whether **va_end** is a macro or an identifier declared with external linkage. If a macro definition is suppressed in order to access an actual function, or a program defines an external identifier with the name **va_end**, the behavior is undefined. The **va_start** and **va_end** macros shall be invoked in the function accepting a varying number of arguments, if access to the varying arguments is desired.

7.8.1.1 The va_start macro

Synopsis

    #include <stdarg.h>
    void va_start(va_list ap, *parmN*);

Description

The **va_start** macro shall be invoked before any access to the unnamed arguments.

The **va_start** macro initializes **ap** for subsequent use by **va_arg** and **va_end**.

The parameter *parmN* is the identifier of the rightmost parameter in the variable parameter list in the function definition (the one just before the , ...). If the parameter *parmN* is declared with the **register** storage class, with a function or array type, or with a type that is not compatible with the type that results after application of the default argument promotions, the behavior is undefined.

Returns

The **va_start** macro returns no value.

7.8.1.2 The va_arg macro

Synopsis

    #include <stdarg.h>
    type va_arg(va_list ap, *type*);

Description

The **va_arg** macro expands to an expression that has the type and value of the next argument in the call. The parameter **ap** shall be the same as the **va_list ap** initialized by **va_start**. Each invocation of **va_arg** modifies **ap** so that the values of successive arguments

(**7.7.2 Send signal**, *continued*)

Here is the output (the value 15 is implementation-specific):

```
 1   2   3   4   5   6   7   8   9   10
11  12  13  14  15  16  17  18  19   20
21  22  23  24  25  26  27  28  29   30
31  32  33  34  35  36  37  38  39   40
41  42  43  44  45  46  47  48  49   50
51  52  53  54  55  56  57  58  59   60
61  62  63  64  65  66  67  68  69   70
71  72  73  74  75  76  77  78  79   80
81  82  83  84  85  86  87  88  89   90
91  92  93  94  95  96  97  98  99  100
```

```
Termination signal 15 received.
```

7.8 Variable arguments <stdarg.h> Although it requires some extra effort on your part, you can create C functions that accept a variable number of arguments. As you probably know, the C standard library contains several of these functions, including **printf()** and **scanf()**. Although the description in the standard is a bit intimidating on this issue, the technique of using variable arguments is quite easy to master. The following discussion explains how to use variable arguments from a more practical perspective.

A function that will accept a variable number of arguments must have at least one actual, known parameter; and it may have more. In either case, the standard refers to the last known parameter as *parmN*. The name of this parameter is used to initialize the variable argument processing system.

All variable argument functions must be prototyped before they are used. The prototype uses an ellipsis to denote a variable-length argument list. For example, here is the prototype for a function that has two actual parameters, consisting of a character pointer and an integer followed by an unknown number of arguments:

    void myfunc(char *str, int count, ...);

In this case, the parameter **count** is the one referred to as *paramN* by the standard.

It is important to understand that a variable-argument function must have some way of determining just how many and what type of arguments it is called with. The number of arguments is often passed to the function in one of its actual parameters. If the variable-length argument list can involve more than one type, the type information is generally passed, as well. The point is this: A function cannot, by itself, know how many arguments it is actually called with or their type.

When a variable-argument function begins, it must first create a special argument pointer, referred to as *ap* by the standard. This pointer is of type **va_list**, and it will be used to access the variable parameters. The *ap* pointer must then be initialized are returned in turn. The parameter *type* is a type name specified such that the type of a pointer to an object that has the specified type can be obtained simply by postfixing a ***** to *type*. If there is no actual next argument, or if *type* is not compatible with the type of the actual next argument (as promoted according to the default argument promotions), the behavior is undefined.

Returns

The first invocation of the **va_arg** macro after that of the **va_start** macro returns the value of the argument after that specified by *parmN*. Successive invocations return the values of the remaining arguments in succession.

7.8.1.3 The va_end macro

Synopsis

```
#include <stdarg.h>
void va_end(va_list ap);
```

Description

The **va_end** macro facilitates a normal return from the function whose variable argument list was referred to by the expansion of **va_start** that initialized the **va_list ap**. The **va_end** macro may modify **ap** so that it is no longer usable (without an intervening invocation of **va_start**). If there is no corresponding invocation of the **va_start** macro, or if the **va_end** macro is not invoked before the return, the behavior is undefined.

Returns

The **va_end** macro returns no value.

Example

The function **f1** gathers into an array a list of arguments that are pointers to strings (but not more than **MAXARGS** arguments), then passes the array as a single argument to function **f2**. The number of pointers is specified by the first argument to **f1**.

```
#include <stdarg.h>
#define MAXARGS    31

void f1(int n_ptrs, ...)
{
        va_list ap;
        char *array[MAXARGS];
        int ptr_no = 0;

        if (n_ptrs > MAXARGS)
              n_ptrs = MAXARGS;
        va_start(ap, n_ptrs);
        while (ptr_no < n_ptrs)
              array[ptr_no++] = va_arg(ap, char *);
        va_end(ap);
        f2(n_ptrs, array);
}
```

Each call to **f1** shall have visible the definition of the function or a declaration such as

```
void f1(int, ...);
```

(7.8 Variable arguments <stdarg.h>, continued)

using a call to the macro **va_start()**. The first parameter to **va_start()** is the pointer variable, and the second is the name of the last parameter before the variable-argument list (that is, *paramN*).

Once the variable-argument system has been initialized, each argument is obtained using a call to the macro **va_arg()**. The first parameter to **va_arg()** is the argument pointer; the second is the type of argument to be retrieved. Each time this macro is called, another argument is obtained. Keep in mind, however, that **va_arg()** has no way of knowing when it reaches the end of the argument list. Therefore, it is imperative that the function be passed the number of parameters it is called with, or some way to determine this. Once you have processed all variable arguments, call **va_end()**.

The following program shows how to create a variable-argument function:

```
/* This program demonstrates variable length arguments. */
#include <stdio.h>
#include <stdarg.h>

int vafunc(int num, ...); /* prototype for variable arg list */

void main(void)
{
  int n;

  n = vafunc(10, 1, 2, 3, 4, 5, 6, 7, 8, 9, 10);
  printf("Sum of args to vafunc() is %d.\n", n);
}

int vafunc(int num, ...)
{
  va_list argptr;
  int sum = 0;
  int i;

  va_start(argptr, num); /* initialize argptr */

  for(i=0 ; i < num; i++)
    sum = sum + va_arg(argptr, int);

  va_end(argptr); /* end variable processing */
  return sum;
}
```

The function **vafunc()** sums the values of a variable number of integer arguments and returns the result. The number of arguments passed to the function is in **num**.

7.9 Input/output <stdio.h>

7.9.1 Introduction

The header **<stdio.h>** declares three types, several macros, and many functions for performing input and output.

The types declared are **size_t** (described in 7.1.6);

FILE

which is an object type capable of recording all the information needed to control a stream, including its file position indicator, a pointer to its associated buffer (if any), an *error indicator* that records whether a read/write error has occurred, and an *end-of-file indicator* that records whether the end of the file has been reached; and

fpos_t

which is an object type capable of recording all the information needed to specify uniquely every position within a file.

The macros are **NULL** (described in 7.1.6);

_IOFBF
_IOLBF
_IONBF

which expand to integral constant expressions with distinct values, suitable for use as the third argument to the **setvbuf** function;

BUFSIZ

which expands to an integral constant expression, which is the size of the buffer used by the **setbuf** function;

EOF

which expands to a negative integral constant expression that is returned by several functions to indicate *end-of-file*, that is, no more input from a stream;

FOPEN_MAX

which expands to an integral constant expression that is the minimum number of files that the implementation guarantees can be open simultaneously;

FILENAME_MAX

which expands to an integral constant expression that is the size needed for an array of **char** large enough to hold the longest file name string that the implementation guarantees can be opened;[110]

L_tmpnam

which expands to an integral constant expression that is the size needed for an array of **char** large enough to hold a temporary file name string generated by the **tmpnam** function;

---

110 If the implementation imposes no practical limit on the length of file name strings, the value of **FILENAME_MAX** should instead be the recommended size of an array intended to hold a file name string. Of course, file name string contents are subject to other system-specific constraints; therefore *all* possible strings of length **FILENAME_MAX** cannot be expected to be opened successfully.

7.9   Input/output <stdio.h> The functions supported by **stdio.h** constitute the largest subsystem in the C standard library and are generally referred to as the *file system*. This subsystem performs I/O operations on the console, files, and other supported devices. A careful reading of the I/O function descriptions is advised, because several nuances of behavior are allowed with which you may not be familiar.

Historical note: Early versions of C defined and supported two distinct file systems, the *UNIX-like* (sometimes called the *unformatted* or *unbuffered*) file system and the *formatted* (also called the *buffered* or *high-level*) file system. The ANSI standard C, however, does not define the UNIX-like file system, but only the formatted file system, which is now called the *ANSI C file system.* There is logical reasoning behind this decision. First, the two file systems were redundant. Second, not all environments are capable of fully supporting the UNIX-like file system. If you have older code to maintain, don't worry. Most compiler implementations still support the UNIX-like I/O system and probably will for quite some time. However, if you are creating new programs, use the ANSI C file system because it is now the standard.

The glue that holds the C file system together is the **FILE** structure. (Though the standard does not require that this object be a structure, in practice it nearly always is.) The **FILE** structure contains information about each open file. The file system functions often take as an argument a pointer to the **FILE** structure associated with each file. A pointer to a **FILE** structure is obtained when a file is opened.

The type **fpos_t** is some type of an unsigned integer. It is guaranteed to be capable of holding the size (in bytes) of the largest file that can be supported by the host environment.

```
SEEK_CUR
SEEK_END
SEEK_SET
```

which expand to integral constant expressions with distinct values, suitable for use as the third argument to the **fseek** function;

```
TMP_MAX
```

which expands to an integral constant expression that is the minimum number of unique file names that shall be generated by the **tmpnam** function;

```
stderr
stdin
stdout
```

which are expressions of type ''pointer to **FILE**'' that point to the **FILE** objects associated, respectively, with the standard error, input, and output streams.

Forward references: files (7.9.3), the **fseek** function (7.9.9.2), streams (7.9.2), the **tmpnam** function (7.9.4.4).

7.9.2 Streams

Input and output, whether to or from physical devices such as terminals and tape drives, or whether to or from files supported on structured storage devices, are mapped into logical data *streams*, whose properties are more uniform than their various inputs and outputs. Two forms of mapping are supported, for *text streams* and for *binary streams*.[111]

A text stream is an ordered sequence of characters composed into *lines*, each line consisting of zero or more characters plus a terminating new-line character. Whether the last line requires a terminating new-line character is implementation-defined. Characters may have to be added, altered, or deleted on input and output to conform to differing conventions for representing text in the host environment. Thus, there need not be a one-to-one correspondence between the characters in a stream and those in the external representation. Data read in from a text stream will necessarily compare equal to the data that were earlier written out to that stream only if: the data consist only of printable characters and the control characters horizontal tab and new-line; no new-line character is immediately preceded by space characters; and the last character is a new-line character. Whether space characters that are written out immediately before a new-line character appear when read in is implementation-defined.

A binary stream is an ordered sequence of characters that can transparently record internal data. Data read in from a binary stream shall compare equal to the data that were earlier written out to that stream, under the same implementation. Such a stream may, however, have an implementation-defined number of null characters appended to the end of the stream.

Environmental limits

An implementation shall support text files with lines containing at least 254 characters, including the terminating new-line character. The value of the macro **BUFSIZ** shall be at least 256.

---

111 An implementation need not distinguish between text streams and binary streams. In such an implementation, there need be no new-line characters in a text stream nor any limit to the length of a line.

When it begins execution, a C program automatically opens three *streams*: **stdin**, **stdout**, and **stderr**. (See section 7.9.2 for additional information about streams.) Generally, these are initially linked to the keyboard, the screen, and the screen, respectively. However, because the C file system can be redirected, they can be linked to other devices. Many compilers have added additional streams that are automatically opened when your program begins execution. For example, most compilers give you access to the printer and to a serial port. Check your compiler user manuals for further information.

7.9.2 Streams The ANSI C file system is based on the concept of a *stream—a logical device* on which your program performs I/O. A stream is linked to a file or another physical device. All devices have different characteristics; streams, however, have similar characteristics, no matter what device they are linked to. The stream handles the low-level details of accessing the physical device, masking the details and differences of the physical devices from the programmer. Thus, by performing I/O operations on streams, your program always has a consistent interface with which to work.

There are two types of streams: text and binary. A *text stream* is designed to handle textual information. As such, it may perform various character translations. For example, a newline character may be converted into a carriage return/line feed sequence. Therefore, a text stream does *not* guarantee a one-to-one mapping between what is written to a file and what is actually stored in that file, and vice versa. In contrast, a *binary stream* does guarantee this one-to-one mapping; that is, a binary stream performs no character translations whatsoever. Binary streams are especially useful when you want to store information in a file using its internal (binary) representation.

Although the standard states that text streams can be organized as lines, it does not designate a maximum line length. The standard also says that the last line need not be terminated by a newline character. Thus, it is permissible for a text stream to treat all characters as part of one long, uninterrupted line, if it so chooses. Put differently, the use of lines in a text file is arbitrary and, essentially, optional.

Whether a stream is binary or text depends upon how it is opened. There is nothing in the standard that prevents a text file from being read by a binary stream or a binary file from being read by a text stream.

7.9.3 Files

A stream is associated with an external file (which may be a physical device) by *opening* a file, which may involve *creating* a new file. Creating an existing file causes its former contents to be discarded, if necessary. If a file can support positioning requests (such as a disk file, as opposed to a terminal), then a *file position indicator*[112] associated with the stream is positioned at the start (character number zero) of the file, unless the file is opened with append mode in which case it is implementation-defined whether the file position indicator is initially positioned at the beginning or the end of the file. The file position indicator is maintained by subsequent reads, writes, and positioning requests, to facilitate an orderly progression through the file. All input takes place as if characters were read by successive calls to the **fgetc** function; all output takes place as if characters were written by successive calls to the **fputc** function.

Binary files are not truncated, except as defined in 7.9.5.3. Whether a write on a text stream causes the associated file to be truncated beyond that point is implementation-defined.

When a stream is *unbuffered*, characters are intended to appear from the source or at the destination as soon as possible. Otherwise characters may be accumulated and transmitted to or from the host environment as a block. When a stream is *fully buffered*, characters are intended to be transmitted to or from the host environment as a block when a buffer is filled. When a stream is *line buffered*, characters are intended to be transmitted to or from the host environment as a block when a new-line character is encountered. Furthermore, characters are intended to be transmitted as a block to the host environment when a buffer is filled, when input is requested on an unbuffered stream, or when input is requested on a line buffered stream that requires the transmission of characters from the host environment. Support for these characteristics is implementation-defined, and may be affected via the **setbuf** and **setvbuf** functions.

A file may be disassociated from a controlling stream by *closing* the file. Output streams are flushed (any unwritten buffer contents are transmitted to the host environment) before the stream is disassociated from the file. The value of a pointer to a **FILE** object is indeterminate after the associated file is closed (including the standard text streams). Whether a file of zero length (on which no characters have been written by an output stream) actually exists is implementation-defined.

The file may be subsequently reopened, by the same or another program execution, and its contents reclaimed or modified (if it can be repositioned at its start). If the **main** function returns to its original caller, or if the **exit** function is called, all open files are closed (hence all output streams are flushed) before program termination. Other paths to program termination, such as calling the **abort** function, need not close all files properly.

The address of the **FILE** object used to control a stream may be significant; a copy of a **FILE** object may not necessarily serve in place of the original.

At program startup, three text streams are predefined and need not be opened explicitly — *standard input* (for reading conventional input), *standard output* (for writing conventional output), and *standard error* (for writing diagnostic output). When opened, the standard error stream is not fully buffered; the standard input and standard output streams are fully buffered if and only if the stream can be determined not to refer to an interactive device.

Functions that open additional (nontemporary) files require a *file name*, which is a string. The rules for composing valid file names are implementation-defined. Whether the same file can be simultaneously open multiple times is also implementation-defined.

---

112 This is described in the Base Document as a *file pointer*. That term is not used in this International Standard to avoid confusion with a pointer to an object that has type **FILE**.

7.9.3   Files   The standard states several items of interest relative to files (although it leaves most implementation details to the host environment). Here is a synopsis.

A file is linked to a stream using an *open* operation, and disassociated from a stream using a *close* operation. If the file supports random access (called *position requests* in the standard), then the file position indicator is set to the start of the file when it is opended. The file position indicator simply defines the point in the file at which the next I/O operation will occur. I/O operations may be unbuffered, line buffered, or fully buffered, as defined in the standard. For interactive environments, I/O is generally unbuffered by default. Often, you can tell the compiler what type of buffering you desire.

Here is a point often overlooked by C programmers: When **main()** returns or when the **exit()** function is executed, all streams are automatically flushed and all files are closed. Thus, although many programmers still manually perform these operations prior to program termination, they will be done automatically for you. Also, closing an output file automatically flushes the output stream associated with that file. No separate flush operation is required.

Flushing a stream causes any contents of that stream still in RAM to be physically written to the device. As you probably know, information written to files is typically buffered in memory until a sector's worth is collected, at which point the buffer is physically written to the file. When a file is closed, it is common for a partially filled buffer to still be residing in memory, waiting to be written. A *flush* operation simply writes that partially filled buffer to the device.

Environmental limits

The value of **FOPEN_MAX** shall be at least eight, including the three standard text streams.

Forward references: the **exit** function (7.10.4.3), the **fgetc** function (7.9.7.1), the **fopen** function (7.9.5.3), the **fputc** function (7.9.7.3), the **setbuf** function (7.9.5.5), the **setvbuf** function (7.9.5.6).

7.9.4 Operations on files

7.9.4.1 The remove function

Synopsis

```
#include <stdio.h>
int remove(const char *filename);
```

Description

The **remove** function causes the file whose name is the string pointed to by **filename** to be no longer accessible by that name. A subsequent attempt to open that file using that name will fail, unless it is created anew. If the file is open, the behavior of the **remove** function is implementation-defined.

Returns

The **remove** function returns zero if the operation succeeds, nonzero if it fails.

7.9.4.2 The rename function

Synopsis

```
#include <stdio.h>
int rename(const char *old, const char *new);
```

Description

The **rename** function causes the file whose name is the string pointed to by **old** to be henceforth known by the name given by the string pointed to by **new**. The file named **old** is no longer accessible by that name. If a file named by the string pointed to by **new** exists prior to the call to the **rename** function, the behavior is implementation-defined.

Returns

The **rename** function returns zero if the operation succeeds, nonzero if it fails,[113] in which case if the file existed previously it is still known by its original name.

7.9.4.3 The tmpfile function

Synopsis

```
#include <stdio.h>
FILE *tmpfile(void);
```

Description

The **tmpfile** function creates a temporary binary file that will automatically be removed when it is closed or at program termination. If the program terminates abnormally, whether an open temporary file is removed is implementation-defined. The file is opened for update with **"wb+"** mode.

---

113 Among the reasons the implementation may cause the **rename** function to fail are that the file is open or that it is necessary to copy its contents to effectuate its renaming.

7.9.4   *Operations on files*   The operations of the functions described in this section are, for the most part, clear. Following are a few additional points to consider.

The standard states that **remove()** causes the file specified by *filename* to be "no longer accessible." In practical terms, this means the file is erased. The purpose of **tmpfile()** is to open a temporary scratch file, using a name not currently in use, that will be erased automatically when your program terminates. The **tmpnam()** function generates a unique file name (one not currently in use) that your program can use to open a temporary file. (You must destroy this temporary file manually.) The following program demonstrates the **remove()**, **rename()**, and **tmpnam()** functions:

```c
/* This program demonstrates remove(), rename(), and
   tmpnam(). */
#include <stdio.h>
#include <stdlib.h>

char tempstr[] = "This is a test file.";

void main(void)
{
  char fname[FILENAME_MAX];
  FILE *fp;

  /* obtain a temporary filename */
  tmpnam(fname);

  if(!(fp=fopen(fname, "w"))) {
    printf("Cannot open file.\n");
    exit(1);
  }
  printf("Opened file named %s.\n", fname);

  /* write something to it */
  fwrite(tempstr, sizeof tempstr, 1, fp);
  fclose(fp); /* close the file */
  printf("Closed %s.\n", fname);

  /* rename file */
  if(rename(fname, "MYFILE")) {
    printf("Cannot rename file.\n");
    exit(1);
  }
  printf("Renamed file.\n");
```

Returns

The **tmpfile** function returns a pointer to the stream of the file that it created. If the file cannot be created, the **tmpfile** function returns a null pointer.

Forward references: the **fopen** function (7.9.5.3).

7.9.4.4 The tmpnam function

Synopsis

```
#include <stdio.h>
char *tmpnam(char *s);
```

Description

The **tmpnam** function generates a string that is a valid file name and that is not the same as the name of an existing file.[114]

The **tmpnam** function generates a different string each time it is called, up to **TMP_MAX** times. If it is called more than **TMP_MAX** times, the behavior is implementation-defined.

The implementation shall behave as if no library function calls the **tmpnam** function.

Returns

If the argument is a null pointer, the **tmpnam** function leaves its result in an internal static object and returns a pointer to that object. Subsequent calls to the **tmpnam** function may modify the same object. If the argument is not a null pointer, it is assumed to point to an array of at least **L_tmpnam char**s; the **tmpnam** function writes its result in that array and returns the argument as its value.

Environmental limits

The value of the macro **TMP_MAX** shall be at least 25.

7.9.5 File access functions

7.9.5.1 The fclose function

Synopsis

```
#include <stdio.h>
int fclose(FILE *stream);
```

Description

The **fclose** function causes the stream pointed to by **stream** to be flushed and the associated file to be closed. Any unwritten buffered data for the stream are delivered to the host environment to be written to the file; any unread buffered data are discarded. The stream is disassociated from the file. If the associated buffer was automatically allocated, it is deallocated.

---

114 Files created using strings generated by the **tmpnam** function are temporary only in the sense that their names should not collide with those generated by conventional naming rules for the implementation. It is still necessary to use the **remove** function to remove such files when their use is ended, and before program termination.

(*7.9.4*   *Operations on files,* continued)

```
/* open file to prove it was renamed */
if(!(fp=fopen("MYFILE", "r"))) {
  printf("Cannot open file.\n");
  exit(1);
}

printf("Contents of MYFILE: ");
/* display the file */
while(!feof(fp)) printf("%c", getc(fp));
printf("\n");
fclose(fp); /* close the file */

/* remove the file */
if(remove("MYFILE")) {
  printf("Cannot erase file.\n");
  exit(1);
}
printf("MYFILE has been erased.\n");

/* try to open file to prove it was removed */
if(!(fp=fopen("MYFILE", "r")))
  printf("Cannot open file because it was erased.\n");
}
```

This program displays the following output (of course, the temporary file name may differ):

```
Opened file named TMP1.$$$.
Closed TMP1.$$$.
Renamed file.
Contents of MYFILE: This is a test file.
MYFILE has been erased.
Cannot open file because it was erased.
```

7.9.5 File access functions The *file access functions* are **fopen()**, **fclose()**, **fflush()**, **freopen()**, **setbuf()**, and **setvbuf()**. Of these, **fopen()**, **fclose()**, and **fflush()** are the most commonly used. The others exist primarily to handle relatively unusual situations.

7.9.5.1 *The fclose function* The **fclose()** function disassociates a stream from a file. Notice that a call to **fclose()** automatically flushes the stream. Therefore, no explicit call to **fflush()** is required before closing a file.

Returns

The **fclose** function returns zero if the stream was successfully closed, or **EOF** if any errors were detected.

7.9.5.2 The **fflush** function

Synopsis

```
#include <stdio.h>
int fflush(FILE *stream);
```

Description

If **stream** points to an output stream or an update stream in which the most recent operation was not input, the **fflush** function causes any unwritten data for that stream to be delivered to the host environment to be written to the file; otherwise, the behavior is undefined.

If **stream** is a null pointer, the **fflush** function performs this flushing action on all streams for which the behavior is defined above.

Returns

The **fflush** function returns **EOF** if a write error occurs, otherwise zero.

Forward references: the **fopen** function (7.9.5.3), the **ungetc** function (7.9.7.11).

7.9.5.3 The **fopen** function

Synopsis

```
#include <stdio.h>
FILE *fopen(const char *filename, const char *mode);
```

Description

The **fopen** function opens the file whose name is the string pointed to by **filename**, and associates a stream with it.

The argument **mode** points to a string beginning with one of the following sequences:[115]

r	open text file for reading
w	truncate to zero length or create text file for writing
a	append; open or create text file for writing at end-of-file
rb	open binary file for reading
wb	truncate to zero length or create binary file for writing
ab	append; open or create binary file for writing at end-of-file
r+	open text file for update (reading and writing)
w+	truncate to zero length or create text file for update
a+	append; open or create text file for update, writing at end-of-file
r+b *or* **rb+**	open binary file for update (reading and writing)
w+b *or* **wb+**	truncate to zero length or create binary file for update
a+b *or* **ab+**	append; open or create binary file for update, writing at end-of-file

Opening a file with read mode (' **r**' as the first character in the **mode** argument) fails if the file does not exist or cannot be read.

Opening a file with append mode (' **a**' as the first character in the **mode** argument) causes all subsequent writes to the file to be forced to the then current end-of-file, regardless of intervening

---

115 Additional characters may follow these sequences.

7.9.5.2   The fflush function   Often, a device requires that data be written in fixed-length units of some sort. For example, disk files are written a sector at a time. For this reason, data written to a stream is generally buffered in RAM until a sector's worth of information has been written, before the data is actually transferred to the physical file. The purpose of **fflush()** is to cause the contents of a partially filled buffer to be transferred to the physical file. Since any partially filled buffer is automatically flushed when the file is closed, **fflush()** is typically used as a safety feature in unstable situations.

7.9.5.3   The fopen function   A stream is linked to a file using **fopen()**. The description of **fopen()** in the standard is quite clear. Here are two other things to remember: First, **fopen()**, if successful, returns a pointer to a **FILE** structure associated with the file, or it returns NULL if the file cannot be opened. When you open a file, you must check the return value, because attempting subsequent I/O operations on a NULL pointer will cause a serious program malfunction (in simple terms, your program could crash!). Second, in addition to the values for the *mode* parameter shown in the standard, your compiler may support additional, implementation-dependent ones. (Of course, using nonstandard values will render your program less portable.)

calls to the **fseek** function. In some implementations, opening a binary file with append mode ('**b**' as the second or third character in the above list of **mode** argument values) may initially position the file position indicator for the stream beyond the last data written, because of null character padding.

When a file is opened with update mode ('**+**' as the second or third character in the above list of **mode** argument values), both input and output may be performed on the associated stream. However, output may not be directly followed by input without an intervening call to the **fflush** function or to a file positioning function (**fseek**, **fsetpos**, or **rewind**), and input may not be directly followed by output without an intervening call to a file positioning function, unless the input operation encounters end-of-file. Opening (or creating) a text file with update mode may instead open (or create) a binary stream in some implementations.

When opened, a stream is fully buffered if and only if it can be determined not to refer to an interactive device. The error and end-of-file indicators for the stream are cleared.

Returns

The **fopen** function returns a pointer to the object controlling the stream. If the open operation fails, **fopen** returns a null pointer.

Forward references: file positioning functions (7.9.9).

7.9.5.4 The **freopen** function

Synopsis

```
#include <stdio.h>
FILE *freopen(const char *filename, const char *mode,
     FILE *stream);
```

Description

The **freopen** function opens the file whose name is the string pointed to by **filename** and associates the stream pointed to by **stream** with it. The **mode** argument is used just as in the **fopen** function.[116]

The **freopen** function first attempts to close any file that is associated with the specified stream. Failure to close the file successfully is ignored. The error and end-of-file indicators for the stream are cleared.

Returns

The **freopen** function returns a null pointer if the open operation fails. Otherwise, **freopen** returns the value of **stream**.

7.9.5.5 The **setbuf** function

Synopsis

```
#include <stdio.h>
void setbuf(FILE *stream, char *buf);
```

---

116 The primary use of the **freopen** function is to change the file associated with a standard text stream (**stderr**, **stdin**, or **stdout**), as those identifiers need not be modifiable lvalues to which the value returned by the **fopen** function may be assigned.

7.9.5.4 The freopen function The **freopen()** function opens the file specified by *filename* and links it to the already existent stream specified by *stream*. The **FILE** structure pointed to by *stream* must either be one of the standard streams or have been obtained by a previous call to **fopen()**. As the footnote explains, the main use of **freopen()** is to redirect the standard streams. Any redirected standard streams are reset when the program terminates.

7.9.5.5 The setbuf function and 7.9.5.6 The setvbuf function The functions, **setbuf()** and **setvbuf()**, change how a stream will be buffered and, optionally, will specify a character array to be used as the I/O buffer associated with the stream. (To review, *full buffering* means data is transferred in fixed length blocks; *line buffering* means data is transferred each time a newline character is encountered; no buffering means characters are transmitted as soon as possible.) **setvbuf()** and **setbuf()** are special-purpose functions that many programmers will never use.

Here is a program that demonstrates **fopen()**, **freopen()**, and **fclose()**:

```
/* This program demonstrates fopen(), freopen(), and
   fclose(). */
#include <stdio.h>
#include <stdlib.h>

char tempstr[] = "This is a test file.";

void main(void)
{
  FILE *fp;

  if(!(fp=fopen("TEST", "w"))) {
    printf("Cannot open file.\n");
    exit(1);
  }

  /* write something to the file */
  fwrite(tempstr, sizeof tempstr, 1, fp);
  fclose(fp); /* close the TEST file */

  /* reopen the stdout and link it to a file */
  if(!(fp=freopen("STANDOUT", "w", stdout))) {
    printf("Cannot reopen stdout.\n");
    exit(1);
  }

  printf("This will go to the file called STANDOUT. ");
```

Description

Except that it returns no value. the **setbuf** function is equivalent to the **setvbuf** function invoked with the values **_IOFBF** for **mode** and **BUFSIZ** for **size**, or (if **buf** is a null pointer). with the value **_IONBF** for **mode**.

Returns

The **setbuf** function returns no value.

Forward references: the **setvbuf** function (7.9.5.6).

7.9.5.6 The setvbuf function

Synopsis

```
#include <stdio.h>
int setvbuf(FILE *stream, char *buf, int mode, size_t size);
```

Description

The **setvbuf** function may be used only after the stream pointed to by **stream** has been associated with an open file and before any other operation is performed on the stream. The argument **mode** determines how **stream** will be buffered, as follows: **_IOFBF** causes input/output to be fully buffered; **_IOLBF** causes input/output to be line buffered; **_IONBF** causes input/output to be unbuffered. If **buf** is not a null pointer. the array it points to may be used instead of a buffer allocated by the **setvbuf** function.[117] The argument **size** specifies the size of the array. The contents of the array at any time are indeterminate.

Returns

The **setvbuf** function returns zero on success, or nonzero if an invalid value is given for **mode** or if the request cannot be honored.

7.9.6 Formatted input/output functions

7.9.6.1 The fprintf function

Synopsis

```
#include <stdio.h>
int fprintf(FILE *stream, const char *format, ...);
```

Description

The **fprintf** function writes output to the stream pointed to by **stream**, under control of the string pointed to by **format** that specifies how subsequent arguments are converted for output. If there are insufficient arguments for the format, the behavior is undefined. If the format is exhausted while arguments remain, the excess arguments are evaluated (as always) but are otherwise ignored. The **fprintf** function returns when the end of the format string is encountered.

The format shall be a multibyte character sequence, beginning and ending in its initial shift state. The format is composed of zero or more directives: ordinary multibyte characters (not **%**). which are copied unchanged to the output stream; and conversion specifications, each of which results in fetching zero or more subsequent arguments. Each conversion specification is introduced by the character **%**. After the **%**, the following appear in sequence:

---

117 The buffer must have a lifetime at least as great as the open stream. so the stream should be closed before a buffer that has automatic storage duration is deallocated upon block exit.

*(**7.9.5.5** and **7.9.5.6**, continued)*

```
    printf("not to the screen.\n");
    fclose(fp); /* close the reopened STANDOUT file */
}
```

7.9.6   Formatted input/output functions The core formatted I/O functions are **printf()** and **scanf()**. Related to these functions are **fprintf()**, **fscanf()**, **sprintf()**, **sscanf()**, **vfprintf()**, **vprintf()**, and **vsprintf()**. Because **fprintf()** and **fscanf()** appear alphabetically first in this section, the formatting features of all of these functions are discussed in the description of **fprintf()** and **fscanf()**.

The term *formatted I/O* is applied to these functions because they operate on human-readable data (that is, ASCII-based text). When **printf()** writes output, it is in text rather than binary form. Also, **scanf()** expects data in its text-based form, not in binary. (To perform I/O on binary data, you will use functions such as **fread()** and **fwrite()**, discussed a little later in this section of the standard.)

For the most part, the standard's descriptions of the formatted I/O functions are clear and easy to understand. Also, since almost all C programmers know, use, and understand **printf()**, **scanf()**, and their derivatives, additional explanation of their basic operation is not needed here. Instead, several example programs are shown which illustrate the use of these functions, and some of their lesser known features are discussed.

There are, however, two general points that bear reinforcement. First, although often ignored, **printf()** (and related functions) returns the number of characters output or a value less than zero if an error occurs. Second, the value returned by **scanf()** (and related functions) is the number of variables successfully assigned a value, or **EOF** if an error occurs before any assignment is made. Notice that the return values of **printf()** and **scanf()** are not precisely parallel.

7.9.6.1   *The fprintf() function* The **fprintf()** function writes output to the stream that is specified by its first parameter (the stream is typically linked to a file). Since **fprintf()** outputs formatted information, the contents of the file will be in a human-readable form.

Note that if *stream* is a pointer to **stdout**, then **fprintf()** behaves exactly like **printf()**.

Description

Except that it returns no value, the **setbuf** function is equivalent to the **setvbuf** function invoked with the values **_IOFBF** for **mode** and **BUFSIZ** for **size**, or (if **buf** is a null pointer), with the value **_IONBF** for **mode**.

Returns

The **setbuf** function returns no value.

Forward references: the **setvbuf** function (7.9.5.6).

7.9.5.6 The **setvbuf** function

Synopsis

```
#include <stdio.h>
int setvbuf(FILE *stream, char *buf, int mode, size_t size);
```

Description

The **setvbuf** function may be used only after the stream pointed to by **stream** has been associated with an open file and before any other operation is performed on the stream. The argument **mode** determines how **stream** will be buffered, as follows: **_IOFBF** causes input/output to be fully buffered; **_IOLBF** causes input/output to be line buffered; **_IONBF** causes input/output to be unbuffered. If **buf** is not a null pointer, the array it points to may be used instead of a buffer allocated by the **setvbuf** function.[117] The argument **size** specifies the size of the array. The contents of the array at any time are indeterminate.

Returns

The **setvbuf** function returns zero on success, or nonzero if an invalid value is given for **mode** or if the request cannot be honored.

7.9.6 Formatted input/output functions

7.9.6.1 The **fprintf** function

Synopsis

```
#include <stdio.h>
int fprintf(FILE *stream, const char *format, ...);
```

Description

The **fprintf** function writes output to the stream pointed to by **stream**, under control of the string pointed to by **format** that specifies how subsequent arguments are converted for output. If there are insufficient arguments for the format, the behavior is undefined. If the format is exhausted while arguments remain, the excess arguments are evaluated (as always) but are otherwise ignored. The **fprintf** function returns when the end of the format string is encountered.

The format shall be a multibyte character sequence, beginning and ending in its initial shift state. The format is composed of zero or more directives: ordinary multibyte characters (not **%**), which are copied unchanged to the output stream; and conversion specifications, each of which results in fetching zero or more subsequent arguments. Each conversion specification is introduced by the character **%**. After the **%**, the following appear in sequence:

---

117 The buffer must have a lifetime at least as great as the open stream, so the stream should be closed before a buffer that has automatic storage duration is deallocated upon block exit.

Here is a program that demonstrates **fprintf()**:

```
/* This program demonstrates fprintf(). */
#include <stdio.h>
#include <stdlib.h>

void main(void)
{
  int i = 100;
  double d = 1234.987;
  char c = 'X';
  char str[] = "This is a string.";
  FILE *fp;

  if(!(fp=fopen("TEST", "w"))) {
    printf("Cannot open file.\n");
    exit(1);
  }

  /* output to file using fprintf() */
  fprintf(fp, "This is the first line in the file.\n");
  fprintf(fp, "A string: %s and a character: %c.\n", str, c);
  fprintf(fp, "An integer: %d and a double: %10.3lf.\n", i, d);

  fclose(fp); /* close the TEST file */
}
```

If you list the contents of the file called TEST, you will see the following:

```
This is the first line in the file.
A string: This is a string. and a character: X.
An integer: 100 and a double:   1234.987.
```

One often-overlooked feature of **printf()** and its derivatives is that either (or both) the minimum field width or precision specifiers may be specified by arguments, rather than as constants within the format string. This is accomplished by using the ***** as a placeholder and specifying the actual value in the argument list at the appropriate point. The following program illustrates the use of the field width and precision specifiers as both constants and as arguments. (Also, remember that when the precision specifier is applied to a string, it acts as a maximum field width specifier, which is also demonstrated by the following program.)

0   For **d, i, o, u, x, X, e, E, f, g**, and **G** conversions, leading zeros (following any indication of sign or base) are used to pad to the field width; no space padding is performed. If the **0** and **−** flags both appear, the **0** flag will be ignored. For **d, i, o, u, x**, and **X** conversions, if a precision is specified, the **0** flag will be ignored. For other conversions, the behavior is undefined.

The conversion specifiers and their meanings are

d,i   The **int** argument is converted to signed decimal in the style *[−]dddd*. The precision specifies the minimum number of digits to appear; if the value being converted can be represented in fewer digits, it will be expanded with leading zeros. The default precision is 1. The result of converting a zero value with a precision of zero is no characters.

o,u,x,X The **unsigned int** argument is converted to unsigned octal (**o**), unsigned decimal (**u**), or unsigned hexadecimal notation (**x** or **X**) in the style *dddd*; the letters **abcdef** are used for **x** conversion and the letters **ABCDEF** for **X** conversion. The precision specifies the minimum number of digits to appear; if the value being converted can be represented in fewer digits, it will be expanded with leading zeros. The default precision is 1. The result of converting a zero value with a precision of zero is no characters.

f   The **double** argument is converted to decimal notation in the style *[−]ddd.ddd*, where the number of digits after the decimal-point character is equal to the precision specification. If the precision is missing, it is taken as 6; if the precision is zero and the **#** flag is not specified, no decimal-point character appears. If a decimal-point character appears, at least one digit appears before it. The value is rounded to the appropriate number of digits.

e,E   The **double** argument is converted in the style *[−]d.ddd e±dd*, where there is one digit before the decimal-point character (which is nonzero if the argument is nonzero) and the number of digits after it is equal to the precision; if the precision is missing, it is taken as 6; if the precision is zero and the **#** flag is not specified, no decimal-point character appears. The value is rounded to the appropriate number of digits. The **E** conversion specifier will produce a number with **E** instead of **e** introducing the exponent. The exponent always contains at least two digits. If the value is zero, the exponent is zero.

g,G   The **double** argument is converted in style **f** or **e** (or in style **E** in the case of a **G** conversion specifier), with the precision specifying the number of significant digits. If the precision is zero, it is taken as 1. The style used depends on the value converted; style **e** (or **E**) will be used only if the exponent resulting from such a conversion is less than −4 or greater than or equal to the precision. Trailing zeros are removed from the fractional portion of the result; a decimal-point character appears only if it is followed by a digit.

c   The **int** argument is converted to an **unsigned char**, and the resulting character is written.

s   The argument shall be a pointer to an array of character type.[119] Characters from the array are written up to (but not including) a terminating null character; if the precision is specified, no more than that many characters are written. If the precision is not specified or is greater than the size of the array, the array shall contain a null character.

---

119 No special provisions are made for multibyte characters.

```
/* This program demonstrates field width and precision when
   using fprintf(). */
#include <stdio.h>
#include <stdlib.h>

void main(void)
{
  char str[] = "This is a string.";
  FILE *fp;

  if(!(fp=fopen("TEST", "w"))) {
    printf("Cannot open file.\n");
    exit(1);
  }

  /* field widths and precisions */
  fprintf(fp, "||%12.5lf||\n", 345.343254);
  fprintf(fp, "||%5.5lf||\n", 345.343254);
  /* use arguments for field width and precision */
  fprintf(fp, "||%*.*lf||\n", 15, 2, 345.34254);
  /* apply minimum field length to string */
  fprintf(fp, "||%50s||\n", str);
  /* apply maximum field width to a string */
  fprintf(fp, "||%.10s||\n", str);

  fclose(fp); /* close the TEST file */
}
```

After the program executes, the TEST file will contain the following:

```
||   345.34325||
||345.34325||
||         345.34||
||                                  This is a string.||
||This is a ||
```

There is one final point to notice about the format conversion specifiers used by **printf()** and its related functions: The **n** specifier causes the integer pointed to by its corresponding argument to be assigned the number of characters written thus far. For example, after this call to **fprintf()**:

```
fprintf(fp, "abcde%n fghi", &i);
```

the integer **i** will contain the value 5.

p   The argument shall be a pointer to **void**. The value of the pointer is converted to a sequence of printable characters, in an implementation-defined manner.

n   The argument shall be a pointer to an integer into which is *written* the number of characters written to the output stream so far by this call to **fprintf**. No argument is converted.

%   A **%** is written. No argument is converted. The complete conversion specification shall be **%%**.

If a conversion specification is invalid, the behavior is undefined.[120]

If any argument is, or points to, a union or an aggregate (except for an array of character type using **%s** conversion, or a pointer using **%p** conversion), the behavior is undefined.

In no case does a nonexistent or small field width cause truncation of a field; if the result of a conversion is wider than the field width, the field is expanded to contain the conversion result.

Returns

The **fprintf** function returns the number of characters transmitted, or a negative value if an output error occurred.

Environmental limit

The minimum value for the maximum number of characters produced by any single conversion shall be 509.

Example

To print a date and time in the form "Sunday, July 3, 10:02" followed by π to five decimal places:

```
#include <math.h>
#include <stdio.h>
/*...*/
char *weekday, *month;      /* pointers to strings */
int day, hour, min;
fprintf(stdout, "%s, %s %d, %.2d:%.2d\n",
        weekday, month, day, hour, min);
fprintf(stdout, "pi = %.5f\n", 4 * atan(1.0));
```

7.9.6.2 The fscanf function

Synopsis

```
#include <stdio.h>
int fscanf(FILE *stream, const char *format, ...);
```

Description

The **fscanf** function reads input from the stream pointed to by **stream**, under control of the string pointed to by **format** that specifies the admissible input sequences and how they are to be converted for assignment, using subsequent arguments as pointers to the objects to receive the converted input. If there are insufficient arguments for the format, the behavior is undefined. If the format is exhausted while arguments remain, the excess arguments are evaluated (as always) but are otherwise ignored.

---

120 See "future library directions" (7.13.6).

7.9.6.2   *The fscanf function* The **fscanf()** function reads input from the stream pointed to by *stream*, which is typically linked to a disk file. For example, here is a program that uses **fscanf()** to read information from the file created by calls to **fprintf()**:

```
/* This program demonstrates fscanf(). */
#include <stdio.h>
#include <stdlib.h>

void main(void)
{
  int i;
  double d;
  char c;
  char str[80];
  FILE *fp;

  if(!(fp=fopen("TEST", "w"))) {
    printf("Cannot open file for output.\n");
    exit(1);
  }

  /* output a string, an integer, a float, and a character
     to file using fprintf() */
  fprintf(fp, "string ");
  fprintf(fp, "%d %lf %c\n", 10, 123.23, 'X');

  /* now, reopen the file and read in the information
     using fscanf() */
  if(!(fp=fopen("TEST", "r"))) {
    printf("Cannot open file for input.\n");
    exit(1);
  }

  fscanf(fp, "%s %d%lf %c", str, &i, &d, &c);

  printf("Here are the values: %s %d %lf %c",
         str, i, d, c);

  fclose(fp); /* close the TEST file */
}
```

When run, this program displays

```
Here are the values: string 10 123.230000 X
```

The format shall be a multibyte character sequence, beginning and ending in its initial shift state. The format is composed of zero or more directives: one or more white-space characters; an ordinary multibyte character (neither % nor a white-space character); or a conversion specification. Each conversion specification is introduced by the character %. After the %, the following appear in sequence:

— An optional assignment-suppressing character *.

— An optional nonzero decimal integer that specifies the maximum field width.

— An optional h, l (ell) or L indicating the size of the receiving object. The conversion specifiers d, i, and n shall be preceded by h if the corresponding argument is a pointer to **short int** rather than a pointer to **int**, or by l if it is a pointer to **long int**. Similarly, the conversion specifiers o, u, and x shall be preceded by h if the corresponding argument is a pointer to **unsigned short int** rather than a pointer to **unsigned int**, or by l if it is a pointer to **unsigned long int**. Finally, the conversion specifiers e, f, and g shall be preceded by l if the corresponding argument is a pointer to **double** rather than a pointer to **float**, or by L if it is a pointer to **long double**. If an h, l, or L appears with any other conversion specifier, the behavior is undefined.

— A character that specifies the type of conversion to be applied. The valid conversion specifiers are described below.

The **fscanf** function executes each directive of the format in turn. If a directive fails, as detailed below, the **fscanf** function returns. Failures are described as input failures (due to the unavailability of input characters), or matching failures (due to inappropriate input).

A directive composed of white-space character(s) is executed by reading input up to the first non-white-space character (which remains unread), or until no more characters can be read.

A directive that is an ordinary multibyte character is executed by reading the next characters of the stream. If one of the characters differs from one comprising the directive, the directive fails, and the differing and subsequent characters remain unread.

A directive that is a conversion specification defines a set of matching input sequences, as described below for each specifier. A conversion specification is executed in the following steps:

Input white-space characters (as specified by the **isspace** function) are skipped, unless the specification includes a [, c, or n specifier.[121]

An input item is read from the stream, unless the specification includes an n specifier. An input item is defined as the longest matching sequence of input characters, unless that exceeds a specified field width, in which case it is the initial subsequence of that length in the sequence. The first character, if any, after the input item remains unread. If the length of the input item is zero, the execution of the directive fails: this condition is a matching failure, unless an error prevented input from the stream, in which case it is an input failure.

Except in the case of a % specifier, the input item (or, in the case of a %n directive, the count of input characters) is converted to a type appropriate to the conversion specifier. If the input item is not a matching sequence, the execution of the directive fails: this condition is a matching failure. Unless assignment suppression was indicated by a *, the result of the conversion is placed in the object pointed to by the first argument following the **format** argument that has not already received a conversion result. If this object does not have an appropriate type, or if the result of the conversion cannot be represented in the space provided, the behavior is undefined.

---

121 These white-space characters are not counted against a specified field width.

(7.9.6.2   The fscanf function, continued)

Here are some things to remember when using **fscanf()** or any related functions:

◆   When inputting a string, input stops when the first white-space character is read. (If you want to read a string that contains white space, use a *scanset*, discussed shortly.)

◆   To read but ignore an item of data, precede the conversion specifier with an *****. For example, this **fscanf** statement causes three characters to be read, the second of which is ignored:

```
fscanf(fp, "%c%*c%c", &c1, &c2);
```

◆   If the format string contains a space, then **fscanf()** (and related functions) will read and discard white space from the input stream until the next nonwhite-space character is read. This implies that you should not end a format string with white space, because it may cause the call to **fscanf()** to "hang," waiting for a nonwhite-space character that never comes.

◆   If the format string contains a nonwhite-space character that is not a conversion code, then **fscanf()** (and related functions) will read and discard a matching character.

One feature of the **fscanf()** family that is unfamiliar to many C programmers is the *scanset*. A scanset defines a set of characters that will be read and stored in the string pointed to by the scanset's corresponding argument. Characters will be read and stored as long as they match those defined by the scanset; as soon as a nonmatching character is read, the scanset stops.

A scanset is created by putting the set of characters inside square brackets. If you begin the scanset with a ^ character, all characters *not* specified are matched. Most (but not all) implementations allow you to specify a range of characters using a construct such as **A-Z**.

One important use of a scanset is to read a string of characters that contains white spaces. (Remember, the %s specifier causes **fscanf()** to stop reading a string when the first white space is encountered.) The following program demonstrates how a scanset can be used to read full English sentences (including spaces) that end in either a period or a question mark:

The following conversion specifiers are valid:

d   Matches an optionally signed decimal integer, whose format is the same as expected for the subject sequence of the **strtol** function with the value 10 for the **base** argument. The corresponding argument shall be a pointer to integer.

i   Matches an optionally signed integer, whose format is the same as expected for the subject sequence of the **strtol** function with the value 0 for the **base** argument. The corresponding argument shall be a pointer to integer.

o   Matches an optionally signed octal integer, whose format is the same as expected for the subject sequence of the **strtoul** function with the value 8 for the **base** argument. The corresponding argument shall be a pointer to unsigned integer.

u   Matches an optionally signed decimal integer, whose format is the same as expected for the subject sequence of the **strtoul** function with the value 10 for the **base** argument. The corresponding argument shall be a pointer to unsigned integer.

x   Matches an optionally signed hexadecimal integer, whose format is the same as expected for the subject sequence of the **strtoul** function with the value 16 for the **base** argument. The corresponding argument shall be a pointer to unsigned integer.

e,f,g Matches an optionally signed floating-point number, whose format is the same as expected for the subject string of the **strtod** function. The corresponding argument shall be a pointer to floating.

s   Matches a sequence of non-white-space characters.[122] The corresponding argument shall be a pointer to the initial character of an array large enough to accept the sequence and a terminating null character, which will be added automatically.

[Matches a nonempty sequence of characters[122] from a set of expected characters (the *scanset*). The corresponding argument shall be a pointer to the initial character of an array large enough to accept the sequence and a terminating null character, which will be added automatically. The conversion specifier includes all subsequent characters in the **format** string, up to and including the matching right bracket (**]**). The characters between the brackets (the *scanlist*) comprise the scanset, unless the character after the left bracket is a circumflex (**^**), in which case the scanset contains all characters that do not appear in the scanlist between the circumflex and the right bracket. If the conversion specifier begins with **[]** or **[^]**, the right bracket character is in the scanlist and the next right bracket character is the matching right bracket that ends the specification; otherwise the first right bracket character is the one that ends the specification. If a – character is in the scanlist and is not the first, nor the second where the first character is a **^**, nor the last character, the behavior is implementation-defined.

c   Matches a sequence of characters[122] of the number specified by the field width (1 if no field width is present in the directive). The corresponding argument shall be a pointer to the initial character of an array large enough to accept the sequence. No null character is added.

p   Matches an implementation-defined set of sequences, which should be the same as the set of sequences that may be produced by the **%p** conversion of the **fprintf** function. The corresponding argument shall be a pointer to a pointer to **void**. The interpretation of the input item is implementation-defined. If the input item is a value converted earlier during the same program execution, the pointer that results shall compare equal to that value; otherwise the behavior of the **%p** conversion is undefined.

---

122 No special provisions are made for multibyte characters.

(7.9.6.2   *The fscanf function,* *continued*)

```
/* This program demonstrates a scanset. */
#include <stdio.h>
#include <stdlib.h>
#include <string.h>

void main(void)
{
  char str[255] = "";

  do {
    printf("Enter a sentence ('stop.' to stop): ");
    fscanf(stdin, "%[^.?]", str);
    fflush(stdin); /* clear crlf from input buffer */
    printf("Here is your sentence: %s\n", str);
  } while(strcmp(str, "stop"));
}
```

This next program uses a scanset to input telephone numbers, which may contain spaces, digits, parentheses, and hyphens. For example, it accommodates the following common telephone number formats:

(111) 555-1234
111 555-1234
111 555 1234

```
/* This program also demonstrates a scanset. */
#include <stdio.h>
#include <stdlib.h>

void main(void)
{
  char str[255] = "";

  do {
    printf("Enter a telephone number (ENTER to stop): ");
    fscanf(stdin, "%[()- 0123456789]", str);
    fflush(stdin); /* clear crlf from input buffer */
    printf("Here is telephone number: %s\n", str);
  } while(*str);
}
```

n   No input is consumed. The corresponding argument shall be a pointer to integer into which is to be written the number of characters read from the input stream so far by this call to the **fscanf** function. Execution of a **%n** directive does not increment the assignment count returned at the completion of execution of the **fscanf** function.

%   Matches a single **%**; no conversion or assignment occurs. The complete conversion specification shall be **%%**.

If a conversion specification is invalid, the behavior is undefined.[123]

The conversion specifiers **E**, **G**, and **X** are also valid and behave the same as, respectively, **e**, **g**, and **x**.

If end-of-file is encountered during input, conversion is terminated. If end-of-file occurs before any characters matching the current directive have been read (other than leading white space, where permitted), execution of the current directive terminates with an input failure; otherwise, unless execution of the current directive is terminated with a matching failure, execution of the following directive (if any) is terminated with an input failure.

If conversion terminates on a conflicting input character, the offending input character is left unread in the input stream. Trailing white space (including new-line characters) is left unread unless matched by a directive. The success of literal matches and suppressed assignments is not directly determinable other than via the **%n** directive.

Returns

The **fscanf** function returns the value of the macro **EOF** if an input failure occurs before any conversion. Otherwise, the **fscanf** function returns the number of input items assigned, which can be fewer than provided for, or even zero, in the event of an early matching failure.

Examples

1. The call:

```
#include <stdio.h>
/*...*/
int n, i; float x; char name[50];
n = fscanf(stdin, "%d%f%s", &i, &x, name);
```

with the input line:

```
25 54.32E-1 thompson
```

will assign to *n* the value **3**, to *i* the value **25**, to *x* the value **5.432**, and *name* will contain **thompson\0**.

2. The call:

```
#include <stdio.h>
/*...*/
int i; float x; char name[50];
fscanf(stdin, "%2d%f%*d %[0123456789]", &i, &x, name);
```

with input:

```
56789 0123 56a72
```

will assign to *i* the value **56** and to *x* the value **789.0**, will skip **0123**, and *name* will contain **56\0**. The next character read from the input stream will be **a**.

---

123 See ''future library directions'' (7.13.6).

(7.9.6.2   The fscanf function, continued)

A commonly overlooked format conversion specifier used by **fscanf()** and its related functions is **n**, which causes the integer pointed to by its corresponding argument to be assigned the number of characters read thus far. For example, after this statement executes:

```
fscanf(fp, "%d%s%n", &i, str, &num);
```

the number of characters input will be in **num**.

3. To accept repeatedly from **stdin** a quantity, a unit of measure and an item name:

```
#include <stdio.h>
/*...*/
int count; float quant; char units[21], item[21];
while (!feof(stdin) && !ferror(stdin)) {
        count = fscanf(stdin, "%f%20s of %20s",
                &quant, units, item);
        fscanf(stdin,"%*[^\n]");
}
```

If the **stdin** stream contains the following lines:

```
2 quarts of oil
-12.8degrees Celsius
lots of luck
10.0LBS        of
dirt
100ergs of energy
```

the execution of the above example will be analogous to the following assignments:

```
quant = 2; strcpy(units, "quarts"); strcpy(item, "oil");
count = 3;
quant = -12.8; strcpy(units, "degrees");
count = 2; /* "C" fails to match "o" */
count = 0; /* "l" fails to match "%f" */
quant = 10.0; strcpy(units, "LBS"); strcpy(item, "dirt");
count = 3;
count = 0; /* "100e" fails to match "%f" */
count = EOF;
```

Forward references: the **strtod** function (7.10.1.4), the **strtol** function (7.10.1.5), the **strtoul** function (7.10.1.6).

7.9.6.3 The printf function
Synopsis

```
#include <stdio.h>
int printf(const char *format, ...);
```

Description

The **printf** function is equivalent to **fprintf** with the argument **stdout** interposed before the arguments to **printf**.

Returns

The **printf** function returns the number of characters transmitted, or a negative value if an output error occurred.

7.9.6.4 The scanf function
Synopsis

```
#include <stdio.h>
int scanf(const char *format, ...);
```

Description

The **scanf** function is equivalent to **fscanf** with the argument **stdin** interposed before the arguments to **scanf**.

7.9.6.3 The printf function* and *7.9.6.4 The scanf function The two functions, **printf()** and **scanf()**, automatically direct their operations to **stdout** and **stdin**, respectively. In all other ways, these functions are equivalent to **fprintf()** and **fscanf()**.

Returns

The **scanf** function returns the value of the macro **EOF** if an input failure occurs before any conversion. Otherwise, the **scanf** function returns the number of input items assigned, which can be fewer than provided for, or even zero, in the event of an early matching failure.

7.9.6.5 The **sprintf** function

Synopsis

```
#include <stdio.h>
int sprintf(char *s, const char *format, ...);
```

Description

The **sprintf** function is equivalent to **fprintf**, except that the argument **s** specifies an array into which the generated output is to be written, rather than to a stream. A null character is written at the end of the characters written; it is not counted as part of the returned sum. If copying takes place between objects that overlap, the behavior is undefined.

Returns

The **sprintf** function returns the number of characters written in the array, not counting the terminating null character.

7.9.6.6 The **sscanf** function

Synopsis

```
#include <stdio.h>
int sscanf(const char *s, const char *format, ...);
```

Description

The **sscanf** function is equivalent to **fscanf**, except that the argument **s** specifies a string from which the input is to be obtained, rather than from a stream. Reaching the end of the string is equivalent to encountering end-of-file for the **fscanf** function. If copying takes place between objects that overlap, the behavior is undefined.

Returns

The **sscanf** function returns the value of the macro **EOF** if an input failure occurs before any conversion. Otherwise, the **sscanf** function returns the number of input items assigned, which can be fewer than provided for, or even žero, in the event of an early matching failure.

7.9.6.7 The **vfprintf** function

Synopsis

```
#include <stdarg.h>
#include <stdio.h>
int vfprintf(FILE *stream, const char *format, va_list arg);
```

Description

The **vfprintf** function is equivalent to **fprintf**, with the variable argument list replaced by **arg**, which shall have been initialized by the **va_start** macro (and possibly subsequent **va_arg** calls). The **vfprintf** function does not invoke the **va_end** macro.[124]

---

124 As the functions **vfprintf**, **vsprintf**, and **vprintf** invoke the **va_arg** macro, the value of **arg** after the return is indeterminate.

7.9.6.5 The sprintf function and 7.9.6.6 The sscanf function The **sprintf()** function operates exactly like **printf()**, except that output is written to the array pointed to by *s* instead of sent to a stream. The **sscanf()** function operates exactly like **scanf()**, except that information is read from the array pointed to by *s* rather than from an input stream.

These functions are handy in several situations. One common use for **sprintf()**, for instance, is to predefine a table of formatted strings that can output with little overhead when needed. Also, some graphics-based operating systems, such as Windows, do not supply a set of formatted output functions. In these cases you must manually create a string that contains the formatted output and then output that string to the window.

The following program illustrates the operation of both **sprintf()** and **sscanf()**:

```c
/* This program demonstrates sprintf() and sscanf(). */
#include <stdio.h>

void main(void)
{
  char buf[255];

  int i;
  double d;
  char c;
  char str[80];

  /* write output to an array */
  sprintf(buf, "%s %d %lf %c", "Hello", 10, 123.23, 'X');
  printf("Here is formatted output: %s\n", buf);

  /* read input from an array */
  sscanf(buf, "%s%d%lf%*c%c", str, &i, &d, &c);

  /* output the variables */
  printf("Here is the information: %s %d %lf %c\n",
       str, i, d, c);
}
```

Returns

The **vfprintf** function returns the number of characters transmitted, or a negative value if an output error occurred.

Example

The following shows the use of the **vfprintf** function in a general error-reporting routine.

```
#include <stdarg.h>
#include <stdio.h>

void error(char *function_name, char *format, ...)
{
        va_list args;

        va_start(args, format);
        /* print out name of function causing error */
        fprintf(stderr, "ERROR in %s: ", function_name);
        /* print out remainder of message */
        vfprintf(stderr, format, args);
        va_end(args);
}
```

7.9.6.8 The **vprintf** function

Synopsis

```
#include <stdarg.h>
#include <stdio.h>
int vprintf(const char *format, va_list arg);
```

Description

The **vprintf** function is equivalent to **printf**, with the variable argument list replaced by **arg**, which shall have been initialized by the **va_start** macro (and possibly subsequent **va_arg** calls). The **vprintf** function does not invoke the **va_end** macro.[124]

Returns

The **vprintf** function returns the number of characters transmitted, or a negative value if an output error occurred.

7.9.6.9 The **vsprintf** function

Synopsis

```
#include <stdarg.h>
#include <stdio.h>
int vsprintf(char *s, const char *format, va_list arg);
```

Description

The **vsprintf** function is equivalent to **sprintf**, with the variable argument list replaced by **arg**, which shall have been initialized by the **va_start** macro (and possibly subsequent **va_arg** calls). The **vsprintf** function does not invoke the **va_end** macro.[124] If copying takes place between objects that overlap, the behavior is undefined.

Returns

The **vsprintf** function returns the number of characters written in the array, not counting the terminating null character.

7.9.6.7 The vfprintf function; 7.9.6.8 The vprintf function; and 7.9.6.9 The vsprintf function   The **vfprintf()** function is the equivalent of **fprintf()**; the **vprintf()** function is the equivalent to **printf()**; and the **vsprintf()** function is the equivalent of **sprintf()**—except that each of these functions takes a variable-length argument list as its final parameter. You must include **stdarg.h** in any program that uses **vfprintf()**, **vprintf()**, or **vsprintf()**. (Refer to Section 7.8 for details on variable-argument processing.) The example of **vfprintf()** in the standard shows a common usage.

7.9.7 Character input/output functions

7.9.7.1 The **fgetc** function

Synopsis

```
#include <stdio.h>
int fgetc(FILE *stream);
```

Description

The **fgetc** function obtains the next character (if present) as an **unsigned char** converted to an **int**, from the input stream pointed to by **stream**, and advances the associated file position indicator for the stream (if defined).

Returns

The **fgetc** function returns the next character from the input stream pointed to by **stream**. If the stream is at end-of-file, the end-of-file indicator for the stream is set and **fgetc** returns **EOF**. If a read error occurs, the error indicator for the stream is set and **fgetc** returns **EOF**.[125]

7.9.7.2 The **fgets** function

Synopsis

```
#include <stdio.h>
char *fgets(char *s, int n, FILE *stream);
```

Description

The **fgets** function reads at most one less than the number of characters specified by **n** from the stream pointed to by **stream** into the array pointed to by **s**. No additional characters are read after a new-line character (which is retained) or after end-of-file. A null character is written immediately after the last character read into the array.

Returns

The **fgets** function returns **s** if successful. If end-of-file is encountered and no characters have been read into the array, the contents of the array remain unchanged and a null pointer is returned. If a read error occurs during the operation, the array contents are indeterminate and a null pointer is returned.

7.9.7.3 The **fputc** function

Synopsis

```
#include <stdio.h>
int fputc(int c, FILE *stream);
```

Description

The **fputc** function writes the character specified by **c** (converted to an **unsigned char**) to the output stream pointed to by **stream**, at the position indicated by the associated file position indicator for the stream (if defined), and advances the indicator appropriately. If the file cannot support positioning requests, or if the stream was opened with append mode, the character is appended to the output stream.

---

125 An end-of-file and a read error can be distinguished by use of the **feof** and **ferror** functions.

7.9.7   *Character input/output functions* A more accurate title for this section might be "Character-based input/output functions," since it includes functions that operate on characters and strings. The *character-based I/O functions* are fundamental and thoroughly familiar to most C programmers, and the standard is clear in its description of them. Here are a few additional tips to remember about their usage:

◆ The functions **fgetc()**, **getc()**, and **getchar()** read the next character from the input stream and return it as an integer value. This means the high-order byte will be zero, and the low-order byte will contain the character code.

◆ The functions **putc()** and **fputc()** are prototyped as taking integer arguments, but only the low-order byte is written to the output stream.

◆ Special keys, such as the arrow keys, function keys, and various editing keys, may not be able to be read using the character-based functions. You may need to use special machine- and compiler-specific functions to read these types of keys.

◆ When outputting only a string, a call to **puts()** may be more efficient than using **printf()**, because **puts()** does not involve the extra overhead incurred by the formatting code contained in **printf()**. (The same principle applies to **fputs()** and **fprintf()**.)

◆ Though most programmers freely use **gets()** to read a string entered by the user at the keyboard, this can cause a problem. Since **gets()** will read a string of any length, it is possible for the user to enter a string longer than what the receiving array can hold. A better solution is to use **fgets()** with the *stream* set to **stdin**, because the maximum length can be set. There is, however, one difference between **gets()** and **fgets()** that may be important: **fgets()** stores the newline character as part of the string, and **gets()** does not. (The second of the two following examples shows how to remove the newline character.)

Returns

The **fputc** function returns the character written. If a write error occurs, the error indicator for the stream is set and **fputc** returns **EOF**.

7.9.7.4 The fputs function

Synopsis

```
#include <stdio.h>
int fputs(const char *s, FILE *stream);
```

Description

The **fputs** function writes the string pointed to by **s** to the stream pointed to by **stream**. The terminating null character is not written.

Returns

The **fputs** function returns **EOF** if a write error occurs; otherwise it returns a nonnegative value.

7.9.7.5 The getc function

Synopsis

```
#include <stdio.h>
int getc(FILE *stream);
```

Description

The **getc** function is equivalent to **fgetc**, except that if it is implemented as a macro, it may evaluate **stream** more than once, so the argument should never be an expression with side effects.

Returns

The **getc** function returns the next character from the input stream pointed to by **stream**. If the stream is at end-of-file, the end-of-file indicator for the stream is set and **getc** returns **EOF**. If a read error occurs, the error indicator for the stream is set and **getc** returns **EOF**.

7.9.7.6 The getchar function

Synopsis

```
#include <stdio.h>
int getchar(void);
```

Description

The **getchar** function is equivalent to **getc** with the argument **stdin**.

Returns

The **getchar** function returns the next character from the input stream pointed to by **stdin**. If the stream is at end-of-file, the end-of-file indicator for the stream is set and **getchar** returns **EOF**. If a read error occurs, the error indicator for the stream is set and **getchar** returns **EOF**.

7.9.7.7 The gets function

Synopsis

```
#include <stdio.h>
char *gets(char *s);
```

(7.9.7   *Character input/output functions,* continued)

Here is a program that uses several of the character-based I/O functions. The program first creates a short text file and then reads (and displays) its contents.

```
/* This program demonstrates fputc(), fgetc(), fputs(),
      fgets(), puts(), and putchar(). */
#include <stdio.h>
#include <stdlib.h>

void main(void)
{
  FILE *fp;
  char str[80] = "This is the first line.";
  char *p;
  char c;

  if(!(fp=fopen("TEST", "w"))) {
    printf("Cannot open file.\n");
    exit(1);
  }

  /* write characters to the file */
  p = str;
  while(*p) {
    fputc(*p, fp); /* write characters */
    p++;
  }
  fputc('\n', fp);
  /* write a string */
  fputs("This is line two.\n", fp);

  /* close and then open as input file */
  fclose(fp);
  if(!(fp=fopen("TEST", "r"))) {
    printf("Cannot open file.\n");
    exit(1);
  }

  /* read characters */
  do {
    c = fgetc(fp);
    putchar(c);
  } while(c!='\n');
```

Description

The **gets** function reads characters from the input stream pointed to by **stdin**, into the array pointed to by **s**, until end-of-file is encountered or a new-line character is read. Any new-line character is discarded, and a null character is written immediately after the last character read into the array.

Returns

The **gets** function returns **s** if successful. If end-of-file is encountered and no characters have been read into the array, the contents of the array remain unchanged and a null pointer is returned. If a read error occurs during the operation, the array contents are indeterminate and a null pointer is returned.

7.9.7.8 The putc function

Synopsis

```
#include <stdio.h>
int putc(int c, FILE *stream);
```

Description

The **putc** function is equivalent to **fputc**, except that if it is implemented as a macro, it may evaluate **stream** more than once, so the argument should never be an expression with side effects.

Returns

The **putc** function returns the character written. If a write error occurs, the error indicator for the stream is set and **putc** returns **EOF**.

7.9.7.9 The putchar function

Synopsis

```
#include <stdio.h>
int putchar(int c);
```

Description

The **putchar** function is equivalent to **putc** with the second argument **stdout**.

Returns

The **putchar** function returns the character written. If a write error occurs, the error indicator for the stream is set and **putchar** returns **EOF**.

7.9.7.10 The puts function

Synopsis

```
#include <stdio.h>
int puts(const char *s);
```

Description

The **puts** function writes the string pointed to by **s** to the stream pointed to by **stdout**, and appends a new-line character to the output. The terminating null character is not written.

Returns

The **puts** function returns **EOF** if a write error occurs; otherwise it returns a nonnegative value.

(7.9.7   Character input/output functions, continued)

```
        /* read a string */
        fgets(str, sizeof str, fp);
        puts(str);

        fclose(fp);
    }
```

This next program shows how to use **fgets()** as a safer alternative to **gets()**. Unlike **gets()**, **fgets()** stores the newline character; thus, it must be removed manually (as the program illustrates) if it is not wanted.

```
    /* This program uses fgets() as a safer alternative
       to gets(). */
    #include <stdio.h>
    #include <string.h>

    void main(void)
    {
      char buf[20];
      int i;

      printf("Enter a string of characters: ");
      fgets(buf, sizeof buf, stdin);

      /* remove newline if present at end */
      i = strlen(buf);
      if(buf[i-1]=='\n') buf[i-1] = '\0'; /* change \n to null */

      /* if more than 20 characters were entered, they
         will have been truncated */
      puts(buf);
    }
```

7.9.7.11 The ungetc function

Synopsis

```
#include <stdio.h>
int ungetc(int c, FILE *stream);
```

Description

The **ungetc** function pushes the character specified by **c** (converted to an **unsigned char**) back onto the input stream pointed to by **stream**. The pushed-back characters will be returned by subsequent reads on that stream in the reverse order of their pushing. A successful intervening call (with the stream pointed to by **stream**) to a file positioning function (**fseek**, **fsetpos**, or **rewind**) discards any pushed-back characters for the stream. The external storage corresponding to the stream is unchanged.

One character of pushback is guaranteed. If the **ungetc** function is called too many times on the same stream without an intervening read or file positioning operation on that stream, the operation may fail.

If the value of **c** equals that of the macro **EOF**, the operation fails and the input stream is unchanged.

A successful call to the **ungetc** function clears the end-of-file indicator for the stream. The value of the file position indicator for the stream after reading or discarding all pushed-back characters shall be the same as it was before the characters were pushed back. For a text stream, the value of its file position indicator after a successful call to the **ungetc** function is unspecified until all pushed-back characters are read or discarded. For a binary stream, its file position indicator is decremented by each successful call to the **ungetc** function; if its value was zero before a call, it is indeterminate after the call.

Returns

The **ungetc** function returns the character pushed back after conversion, or **EOF** if the operation fails.

Forward references: file positioning functions (7.9.9).

7.9.8 Direct input/output functions

7.9.8.1 The fread function

Synopsis

```
#include <stdio.h>
size_t fread(void *ptr, size_t size, size_t nmemb,
     FILE *stream);
```

Description

The **fread** function reads, into the array pointed to by **ptr**, up to **nmemb** elements whose size is specified by **size**, from the stream pointed to by **stream**. The file position indicator for the stream (if defined) is advanced by the number of characters successfully read. If an error occurs, the resulting value of the file position indicator for the stream is indeterminate. If a partial element is read, its value is indeterminate.

Returns

The **fread** function returns the number of elements successfully read, which may be less than **nmemb** if a read error or end-of-file is encountered. If **size** or **nmemb** is zero, **fread** returns zero and the contents of the array and the state of the stream remain unchanged.

7.9.7.11   *The ungetc function*   The **ungetc()** function returns the character specified by *c* to the stream specified by *stream*. The standard states that a conforming implementation need only be able to return one character to the stream, and for the sake of portability, it is best to heed this limitation. Notice that any file position requests nullify the effects of **ungetc()**.

One important purpose of **ungetc()** is to support *one-character look-ahead*. As you may know, many routines base their next operation upon the nature of the next character from the input stream. For many of these routines, it is helpful to look ahead to the next character and then return it to the stream for later processing by an appropriate subroutine. Thus, a **fgetc()** followed by an **ungetc()** effectively creates a *peek* operation.

7.9.8   *Direct input/output functions*   The *direct input/output functions* are **fread()** and **fwrite()**, which read or write blocks of data. They are typically used to perform I/O operations on binary, rather than textual, data. These functions perform no formatting; therefore, a file that contains data written by **fwrite()**, for example, will not always be in human-readable form. Instead, it will be a mirror image of the binary representation of the data written.

Caution: The **fread()** function returns the number of items read, *not* the number of characters; **fwrite()** returns the number of items written, *not* the number of characters. Forgetting this is a common programming error.

7.9.8.2 The `fwrite` function

Synopsis

```
#include <stdio.h>
size_t fwrite(const void *ptr, size_t size, size_t nmemb,
     FILE *stream);
```

Description

The **fwrite** function writes, from the array pointed to by **ptr**, up to **nmemb** elements whose size is specified by **size**, to the stream pointed to by **stream**. The file position indicator for the stream (if defined) is advanced by the number of characters successfully written. If an error occurs, the resulting value of the file position indicator for the stream is indeterminate.

Returns

The **fwrite** function returns the number of elements successfully written, which will be less than **nmemb** only if a write error is encountered.

7.9.9 File positioning functions

7.9.9.1 The `fgetpos` function

Synopsis

```
#include <stdio.h>
int fgetpos(FILE *stream, fpos_t *pos);
```

Description

The **fgetpos** function stores the current value of the file position indicator for the stream pointed to by **stream** in the object pointed to by **pos**. The value stored contains unspecified information usable by the **fsetpos** function for repositioning the stream to its position at the time of the call to the **fgetpos** function.

Returns

If successful, the **fgetpos** function returns zero; on failure, the **fgetpos** function returns nonzero and stores an implementation-defined positive value in **errno**.

Forward references: the **fsetpos** function (7.9.9.3).

7.9.9.2 The `fseek` function

Synopsis

```
#include <stdio.h>
int fseek(FILE *stream, long int offset, int whence);
```

Description

The **fseek** function sets the file position indicator for the stream pointed to by **stream**.

For a binary stream, the new position, measured in characters from the beginning of the file, is obtained by adding **offset** to the position specified by **whence**. The specified position is the beginning of the file if **whence** is **SEEK_SET**, the current value of the file position indicator if **SEEK_CUR**, or end-of-file if **SEEK_END**. A binary stream need not meaningfully support **fseek** calls with a **whence** value of **SEEK_END**.

For a text stream, either **offset** shall be zero, or **offset** shall be a value returned by an earlier call to the **ftell** function on the same stream and **whence** shall be **SEEK_SET**.

A successful call to the **fseek** function clears the end-of-file indicator for the stream and undoes any effects of the **ungetc** function on the same stream. After an **fseek** call, the next operation on an update stream may be either input or output.

(7.9.8   Direct input/output functions, *continued*)

The following program uses **fwrite()** to write an array of floating–point values to a file, and **fread()** to read them back again. Notice that the entire array is written and read as one single block of memory, not as individual values.

```
/* This program demonstrates fread() and fwrite(). */
#include <stdio.h>
#include <stdlib.h>

void main(void)
{
  FILE *fp;
  double count[10] = {1.1, 2.2, 3.3, 4.4, 5.5,
                      6.6, 7.7, 8.8, 9.9, 10.1};
  int i;

  /* open a binary output file */
  if(!(fp=fopen("TEST", "wb"))) {
    printf("Cannot open file.\n");
    exit(1);
  }
  /* write data */
  if(fwrite(count, sizeof count, 1, fp)!=1) {
    printf("Write error!\n");
    exit(1);
  }
  /* close and reopen for binary input */
  fclose(fp);
  if(!(fp=fopen("TEST", "rb"))) {
    printf("Cannot open file.\n");
    exit(1);
  }
  /* read in the array */
  if(fread(count, sizeof count, 1, fp)!=1) {
    printf("Read error!\n");
    exit(1);
  }
  for(i=0; i<10; i++)
    printf("%6.21f", count[i]);
  fclose(fp);
}
```

7.9.9   File positioning functions You can perform random access I/O using the ANSI C file system with the *file-positioning functions*.

Returns

The **fseek** function returns nonzero only for a request that cannot be satisfied.

Forward references: the **ftell** function (7.9.9.4).

7.9.9.3 The **fsetpos** function

Synopsis

```
#include <stdio.h>
int fsetpos(FILE *stream, const fpos_t *pos);
```

Description

The **fsetpos** function sets the file position indicator for the stream pointed to by **stream** according to the value of the object pointed to by **pos**, which shall be a value obtained from an earlier call to the **fgetpos** function on the same stream.

A successful call to the **fsetpos** function clears the end-of-file indicator for the stream and undoes any effects of the **ungetc** function on the same stream. After an **fsetpos** call, the next operation on an update stream may be either input or output.

Returns

If successful, the **fsetpos** function returns zero; on failure, the **fsetpos** function returns nonzero and stores an implementation-defined positive value in **errno**.

7.9.9.4 The **ftell** function

Synopsis

```
#include <stdio.h>
long int ftell(FILE *stream);
```

Description

The **ftell** function obtains the current value of the file position indicator for the stream pointed to by **stream**. For a binary stream, the value is the number of characters from the beginning of the file. For a text stream, its file position indicator contains unspecified information, usable by the **fseek** function for returning the file position indicator for the stream to its position at the time of the **ftell** call; the difference between two such return values is not necessarily a meaningful measure of the number of characters written or read.

Returns

If successful, the **ftell** function returns the current value of the file position indicator for the stream. On failure, the **ftell** function returns −1L and stores an implementation-defined positive value in **errno**.

7.9.9.5 The **rewind** function

Synopsis

```
#include <stdio.h>
void rewind(FILE *stream);
```

Description

The **rewind** function sets the file position indicator for the stream pointed to by **stream** to the beginning of the file. It is equivalent to

```
(void)fseek(stream, 0L, SEEK_SET)
```

except that the error indicator for the stream is also cleared.

(*7.9.9 File positioning functions, continued*)

Notice that **fgetpos()** and **fsetpos()** are designed to work together. The **fgetpos()** function obtains the current position of the file associated with *stream* and stores it in the object pointed to by *pos*. **fsetpos()** sets the current position to that specified in the object pointed to by *pos*, which must have been previously obtained by calling **fgetpos()**. As the standard states, the contents of the object pointed to by *pos* is "unspecified," which means, in essence, that it is intended only to be filled by **fgetpos()** for later use by **fsetpos()** and not to be created or modified by your program. One use for these functions is to allow a quick means by which you can reset the current position to a previous point in a file.

Another set of complementary functions is **fseek()** and **ftell()**. **fseek()** is C's general-purpose random access function. Because character translations can affect the apparent positioning, **fseek()** is generally applied to files opened for binary operations. (Remember, a file containing text can be opened as a binary file, in which case no character translations will occur.) The operation of **fseek()** depends on a combination of *offset* and the value of *whence*. The valid values of *whence* (defined in **stdio.h**) are

SEEK_SET   Seeks *offset* bytes from start of file

SEEK_CUR   Seeks *offset* bytes from current location

SEEK_END   Seeks *offset* bytes from end of file

For example, assume that **fp** is a valid file pointer. To seek 10 bytes from the start of the file, use this statement:

```
fseek(fp, 10, SEEK_SET);
```

To seek 3 bytes from the current location, use this statement:

```
fseek(fp, 3, SEEK_CUR);
```

The value of *offset* may be positive or negative. For example, to seek to a position 15 bytes *before* the end, use this statement:

```
fseek(fp, -15, SEEK_END);
```

The **ftell()** function returns the location of the current position indicator as the number of bytes from the start of the file. This value can be used in a call to **fseek()** to return to a previous location, even if the file is opened as text instead of binary.

The **rewind()** function resets the file and returns the file position indicator to the beginning.

Returns

The **rewind** function returns no value.

7.9.10 Error-handling functions

7.9.10.1 The clearerr function

Synopsis

```
#include <stdio.h>
void clearerr(FILE *stream);
```

Description

The **clearerr** function clears the end-of-file and error indicators for the stream pointed to by **stream**.

Returns

The **clearerr** function returns no value.

7.9.10.2 The feof function

Synopsis

```
#include <stdio.h>
int feof(FILE *stream);
```

Description

The **feof** function tests the end-of-file indicator for the stream pointed to by **stream**.

Returns

The **feof** function returns nonzero if and only if the end-of-file indicator is set for **stream**.

7.9.10.3 The ferror function

Synopsis

```
#include <stdio.h>
int ferror(FILE *stream);
```

Description

The **ferror** function tests the error indicator for the stream pointed to by **stream**.

Returns

The **ferror** function returns nonzero if and only if the error indicator is set for **stream**.

7.9.10.4 The perror function

Synopsis

```
#include <stdio.h>
void perror(const char *s);
```

Description

The **perror** function maps the error number in the integer expression **errno** to an error message. It writes a sequence of characters to the standard error stream thus: first (if **s** is not a null pointer and the character pointed to by **s** is not the null character), the string pointed to by **s** followed by a colon (:) and a space: then an appropriate error message string followed by a new-line character. The contents of the error message strings are the same as those returned by the **strerror** function with argument **errno**, which are implementation-defined.

7.9.10 Error-handling functions These functions are quite straightforward. Following are some usage considerations for **feof()** and **ferror()**.

7.9.10.2 The feof function The standard defines four *error-handling functions*, including **feof()**—though most programmers do not consider **feof()** an error-handling function. Reaching an unexpected end-of-file can be an error, but most often **feof()** is used simply as a way to check if the end of the file has been reached. For example, you can use **feof()** to determine when the entire contents of an arbitrarily long file have been read. The following fragment illustrates how files are commonly read:

```
do {
  ch = fgetc(fp);
  /* ... */
} while(!feof(fp));
```

7.9.10.3 The ferror function Functions such as **fgetc()** return EOF when the end of the file is encountered *and* when an error occurs. Also, for files opened for binary operations, EOF is a valid binary value and does not necessarily indicate an error or end-of-file condition. For these reasons, the best way to determine if an error has occurred is to call the **ferror()** function immediately after each file operation.

As an example of how error checking can be applied, the following program copies the contents of one file to another with complete error checking:

```
/* This program copies a file and illustrates
   error checking. */
#include <stdio.h>
#include <stdlib.h>

int main(int argc, char *argv[])
{
  FILE *in, *out;
  unsigned char ch;

  if(argc!=3) {
    printf("Usage: COPYFILE <source> <target>\n");
    exit(1);
  }
```

Returns

The **perror** function returns no value.

Forward references: the **strerror** function (7.11.6.2).

(7.9.10.3   The ferror function, continued)

```c
/* open source file for binary input */
if(!(in=fopen(argv[1], "rb"))) {
  printf("Cannot open input file.\n");
  exit(1);
}

/* open target file for binary output */
if(!(out=fopen(argv[2], "wb"))) {
  printf("Cannot open output file.\n");
  exit(1);
}

/* copy the file */
do {
  ch = fgetc(in);
  if(ferror(in)) {
    printf("Error reading source file.\n");
    exit(1);
  }
  if(!feof(in)) fputc(ch, out);
  if(ferror(out)) {
    printf("Error writing target file.\n");
    exit(1);
  }
} while(!feof(in));

if(fclose(in)) {
  printf("Error closing source file.\n");
  exit(1);
}
if(fclose(out)) {
  printf("Error closing target file.\n");
  exit(1);
}

return 0; /* no errors copying file */
}
```

7.10 General utilities <stdlib.h>

The header **<stdlib.h>** declares four types and several functions of general utility. and defines several macros.[126]

The types declared are **size_t** and **wchar_t** (both described in 7.1.6).

div_t

which is a structure type that is the type of the value returned by the **div** function, and

ldiv_t

which is a structure type that is the type of the value returned by the **ldiv** function.

The macros defined are **NULL** (described in 7.1.6):

EXIT_FAILURE

and

EXIT_SUCCESS

which expand to integral expressions that may be used as the argument to the **exit** function to return unsuccessful or successful termination status, respectively, to the host environment;

RAND_MAX

which expands to an integral constant expression, the value of which is the maximum value returned by the **rand** function; and

MB_CUR_MAX

which expands to a positive integer expression whose value is the maximum number of bytes in a multibyte character for the extended character set specified by the current locale (category **LC_CTYPE**), and whose value is never greater than **MB_LEN_MAX**.

7.10.1 String conversion functions

The functions **atof**, **atoi**, and **atol** need not affect the value of the integer expression **errno** on an error. If the value of the result cannot be represented, the behavior is undefined.

7.10.1.1 The atof function

Synopsis

```
#include <stdlib.h>
double atof(const char *nptr);
```

Description

The **atof** function converts the initial portion of the string pointed to by **nptr** to **double** representation. Except for the behavior on error, it is equivalent to

```
strtod(nptr, (char **)NULL)
```

Returns

The **atof** function returns the converted value.

Forward references: the **strtod** function (7.10.1.4).

---

126 See ''future library directions'' (7.13.7).

7.10 **General utilities <stdlib.h>** This section describes library functions that don't fit into any of the major categories. Some of these are very useful and powerful, including the C dynamic allocation functions, several conversion functions, and C's sorting function, **qsort()**.

7.10.1 **String conversion functions** The *string conversion functions* convert a string containing a numeric value into the internal representation of that value. The standard defines six string conversion functions, but only three are actually needed. As the standard states, the functions **atof()**, **atoi()**, and **atol()** are, for the most part, shorthand for calls to the more general functions **strtod()** and **strtol()**.

Notice that all of these functions utilize only the initial part of the string to be converted that contains a valid numeric value. For example, when **atoi()** is called with the string "987XYZ", only the beginning part of the string, the number 987, is converted; the rest of the string is ignored. It is important to understand that calling one of the string conversion functions with a string such as "987XYZ" is not an error.

Also, remember that if the string does not contain a valid numeric value as defined by the function, then 0 is returned. Although **strtod()**, **strtol()**, and **strtoul()** set **errno** when an out-of-range condition exists, there is no requirement that **errno** be set when the string does not contain a number. Thus, if this is important to your program, you must manually check for the presence of a number before calling one of the conversion functions.

Here is a program that demonstrates **atoi()**, **atof()**, and **atol()**:

```
/* This program demonstrates atof(), atoi(), and atol(). */
#include <stdio.h>
#include <stdlib.h>

void main(void)
{
  int i;
  double d;
  long l;

  i = atoi("100");
  d = atof("100.232");
  l = atol("100000");

  printf("%d %lf %ld\n", i, d, l);
}
```

7.10.1.2 The `atoi` function
Synopsis

```
#include <stdlib.h>
int atoi(const char *nptr);
```

Description

The **atoi** function converts the initial portion of the string pointed to by **nptr** to **int** representation. Except for the behavior on error, it is equivalent to

```
(int)strtol(nptr, (char **)NULL, 10)
```

Returns

The **atoi** function returns the converted value.

Forward references: the **strtol** function (7.10.1.5).

7.10.1.3 The `atol` function
Synopsis

```
#include <stdlib.h>
long int atol(const char *nptr);
```

Description

The **atol** function converts the initial portion of the string pointed to by **nptr** to **long int** representation. Except for the behavior on error, it is equivalent to

```
strtol(nptr, (char **)NULL, 10)
```

Returns

The **atol** function returns the converted value.

Forward references: the **strtol** function (7.10.1.5).

7.10.1.4 The `strtod` function
Synopsis

```
#include <stdlib.h>
double strtod(const char *nptr, char **endptr);
```

Description

The **strtod** function converts the initial portion of the string pointed to by **nptr** to **double** representation. First, it decomposes the input string into three parts: an initial, possibly empty, sequence of white-space characters (as specified by the **isspace** function), a subject sequence resembling a floating-point constant; and a final string of one or more unrecognized characters, including the terminating null character of the input string. Then, it attempts to convert the subject sequence to a floating-point number, and returns the result.

The expected form of the subject sequence is an optional plus or minus sign, then a nonempty sequence of digits optionally containing a decimal-point character, then an optional exponent part as defined in 6.1.3.1, but no floating suffix. The subject sequence is defined as the longest initial subsequence of the input string, starting with the first non-white-space character, that is of the expected form. The subject sequence contains no characters if the input string is empty or consists entirely of white space, or if the first non-white-space character is other than a sign, a digit, or a decimal-point character.

If the subject sequence has the expected form, the sequence of characters starting with the first digit or the decimal-point character (whichever occurs first) is interpreted as a floating constant according to the rules of 6.1.3.1, except that the decimal-point character is used in place

(*7.10.1   String conversion functions, continued*)

This program displays **100 100.232000 100000**. Remember, only the initial portion of the string that contains a valid numeric value is used. For example, this line

```
i = atoi("100ABC");
```

also assigns **i** the value 100 and ignores the rest of the string.

This next program demonstrates the use of **strtod()**. Notice that after the call, **endptr** points to the remainder of the string, which may be processed further as needed. Pay special attention to how **endptr** is declared and passed to **strtod()**: The second parameter to **strtod()** is a pointer to a character pointer; thus, **endptr** is declared as a character pointer and its address is passed to **strtod()**.

```
/* This program demonstrates strtod(). */
#include <stdio.h>
#include <stdlib.h>
#include <string.h>

void main(void)
{
  char str[] = "98.6 is your temperature";
  char *endptr;
  double temp;

  temp = strtod(str, &endptr);

  printf("Temperature: %lf\n", temp);
  printf("Remainder of string: %s\n", endptr);
}
```

The foregoing program displays

```
Temperature: 98.600000
Remainder of string:  is your temperature
```

of a period, and that if neither an exponent part nor a decimal-point character appears, a decimal point is assumed to follow the last digit in the string. If the subject sequence begins with a minus sign, the value resulting from the conversion is negated. A pointer to the final string is stored in the object pointed to by **endptr**, provided that **endptr** is not a null pointer.

In other than the **"C"** locale, additional implementation-defined subject sequence forms may be accepted.

If the subject sequence is empty or does not have the expected form, no conversion is performed; the value of **nptr** is stored in the object pointed to by **endptr**, provided that **endptr** is not a null pointer.

Returns

The **strtod** function returns the converted value, if any. If no conversion could be performed, zero is returned. If the correct value is outside the range of representable values, plus or minus **HUGE_VAL** is returned (according to the sign of the value), and the value of the macro **ERANGE** is stored in **errno**. If the correct value would cause underflow, zero is returned and the value of the macro **ERANGE** is stored in **errno**.

7.10.1.5 The **strtol** function

Synopsis

```
#include <stdlib.h>
long int strtol(const char *nptr, char **endptr, int base);
```

Description

The **strtol** function converts the initial portion of the string pointed to by **nptr** to **long int** representation. First, it decomposes the input string into three parts: an initial, possibly empty, sequence of white-space characters (as specified by the **isspace** function), a subject sequence resembling an integer represented in some radix determined by the value of **base**, and a final string of one or more unrecognized characters, including the terminating null character of the input string. Then, it attempts to convert the subject sequence to an integer, and returns the result.

If the value of **base** is zero, the expected form of the subject sequence is that of an integer constant as described in 6.1.3.2, optionally preceded by a plus or minus sign, but not including an integer suffix. If the value of **base** is between 2 and 36, the expected form of the subject sequence is a sequence of letters and digits representing an integer with the radix specified by **base**, optionally preceded by a plus or minus sign, but not including an integer suffix. The letters from **a** (or **A**) through **z** (or **Z**) are ascribed the values 10 to 35; only letters whose ascribed values are less than that of **base** are permitted. If the value of **base** is 16, the characters **0x** or **0X** may optionally precede the sequence of letters and digits, following the sign if present.

The subject sequence is defined as the longest initial subsequence of the input string, starting with the first non-white-space character, that is of the expected form. The subject sequence contains no characters if the input string is empty or consists entirely of white space, or if the first non-white-space character is other than a sign or a permissible letter or digit.

If the subject sequence has the expected form and the value of **base** is zero, the sequence of characters starting with the first digit is interpreted as an integer constant according to the rules of 6.1.3.2. If the subject sequence has the expected form and the value of **base** is between 2 and 36, it is used as the base for conversion, ascribing to each letter its value as given above. If the subject sequence begins with a minus sign, the value resulting from the conversion is negated. A pointer to the final string is stored in the object pointed to by **endptr**, provided that **endptr** is not a null pointer.

(7.10.1   String conversion functions, continued)

The **strtol()** and **strtoul()** functions, demonstrated in the following program, both allow you to specify the base of the string being converted. Notice that the *endptr* parameter may be NULL when the remainder of the conversion string is not needed.

```
/* This program demonstrates strtol() and strtoul(). */
#include <stdio.h>
#include <stdlib.h>

void main(void)
{
  long l;
  unsigned long u;

  /* convert from base 10 */
  l = strtol("10", NULL, 10);
  printf("Converting from base 10:  %ld\n", l);
  /* convert from binary */
  l = strtol("10", NULL, 2);
  printf("Converting from base 2:  %ld\n", l);

  /* convert from base 10 */
  u = strtoul("101010101", NULL, 10);
  printf("Converting from base 10:  %lu\n", u);
  /* convert from binary */
  u = strtoul("101010101", NULL, 2);
  printf("Converting from base 2:  %lu\n", u);
}
```

Here is the output from the foregoing program:

```
Converting from base 10:  10
Converting from base 2:  2
Converting from base 10:  101010101
Converting from base 2:  341
```

In other than the "C" locale, additional implementation-defined subject sequence forms may be accepted.

If the subject sequence is empty or does not have the expected form, no conversion is performed; the value of **nptr** is stored in the object pointed to by **endptr**, provided that **endptr** is not a null pointer.

Returns

The **strtol** function returns the converted value, if any. If no conversion could be performed, zero is returned. If the correct value is outside the range of representable values, **LONG_MAX** or **LONG_MIN** is returned (according to the sign of the value), and the value of the macro **ERANGE** is stored in **errno**.

7.10.1.6 The **strtoul** function

Synopsis

```
#include <stdlib.h>
unsigned long int strtoul(const char *nptr, char **endptr,
        int base);
```

Description

The **strtoul** function converts the initial portion of the string pointed to by **nptr** to **unsigned long int** representation. First, it decomposes the input string into three parts: an initial, possibly empty, sequence of white-space characters (as specified by the **isspace** function), a subject sequence resembling an unsigned integer represented in some radix determined by the value of **base**, and a final string of one or more unrecognized characters, including the terminating null character of the input string. Then, it attempts to convert the subject sequence to an unsigned integer, and returns the result.

If the value of **base** is zero, the expected form of the subject sequence is that of an integer constant as described in 6.1.3.2, optionally preceded by a plus or minus sign, but not including an integer suffix. If the value of **base** is between 2 and 36, the expected form of the subject sequence is a sequence of letters and digits representing an integer with the radix specified by **base**, optionally preceded by a plus or minus sign, but not including an integer suffix. The letters from **a** (or **A**) through **z** (or **Z**) are ascribed the values 10 to 35; only letters whose ascribed values are less than that of **base** are permitted. If the value of **base** is 16, the characters **0x** or **0X** may optionally precede the sequence of letters and digits, following the sign if present.

The subject sequence is defined as the longest initial subsequence of the input string, starting with the first non-white-space character, that is of the expected form. The subject sequence contains no characters if the input string is empty or consists entirely of white space, or if the first non-white-space character is other than a sign or a permissible letter or digit.

If the subject sequence has the expected form and the value of **base** is zero, the sequence of characters starting with the first digit is interpreted as an integer constant according to the rules of 6.1.3.2. If the subject sequence has the expected form and the value of **base** is between 2 and 36, it is used as the base for conversion, ascribing to each letter its value as given above. If the subject sequence begins with a minus sign, the value resulting from the conversion is negated. A pointer to the final string is stored in the object pointed to by **endptr**, provided that **endptr** is not a null pointer.

In other than the "C" locale, additional implementation-defined subject sequence forms may be accepted.

If the subject sequence is empty or does not have the expected form, no conversion is performed; the value of **nptr** is stored in the object pointed to by **endptr**, provided that **endptr** is not a null pointer.

There are no annotations for page 152.

Returns

The **strtoul** function returns the converted value, if any. If no conversion could be performed, zero is returned. If the correct value is outside the range of representable values, **ULONG_MAX** is returned, and the value of the macro **ERANGE** is stored in **errno**.

7.10.2 Pseudo-random sequence generation functions

7.10.2.1 The rand function

Synopsis

```
#include <stdlib.h>
int rand(void);
```

Description

The **rand** function computes a sequence of pseudo-random integers in the range 0 to **RAND_MAX**.

The implementation shall behave as if no library function calls the **rand** function.

Returns

The **rand** function returns a pseudo-random integer.

Environmental limit

The value of the **RAND_MAX** macro shall be at least 32767.

7.10.2.2 The srand function

Synopsis

```
#include <stdlib.h>
void srand(unsigned int seed);
```

Description

The **srand** function uses the argument as a seed for a new sequence of pseudo-random numbers to be returned by subsequent calls to **rand**. If **srand** is then called with the same seed value, the sequence of pseudo-random numbers shall be repeated. If **rand** is called before any calls to **srand** have been made, the same sequence shall be generated as when **srand** is first called with a seed value of 1.

The implementation shall behave as if no library function calls the **srand** function.

Returns

The **srand** function returns no value.

Example

The following functions define a portable implementation of **rand** and **srand**.

7.10.2 *Pseudo-random sequence generation functions* The operation of these functions is clearly described in the standard.

The following program illustrates a useful technique that uses the current system time as a seed value. Using this method prevents multiple program runs from using the same random number sequence. (The time functions are discussed in Section 7.12, and the value **INT_MAX** is defined in **limits.h**.)

```
/* This program seeds the random number generator using
   the system time. */
#include <stdio.h>
#include <stdlib.h>
#include <time.h>
#include <limits.h>

void main(void)
{
  unsigned seed;
  long curtime;
  int i;

  /* get the current system time */
  curtime = time(NULL);
  seed = (unsigned) curtime % INT_MAX;
  srand(seed);

  for(i=0; i<10; i++) printf("%d ", rand());
}
```

Each time you run this program, the system time will be different and a new seed value will be used to initialize the random number generator. This will produce a new sequence of numbers.

```
static unsigned long int next = 1;

int rand(void)    /* RAND_MAX assumed to be 32767 */
{
       next = next * 1103515245 + 12345;
       return (unsigned int)(next/65536) % 32768;
}

void srand(unsigned int seed)
{
       next = seed;
}
```

7.10.3 Memory management functions

The order and contiguity of storage allocated by successive calls to the **calloc**, **malloc**, and **realloc** functions is unspecified. The pointer returned if the allocation succeeds is suitably aligned so that it may be assigned to a pointer to any type of object and then used to access such an object or an array of such objects in the space allocated (until the space is explicitly freed or reallocated). Each such allocation shall yield a pointer to an object disjoint from any other object. The pointer returned points to the start (lowest byte address) of the allocated space. If the space cannot be allocated, a null pointer is returned. If the size of the space requested is zero, the behavior is implementation-defined; the value returned shall be either a null pointer or a unique pointer. The value of a pointer that refers to freed space is indeterminate.

7.10.3.1 The calloc function

Synopsis

```
#include <stdlib.h>
void *calloc(size_t nmemb, size_t size);
```

Description

The **calloc** function allocates space for an array of **nmemb** objects, each of whose size is **size**. The space is initialized to all bits zero.[127]

Returns

The **calloc** function returns either a null pointer or a pointer to the allocated space.

7.10.3.2 The free function

Synopsis

```
#include <stdlib.h>
void free(void *ptr);
```

Description

The **free** function causes the space pointed to by **ptr** to be deallocated, that is, made available for further allocation. If **ptr** is a null pointer, no action occurs. Otherwise, if the argument does not match a pointer earlier returned by the **calloc**, **malloc**, or **realloc** function, or if the space has been deallocated by a call to **free** or **realloc**, the behavior is undefined.

---

127 Note that this need not be the same as the representation of floating-point zero or a null pointer constant.

7.10.3 Memory management functions What the standard calls *memory management functions*, most C programmers refer to as the *dynamic allocation system*. Even though this system contains only four functions (although many compilers supply several additional variations), it is one of the most important systems in the C library. Its purpose is to allow your program to allocate memory while it is running. Dynamically allocated memory can be used to hold any type of data and to support various data structures. For example, it is commonly used to implement linked lists, binary trees, stacks, and queues.

Notice that the standard explicitly *does not* state how dynamic allocation will be implemented. This allows compiler implementors to use dynamic allocation as deemed best for the compiler's execution environment. However, dynamically allocated memory is usually obtained from the *heap,* a region of memory that lies between your program's code (and static data area) and the stack. Since memory is a finite resource it is possible that the heap may be used up, and no further memory can be allocated. In some cases, the stack and heap may encounter each other. This is called a *heap-stack collision* and is generally a fatal run-time error.

In addition to the standard's description of the dynamic allocation functions, here are a few points to which you should pay special attention. First, the amount of memory allocated by **malloc()** is specified in bytes. Second, **malloc()** returns a pointer to the start of that memory, or NULL if the allocation request cannot be filled. For this reason it is critical that you check the return value of **malloc()** (or **realloc()**) before attempting to use it. Third, you must only call **free()** with a pointer to previously allocated memory. Calling it with any other type of memory address may cause the dynamic allocation system to crash. Finally, once you free a portion of memory, it is available for reallocation. Therefore, once you free an object, you must consider it destroyed and not attempt to use it for any other purpose.

The following program illustrates **malloc()** and **free()**. It allocates sufficient memory to hold a string of up to 80 characters; it also allocates an array of 10 integers. Finally, for the sake of illustration, it frees both regions of memory. (Since all memory is freed when a program terminates, the calls to **free()** in this example are technically unnecessary.)

```
/* This program demonstrates malloc() and free(). */
#include <stdio.h>
#include <stdlib.h>
#include <string.h>

void main(void)
{
  int i;
  char *p;
```

Returns

The **free** function returns no value.

7.10.3.3 The `malloc` function

Synopsis

```
#include <stdlib.h>
void *malloc(size_t size);
```

Description

The **malloc** function allocates space for an object whose size is specified by **size** and whose value is indeterminate.

Returns

The **malloc** function returns either a null pointer or a pointer to the allocated space.

7.10.3.4 The `realloc` function

Synopsis

```
#include <stdlib.h>
void *realloc(void *ptr, size_t size);
```

Description

The **realloc** function changes the size of the object pointed to by **ptr** to the size specified by **size**. The contents of the object shall be unchanged up to the lesser of the new and old sizes. If the new size is larger, the value of the newly allocated portion of the object is indeterminate. If **ptr** is a null pointer, the **realloc** function behaves like the **malloc** function for the specified size. Otherwise, if **ptr** does not match a pointer earlier returned by the **calloc**, **malloc**, or **realloc** function, or if the space has been deallocated by a call to the **free** or **realloc** function, the behavior is undefined. If the space cannot be allocated, the object pointed to by **ptr** is unchanged. If **size** is zero and **ptr** is not a null pointer, the object it points to is freed.

Returns

The **realloc** function returns either a null pointer or a pointer to the possibly moved allocated space.

7.10.4 Communication with the environment

7.10.4.1 The `abort` function

Synopsis

```
#include <stdlib.h>
void abort(void);
```

Description

The **abort** function causes abnormal program termination to occur, unless the signal **SIGABRT** is being caught and the signal handler does not return. Whether open output streams are flushed or open streams closed or temporary files removed is implementation-defined. An implementation-defined form of the status *unsuccessful termination* is returned to the host environment by means of the function call **raise(SIGABRT)**.

Returns

The **abort** function cannot return to its caller.

(7.10.3   Memory management functions, continued)

```
int *ip;
float *fp;

/* allocate an array of characters */
p = malloc(80);
if(!p) { /* if request fails */
  printf("Cannot allocate string.\n");
  exit(1);
}

/* allocate an array of integers */
ip = malloc(10 * sizeof (int));
if(!ip) { /* if request fails */
  printf("Cannot allocate array of integers.\n");
  exit(1);
}

/* allocate space for a float */
fp = malloc(sizeof (float));
if(!p) { /* if request fails */
  printf("Cannot allocate float.\n");
  exit(1);
}

/* use the dynamically allocated memory */
*fp = 123.25;
strcpy(p, "This is a test.\n");
for(i=0; i<10; i++) ip[i] = i;

printf("float: %f\n", *fp);
printf("String: %s", p);
printf("Integer array: ");
for(i=0; i<10; i++) printf("%4d", ip[i]);

/* free the memory */
free(p);
free(ip);
free(fp);
}
```

7.10.4   Communication with the environment The standard library defines several functions that enable communication with the host environment. The operation of **abort()** and **exit()** is straightforward. **atexit()**, **getenv()**, and **system()** are examined further here.

7.10.4.2 The `atexit` function

Synopsis

```
#include <stdlib.h>
int atexit(void (*func)(void));
```

Description

The **atexit** function registers the function pointed to by **func**, to be called without arguments at normal program termination.

Implementation limits

The implementation shall support the registration of at least 32 functions.

Returns

The **atexit** function returns zero if the registration succeeds, nonzero if it fails.

Forward references: the **exit** function (7.10.4.3).

7.10.4.3 The `exit` function

Synopsis

```
#include <stdlib.h>
void exit(int status);
```

Description

The **exit** function causes normal program termination to occur. If more than one call to the **exit** function is executed by a program, the behavior is undefined.

First, all functions registered by the **atexit** function are called, in the reverse order of their registration.[128]

Next, all open streams with unwritten buffered data are flushed, all open streams are closed, and all files created by the **tmpfile** function are removed.

Finally, control is returned to the host environment. If the value of **status** is zero or **EXIT_SUCCESS**, an implementation-defined form of the status *successful termination* is returned. If the value of **status** is **EXIT_FAILURE**, an implementation-defined form of the status *unsuccessful termination* is returned. Otherwise the status returned is implementation-defined.

Returns

The **exit** function cannot return to its caller.

7.10.4.4 The `getenv` function

Synopsis

```
#include <stdlib.h>
char *getenv(const char *name);
```

Description

The **getenv** function searches an *environment list*, provided by the host environment, for a string that matches the string pointed to by **name**. The set of environment names and the method for altering the environment list are implementation-defined.

---

128 Each function is called as many times as it was registered.

7.10.4.2   The atexit function   The **atexit()** function is used to register functions that are called when a program is terminating normally. Put differently, using **atexit()** you can tell the compiler to include the function pointed to by *func* in a list of functions called just before the program returns to the operating system. At least 32 *termination functions* can be registered, and they are called in first-in, last-out order. Termination functions are typically used to clean up any "messes" left by the program. For example, a file transfer program might use a termination function to send a disconnect message to the remote computer.

The following program demonstrates **atexit()**:

```c
/* This program demonstrates atexit(). */
#include <stdio.h>
#include <stdlib.h>

void term1(void);
void term2(void);

void main(void)
{
  atexit(term2); /* register 2nd termination function */
  atexit(term1); /* register 1st termination function */

  printf("Program now terminating...\n");
}

void term1(void)
{
  printf("This is printed by 1st termination function.\n");
}

void term2(void)
{
  printf("This is printed by 2nd termination function.\n");
}
```

The foregoing program produces the following output:

```
Program now terminating...
This is printed by 1st termination function.
This is printed by 2nd termination function.
```

The implementation shall behave as if no library function calls the **getenv** function.

Returns

The **getenv** function returns a pointer to a string associated with the matched list member. The string pointed to shall not be modified by the program, but may be overwritten by a subsequent call to the **getenv** function. If the specified **name** cannot be found, a null pointer is returned.

7.10.4.5 The system function

Synopsis

```
#include <stdlib.h>
int system(const char *string);
```

Description

The **system** function passes the string pointed to by **string** to the host environment to be executed by a *command processor* in an implementation-defined manner. A null pointer may be used for **string** to inquire whether a command processor exists.

Returns

If the argument is a null pointer, the **system** function returns nonzero only if a command processor is available. If the argument is not a null pointer, the **system** function returns an implementation-defined value.

7.10.5 Searching and sorting utilities

7.10.5.1 The bsearch function

Synopsis

```
#include <stdlib.h>
void *bsearch(const void *key, const void *base,
        size_t nmemb, size_t size,
        int (*compar)(const void *, const void *));
```

Description

The **bsearch** function searches an array of **nmemb** objects, the initial element of which is pointed to by **base**, for an element that matches the object pointed to by **key**. The size of each element of the array is specified by **size**.

The comparison function pointed to by **compar** is called with two arguments that point to the **key** object and to an array element, in that order. The function shall return an integer less than, equal to, or greater than zero if the **key** object is considered, respectively, to be less than, to match, or to be greater than the array element. The array shall consist of: all the elements that compare less than, all the elements that compare equal to, and all the elements that compare greater than the **key** object, in that order.[129]

Returns

The **bsearch** function returns a pointer to a matching element of the array, or a null pointer if no match is found. If two elements compare as equal, which element is matched is unspecified.

---

129 In practice, the entire array is sorted according to the comparison function.

7.10.4.4 *The getenv function and 7.10.4.5   The system function* Most operating systems support environment variables that define or describe various aspects of the execution context. For example, an operating system may use the variable PATH to describe a standard directory search path. The **getenv()** function returns a pointer to the string associated with the environmental variable that it is called with. Your program is then free to use this information as required. The **system()** function passes a command to the command processor of the operating system. Typically, this command will be executed as if you entered it from the command prompt.

This next program demonstrates the **getenv()** and **system()** functions. Notice that it first confirms that a command processor is available before calling **system()** with actual commands.

```
/* This program demonstrates getenv() and system(). This
   program assumes a DOS or WINDOWS environment. */
#include <stdio.h>
#include <stdlib.h>

void main(void)
{
  /* display the info associated with PATH */
  printf("Current path is: %s\n", getenv("PATH"));

  /* see if command processor is present */
  if(!system(NULL)) {
    printf("No command processor present.\n");
    exit(1);
  }

  system("DIR"); /* display the directory */
  system("TIME"); /* set the time */
  system("CHKDSK"); /* check the disk */

  printf("Program terminating\n");
}
```

7.10.5 *Searching and sorting utilities* The functions **bsearch()** and **qsort()** are C's *searching and sorting routines*. Though not actually specified by the standard, **qsearch()** typically performs a binary search (thus, the array must be in sorted order); and **qsort()** is generally implemented using the Quicksort algorithm.

The key to using these two functions is the **compar()** function, which your program must create. The **compar()** function must have this prototype:

int compar(const void *arg1, const void *arg2);

7.10.5.2 The qsort function

Synopsis

```
#include <stdlib.h>
void qsort(void *base, size_t nmemb, size_t size,
        int (*compar)(const void *, const void *));
```

Description

The **qsort** function sorts an array of **nmemb** objects, the initial element of which is pointed to by **base**. The size of each object is specified by **size**.

The contents of the array are sorted into ascending order according to a comparison function pointed to by **compar**, which is called with two arguments that point to the objects being compared. The function shall return an integer less than, equal to, or greater than zero if the first argument is considered to be respectively less than, equal to, or greater than the second.

If two elements compare as equal, their order in the sorted array is unspecified.

Returns

The **qsort** function returns no value.

7.10.6 Integer arithmetic functions

7.10.6.1 The abs function

Synopsis

```
#include <stdlib.h>
int abs(int j);
```

Description

The **abs** function computes the absolute value of an integer **j**. If the result cannot be represented, the behavior is undefined.[130]

Returns

The **abs** function returns the absolute value.

7.10.6.2 The div function

Synopsis

```
#include <stdlib.h>
div_t div(int numer, int denom);
```

Description

The **div** function computes the quotient and remainder of the division of the numerator **numer** by the denominator **denom**. If the division is inexact, the resulting quotient is the integer of lesser magnitude that is the nearest to the algebraic quotient. If the result cannot be represented, the behavior is undefined; otherwise, **quot * denom + rem** shall equal **numer**.

Returns

The **div** function returns a structure of type **div_t**, comprising both the quotient and the remainder. The structure shall contain the following members, in either order:

---

130 The absolute value of the most negative number cannot be represented in two's complement.

(7.10.5   Searching and sorting utilities, continued)

This function compares the key with elements of the array. It must return the following values:

If $*arg1 < *arg2$ return less than zero.

If $*arg1 == *arg2$ return zero.

If $*arg1 > *arg2$ return greater than zero.

The following program demonstrates **bsearch()** and **qsort()**. Notice how **compar()** is implemented. Because its parameters are declared as **void *** pointers, you will need to type cast them into a type compatible with your data.

```c
/* This program demonstrates bsearch() and qsort(). */
#include <stdio.h>
#include <stdlib.h>

#define SIZE 10

double nums[10] = {123.23, 43.3, 2.23, 88.34, 1.1,
                   -12.22, 0.09, 120.2, 99.0, 3.3};

int compar(const void *arg1, const void *arg2);

void main(void)
{
  int i;
  double *dp, key;

  qsort(nums, SIZE, sizeof (double), compar);

  printf("Here is sorted array:\n");
  for(i=0; i<SIZE; i++) printf("%7.2lf", nums[i]);

  printf("\nSearching for 2.23.\n");
  key = 2.23;
  dp = bsearch(&key, nums, SIZE, sizeof (double), compar);
  if(dp) printf("Found: %lf\n", *dp);
  else printf("Not found.\n");
}

/* Compare values for bsearch() and qsort(). */
int compar(const void *arg1, const void *arg2)
{
```

```
int quot;     /* quotient */
int rem;      /* remainder */
```

7.10.6.3 The labs function

Synopsis

```
#include <stdlib.h>
long int labs(long int j);
```

Description

The **labs** function is similar to the **abs** function, except that the argument and the returned value each have type **long int**.

7.10.6.4 The ldiv function

Synopsis

```
#include <stdlib.h>
ldiv_t ldiv(long int numer, long int denom);
```

Description

The **ldiv** function is similar to the **div** function, except that the arguments and the members of the returned structure (which has type **ldiv_t**) all have type **long int**.

7.10.7 Multibyte character functions

The behavior of the multibyte character functions is affected by the **LC_CTYPE** category of the current locale. For a state-dependent encoding, each function is placed into its initial state by a call for which its character pointer argument, **s**, is a null pointer. Subsequent calls with **s** as other than a null pointer cause the internal state of the function to be altered as necessary. A call with **s** as a null pointer causes these functions to return a nonzero value if encodings have state dependency, and zero otherwise.[131] Changing the **LC_CTYPE** category causes the shift state of these functions to be indeterminate.

7.10.7.1 The mblen function

Synopsis

```
#include <stdlib.h>
int mblen(const char *s, size_t n);
```

Description

If **s** is not a null pointer, the **mblen** function determines the number of bytes contained in the multibyte character pointed to by **s**. Except that the shift state of the **mbtowc** function is not affected, it is equivalent to

```
mbtowc((wchar_t *)0, s, n);
```

The implementation shall behave as if no library function calls the **mblen** function.

Returns

If **s** is a null pointer, the **mblen** function returns a nonzero or zero value, if multibyte character encodings, respectively, do or do not have state-dependent encodings. If **s** is not a null pointer, the **mblen** function either returns 0 (if **s** points to the null character), or returns the

---

131 If the implementation employs special bytes to change the shift state, these bytes do not produce separate wide character codes, but are grouped with an adjacent multibyte character.

```
    if(*(double *) arg1 < *(double *) arg2) return -1;
    else if(*(double *) arg1 == *(double *) arg2) return 0;
    else return 1;
}
```

7.10.6 *Integer arithmetic functions* The *integer arithmetic functions* are straightforward; here is a program that demonstrates them:

```
#include <stdio.h>
#include <stdlib.h>

void main(void)
{
    int i;
    long l;
    div_t result;
    ldiv_t lresult;

    result = div(10, 3);
    printf("10 div 3: quotient is %d, remainder is %d\n",
            result.quot, result.rem);

    lresult = ldiv(100000, 3L);
    printf("100000 ldiv 3: quotient is %ld, remainder is %ld\n",
            lresult.quot, lresult.rem);

    i = abs(-10);
    l = labs(-100323);
    printf("Absolute values: %d %ld\n", i, l);
}
```

The foregoing program displays

```
10 div 3: quotient is 3, remainder is 1
100000 ldiv 3: quotient is 33333, remainder is 1
Absolute values: 10 100323
```

7.10.7 *Multibyte character functions* The *multibyte character functions* form a bridge between multibyte characters and wide characters. A *wide character* is an integer type that contains a unique code corresponding to a specific multibyte character. A *multibyte character* consists of one or more bytes. Typically, multibyte characters are used to hold the larger character sets associated with languages such as Chinese.

These functions are clearly explained in the standard. However, since multibyte characters are implementation-specific, you should refer to your compiler's user manual for details.

The standard uses the term *shift state*, which is essentially a context that can be altered using some sort of escape sequence.

number of bytes that are contained in the multibyte character (if the next **n** or fewer bytes form a valid multibyte character), or returns −1 (if they do not form a valid multibyte character).

Forward references: the **mbtowc** function (7.10.7.2).

7.10.7.2 The mbtowc function

Synopsis

```
#include <stdlib.h>
int mbtowc(wchar_t *pwc, const char *s, size_t n);
```

Description

If **s** is not a null pointer, the **mbtowc** function determines the number of bytes that are contained in the multibyte character pointed to by **s**. It then determines the code for the value of type **wchar_t** that corresponds to that multibyte character. (The value of the code corresponding to the null character is zero.) If the multibyte character is valid and **pwc** is not a null pointer, the **mbtowc** function stores the code in the object pointed to by **pwc**. At most **n** bytes of the array pointed to by **s** will be examined.

The implementation shall behave as if no library function calls the **mbtowc** function.

Returns

If **s** is a null pointer, the **mbtowc** function returns a nonzero or zero value, if multibyte character encodings, respectively, do or do not have state-dependent encodings. If **s** is not a null pointer, the **mbtowc** function either returns 0 (if **s** points to the null character), or returns the number of bytes that are contained in the converted multibyte character (if the next **n** or fewer bytes form a valid multibyte character), or returns −1 (if they do not form a valid multibyte character).

In no case will the value returned be greater than **n** or the value of the **MB_CUR_MAX** macro.

7.10.7.3 The wctomb function

Synopsis

```
#include <stdlib.h>
int wctomb(char *s, wchar_t wchar);
```

Description

The **wctomb** function determines the number of bytes needed to represent the multibyte character corresponding to the code whose value is **wchar** (including any change in shift state). It stores the multibyte character representation in the array object pointed to by **s** (if **s** is not a null pointer). At most **MB_CUR_MAX** characters are stored. If the value of **wchar** is zero, the **wctomb** function is left in the initial shift state.

The implementation shall behave as if no library function calls the **wctomb** function.

Returns

If **s** is a null pointer, the **wctomb** function returns a nonzero or zero value, if multibyte character encodings, respectively, do or do not have state-dependent encodings. If **s** is not a null pointer, the **wctomb** function returns −1 if the value of **wchar** does not correspond to a valid multibyte character, or returns the number of bytes that are contained in the multibyte character corresponding to the value of **wchar**.

In no case will the value returned be greater than the value of the **MB_CUR_MAX** macro.

There are no annotations for page 160.

7.10.8 Multibyte string functions

The behavior of the multibyte string functions is affected by the **LC_CTYPE** category of the current locale.

7.10.8.1 The mbstowcs function

Synopsis

```
#include <stdlib.h>
size_t mbstowcs(wchar_t *pwcs, const char *s, size_t n);
```

Description

The **mbstowcs** function converts a sequence of multibyte characters that begins in the initial shift state from the array pointed to by **s** into a sequence of corresponding codes and stores not more than **n** codes into the array pointed to by **pwcs**. No multibyte characters that follow a null character (which is converted into a code with value zero) will be examined or converted. Each multibyte character is converted as if by a call to the **mbtowc** function, except that the shift state of the **mbtowc** function is not affected.

No more than **n** elements will be modified in the array pointed to by **pwcs**. If copying takes place between objects that overlap, the behavior is undefined.

Returns

If an invalid multibyte character is encountered, the **mbstowcs** function returns **(size_t)-1**. Otherwise, the **mbstowcs** function returns the number of array elements modified, not including a terminating zero code, if any.[132]

7.10.8.2 The wcstombs function

Synopsis

```
#include <stdlib.h>
size_t wcstombs(char *s, const wchar_t *pwcs, size_t n);
```

Description

The **wcstombs** function converts a sequence of codes that correspond to multibyte characters from the array pointed to by **pwcs** into a sequence of multibyte characters that begins in the initial shift state and stores these multibyte characters into the array pointed to by **s**, stopping if a multibyte character would exceed the limit of **n** total bytes or if a null character is stored. Each code is converted as if by a call to the **wctomb** function, except that the shift state of the **wctomb** function is not affected.

No more than **n** bytes will be modified in the array pointed to by **s**. If copying takes place between objects that overlap, the behavior is undefined.

Returns

If a code is encountered that does not correspond to a valid multibyte character, the **wcstombs** function returns **(size_t)-1**. Otherwise, the **wcstombs** function returns the number of bytes modified, not including a terminating null character, if any.[132]

---

132 The array will not be null- or zero-terminated if the value returned is **n**.

7.10.8 **_Multibyte string functions_** Like the multibyte character functions, the _multibyte string functions_ provide a transition between wide characters and multibyte characters. Since multibyte characters are implementation-specific, you should refer to your compiler's user manual for details.

7.11 String handling <string.h>

7.11.1 String function conventions

The header **<string.h>** declares one type and several functions. and defines one macro useful for manipulating arrays of character type and other objects treated as arrays of character type.[133] The type is **size_t** and the macro is **NULL** (both described in 7.1.6). Various methods are used for determining the lengths of the arrays, but in all cases a **char *** or **void *** argument points to the initial (lowest addressed) character of the array. If an array is accessed beyond the end of an object, the behavior is undefined.

7.11.2 Copying functions

7.11.2.1 The memcpy function

Synopsis

```
#include <string.h>
void *memcpy(void *s1, const void *s2, size_t n);
```

Description

The **memcpy** function copies **n** characters from the object pointed to by **s2** into the object pointed to by **s1**. If copying takes place between objects that overlap, the behavior is undefined.

Returns

The **memcpy** function returns the value of **s1**.

7.11.2.2 The memmove function

Synopsis

```
#include <string.h>
void *memmove(void *s1, const void *s2, size_t n);
```

Description

The **memmove** function copies **n** characters from the object pointed to by **s2** into the object pointed to by **s1**. Copying takes place as if the **n** characters from the object pointed to by **s2** are first copied into a temporary array of **n** characters that does not overlap the objects pointed to by **s1** and **s2**, and then the **n** characters from the temporary array are copied into the object pointed to by **s1**.

Returns

The **memmove** function returns the value of **s1**.

7.11.2.3 The strcpy function

Synopsis

```
#include <string.h>
char *strcpy(char *s1, const char *s2);
```

Description

The **strcpy** function copies the string pointed to by **s2** (including the terminating null character) into the array pointed to by **s1**. If copying takes place between objects that overlap, the behavior is undefined.

---

133 See "future library directions" (7.13.8).

7.11 *String handling <string.h>* Most programmers consider C's string handling approach to be among its finest traits. As you know, in C a string is a null-terminated array of characters. The null terminator is crucial to the operation of the string functions because it marks the end of the string. In addition, in the string handling category, the standard includes a number of functions that operate on objects that may or may not be strings because they are not necessarily null-terminated. These functions begin with the prefix **mem**, rather than the **str** that is used for the actual string functions.

7.11.2 *Copying functions* These functions all copy characters from one object to another. The key difference between them is what determines how many characters get copied.

For **strcpy()**, the entire string pointed to by *s2* is copied into the array pointed to by *s1*, and the result is a null-terminated string. The **strncpy()** function is the same as **strcpy()**, except that only a specified number of characters are copied. If the null terminator is not copied, then the result will not be null terminated; otherwise, the result is a null-terminated string. In contrast, **memcpy()** and **memmove()** are called with the number of bytes to copy, and neither makes use of a null character as a terminator. The only difference between **memcpy()** and **memmove()** is that **memmove()** may be used on overlapping objects.

For all four copying functions, there must be sufficient room in the destination object to hold the number of characters copied to it. If you overflow the target object, a program crash is likely. Remember, except for **memmove()**, the source and destination objects must not overlap.

Here is a program that demonstrates the copying functions:

```
/* This program demonstrates memcpy(), memmove(),
   strcpy(), and strncpy(). */
#include <stdio.h>
#include <string.h>

void main(void)
{
  int i;
  char str1[80] = "I like C.";
  char str2[80];
  float obj1[5] = {12.2, 3.4, 94.4, 33.903, 10.1};
  float obj2[5];
  float obj3[5] = {0.0, 0.0, 0.0, 0.0, 0.0};
```

Returns

The **strcpy** function returns the value of **s1**.

7.11.2.4 The **strncpy** function

Synopsis

```
#include <string.h>
char *strncpy(char *s1, const char *s2, size_t n);
```

Description

The **strncpy** function copies not more than **n** characters (characters that follow a null character are not copied) from the array pointed to by **s2** to the array pointed to by **s1**.[134] If copying takes place between objects that overlap, the behavior is undefined.

If the array pointed to by **s2** is a string that is shorter than **n** characters, null characters are appended to the copy in the array pointed to by **s1**, until **n** characters in all have been written.

Returns

The **strncpy** function returns the value of **s1**.

7.11.3 Concatenation functions

7.11.3.1 The **strcat** function

Synopsis

```
#include <string.h>
char *strcat(char *s1, const char *s2);
```

Description

The **strcat** function appends a copy of the string pointed to by **s2** (including the terminating null character) to the end of the string pointed to by **s1**. The initial character of **s2** overwrites the null character at the end of **s1**. If copying takes place between objects that overlap, the behavior is undefined.

Returns

The **strcat** function returns the value of **s1**.

7.11.3.2 The **strncat** function

Synopsis

```
#include <string.h>
char *strncat(char *s1, const char *s2, size_t n);
```

Description

The **strncat** function appends not more than **n** characters (a null character and characters that follow it are not appended) from the array pointed to by **s2** to the end of the string pointed to by **s1**. The initial character of **s2** overwrites the null character at the end of **s1**. A terminating null character is always appended to the result.[135] If copying takes place between objects that overlap, the behavior is undefined.

---

134 Thus, if there is no null character in the first **n** characters of the array pointed to by **s2**, the result will not be null-terminated.

135 Thus, the maximum number of characters that can end up in the array pointed to by **s1** is **strlen(s1)+n+1**.

(*7.11.2   Copying functions,* continued)

```
        strcpy(str2, str1); /* copy a string */
        printf("str1: %s str2: %s\n", str1, str2);

        strncpy(str1, "Hi---", 5); /* copy part of a string */
        printf("str1: %s\n", str1);

        /* copy an object */
        memcpy(obj2, obj1, sizeof obj1);
        for(i=0; i<5; i++) printf("%6.2f", obj2[i]);

        printf("\n");

        /* move only part of an object */
        memmove(obj3, obj1, 2 * sizeof (float));
        for(i=0; i<5; i++) printf("%6.2f", obj3[i]);
    }
```

The foregoing program displays

```
    str1: I like C. str2: I like C.
    str1: Hi---e C.
     12.20   3.40 94.40 33.90 10.10
     12.20   3.40  0.00  0.00  0.00
```

7.11.3 Concatenation functions The **strcat()** and **strncat()** functions concatenate one string onto the end of another. The only difference between the two functions is that **strcat()** appends the entire string pointed to by *s2*, and **strncat()** appends up to *n* characters of the string pointed to by *s2*. In both cases, the result is a null-terminated string.

For both the concatenation functions, there must be sufficient room in the destination string to hold the number of characters appended. If you overflow the string, a program crash is likely. Also, the source and destination strings must not overlap.

For example, given the following:

```
    char str1[80] = "Hello ";
    char str2[80] = "there";
```

after this statement:

```
    strcat(str1, str2);
```

str1 will contain the string "Hello there".

Returns

The **strncat** function returns the value of **s1**.

Forward references: the **strlen** function (7.11.6.3).

7.11.4 Comparison functions

The sign of a nonzero value returned by the comparison functions **memcmp**, **strcmp**, and **strncmp** is determined by the sign of the difference between the values of the first pair of characters (both interpreted as **unsigned char**) that differ in the objects being compared.

7.11.4.1 The memcmp function

Synopsis

```
#include <string.h>
int memcmp(const void *s1, const void *s2, size_t n);
```

Description

The **memcmp** function compares the first **n** characters of the object pointed to by **s1** to the first **n** characters of the object pointed to by **s2**.[136]

Returns

The **memcmp** function returns an integer greater than, equal to, or less than zero, accordingly as the object pointed to by **s1** is greater than, equal to, or less than the object pointed to by **s2**.

7.11.4.2 The strcmp function

Synopsis

```
#include <string.h>
int strcmp(const char *s1, const char *s2);
```

Description

The **strcmp** function compares the string pointed to by **s1** to the string pointed to by **s2**.

Returns

The **strcmp** function returns an integer greater than, equal to, or less than zero, accordingly as the string pointed to by **s1** is greater than, equal to, or less than the string pointed to by **s2**.

7.11.4.3 The strcoll function

Synopsis

```
#include <string.h>
int strcoll(const char *s1, const char *s2);
```

Description

The **strcoll** function compares the string pointed to by **s1** to the string pointed to by **s2**, both interpreted as appropriate to the **LC_COLLATE** category of the current locale.

---

136 The contents of "holes" used as padding for purposes of alignment within structure objects are indeterminate. Strings shorter than their allocated space and unions may also cause problems in comparison.

7.11.4 *Comparison functions* The comparison functions are clearly described and, in general, easy to understand. Following are a few additional notes:

◆ The **memcmp()** function is used to compare two regions of memory that need not be null terminated. The size of each region is specified by *n*.

◆ The only difference between **strcmp()** and **strncmp()** is that you can specify a maximum number of characters to compare using the latter.

◆ The **strcoll()** function compares two strings, taking into consideration any differences in the collating sequence specified by the locale environment and the normal ordering of the execution character set.

◆ Notice that the standard does not say that a string transformed using **strxfrm()** is meaningful in any way other than for use with **strcmp()**. Since **strxfrm()** is likely to rearrange the characters in the string, the outcome may not be related to the original string in any other way. Also, make sure that the string pointed to by *s1* is large enough to hold the transformed string pointed to by *s2*, and that the two strings do not overlap.

Here is a program that demonstrates **memcmp()**, **strcmp()**, and **strncmp()**:

```
/* This program demonstrates memcmp(), strcmp(),
   and strncmp(). */
#include <stdio.h>
#include <string.h>

void main(void)
{
  int result;

  char str1[80] = "ABCDEFGHIJKL";
  char str2[80] = "ABCDEFGHIJKLMNOP";
  float obj1[5] = {12.2, 3.4, 94.4, 33.903, 10.1};
  float obj2[5] = {0.0, 0.0, 0.0, 0.0, 0.0};

  /* compare strings */
  result = strcmp(str1, str2);
  if(result<0) printf("%s < %s\n", str1, str2);
  else if(result>0) printf("%s > %s\n", str1, str2);
  else printf("Strings are the same.\n");

  /* compare part of two strings */
  result = strncmp(str1, str2, 10);
```

Returns

The **strcoll** function returns an integer greater than, equal to, or less than zero, accordingly as the string pointed to by **s1** is greater than, equal to, or less than the string pointed to by **s2** when both are interpreted as appropriate to the current locale.

7.11.4.4 The **strncmp** function

Synopsis

```
#include <string.h>
int strncmp(const char *s1, const char *s2, size_t n);
```

Description

The **strncmp** function compares not more than **n** characters (characters that follow a null character are not compared) from the array pointed to by **s1** to the array pointed to by **s2**.

Returns

The **strncmp** function returns an integer greater than, equal to, or less than zero, accordingly as the possibly null-terminated array pointed to by **s1** is greater than, equal to, or less than the possibly null-terminated array pointed to by **s2**.

7.11.4.5 The **strxfrm** function

Synopsis

```
#include <string.h>
size_t strxfrm(char *s1, const char *s2, size_t n);
```

Description

The **strxfrm** function transforms the string pointed to by **s2** and places the resulting string into the array pointed to by **s1**. The transformation is such that if the **strcmp** function is applied to two transformed strings, it returns a value greater than, equal to, or less than zero, corresponding to the result of the **strcoll** function applied to the same two original strings. No more than **n** characters are placed into the resulting array pointed to by **s1**, including the terminating null character. If **n** is zero, **s1** is permitted to be a null pointer. If copying takes place between objects that overlap, the behavior is undefined.

Returns

The **strxfrm** function returns the length of the transformed string (not including the terminating null character). If the value returned is **n** or more, the contents of the array pointed to by **s1** are indeterminate.

Example

The value of the following expression is the size of the array needed to hold the transformation of the string pointed to by **s**.

```
1 + strxfrm(NULL, s, 0)
```

7.11.5 Search functions

7.11.5.1 The **memchr** function

Synopsis

```
#include <string.h>
void *memchr(const void *s, int c, size_t n);
```

```
if(!result)
   printf("1st 10 bytes of each string are the same.\n");

/* compare two objects */
result = memcmp(obj1, obj2, sizeof obj1);
if(result<0) printf("obj1 < obj2\n");
else if(result>0) printf("obj1 > obj2\n");
else printf("Objects are the same.\n");

}
```

The output of this program is

```
ABCDEFGHIJKL < ABCDEFGHIJKLMNOP
1st 10 bytes of each string are the same.
obj1 > obj2
```

7.11.5 Search functions The C standard library contains several string and memory searching functions, which fall into two major categories: functions that search a string or memory for a character (or characters), and functions that search a string for another string. For the most part, these functions are easy to understand and use. Here are a few additional points:

◆ The **memchr()**, **strchr()**, and **strrchr()** functions specify an integer as their second argument; however, only the low-order byte is used.

◆ The standard's descriptions of **strcspn()** and **strspn()** might be somewhat confusing. Here is another explanation: The **strcspn()** function returns the index of the first character in the string pointed to by *s1* that matches any character in the string pointed to by *s2*. The **strspn()** function returns the index of the first character in the string pointed to by *s1* that does *not* match any character in the string pointed to by *s2*.

◆ Another way to look at **strrchr()** is that it returns a pointer to the first occurrence (if any), starting from the *end of the string,* of the character specified in *c* in the string pointed to by *s*.

◆ The **strtok()** function *tokenizes* the string pointed to by *s1*. The characters that delimit each token are specified in the string pointed to by *s2*. Remember, for each string you want to tokenize, first call **strtok()** once using the string as the first parameter. Then, in each subsequent call, use NULL as the first parameter until the entire string has been tokenized.

Description

The **memchr** function locates the first occurrence of **c** (converted to an **unsigned char**) in the initial **n** characters (each interpreted as **unsigned char**) of the object pointed to by **s**.

Returns

The **memchr** function returns a pointer to the located character, or a null pointer if the character does not occur in the object.

7.11.5.2 The strchr function

Synopsis

```
#include <string.h>
char *strchr(const char *s, int c);
```

Description

The **strchr** function locates the first occurrence of **c** (converted to a **char**) in the string pointed to by **s**. The terminating null character is considered to be part of the string.

Returns

The **strchr** function returns a pointer to the located character, or a null pointer if the character does not occur in the string.

7.11.5.3 The strcspn function

Synopsis

```
#include <string.h>
size_t strcspn(const char *s1, const char *s2);
```

Description

The **strcspn** function computes the length of the maximum initial segment of the string pointed to by **s1** which consists entirely of characters *not* from the string pointed to by **s2**.

Returns

The **strcspn** function returns the length of the segment.

7.11.5.4 The strpbrk function

Synopsis

```
#include <string.h>
char *strpbrk(const char *s1, const char *s2);
```

Description

The **strpbrk** function locates the first occurrence in the string pointed to by **s1** of any character from the string pointed to by **s2**.

Returns

The **strpbrk** function returns a pointer to the character, or a null pointer if no character from **s2** occurs in **s1**.

7.11.5.5 The strrchr function

Synopsis

```
#include <string.h>
char *strrchr(const char *s, int c);
```

7.11.5.1 *The memchr function through* **7.11.7** *The strstr function* The following program illustrates the string search functions, except for **strtok()**:

```
/* This program demonstrates the string search functions,
   except for strtok(). */
#include <stdio.h>
#include <string.h>

char str[] = "This is a sample string.";

void main(void)
{
  char *p;
  int index;

  /* find first occurrence of a */
  p = strchr(str, 'a');
  if(p) printf("First match of 'a' found: %s\n", p);

  /* find first occurrence of a using memchr() */
  p = memchr(str, 'a', sizeof str);
  if(p) printf("Using memchr(), match of 'a' found: %s\n", p);

  /* find last occurrence of a */
  p = strrchr(str, 'a');
  if(p) printf("Last match of 'a' found: %s\n", p);

  /* find index of matching character */
  index = strcspn(str, "a");
  printf("Index of first 'a' is: %d, found at: %s\n",
         index, &str[index]);

  /* find first occurrence of a or m */
  p = strpbrk(str, "am");
  if(p) printf("First match of 'a' or 'm' found: %s\n", p);

  /* find first occurrence of 'ple' */
  p = strstr(str, "ple");
  if(p) printf("Match of 'ple' found: %s\n", p);

  /* find first non-match of 'ishT ' */
  index = strspn(str, "ishT ");
  printf("Index of first mismatch is: %d, found at: %s\n",
         index, &str[index]);
}
```

Description

The **strrchr** function locates the last occurrence of **c** (converted to a **char**) in the string pointed to by **s**. The terminating null character is considered to be part of the string.

Returns

The **strrchr** function returns a pointer to the character, or a null pointer if **c** does not occur in the string.

7.11.5.6 The `strspn` function

Synopsis

```
#include <string.h>
size_t strspn(const char *s1, const char *s2);
```

Description

The **strspn** function computes the length of the maximum initial segment of the string pointed to by **s1** which consists entirely of characters from the string pointed to by **s2**.

Returns

The **strspn** function returns the length of the segment.

7.11.5.7 The `strstr` function

Synopsis

```
#include <string.h>
char *strstr(const char *s1, const char *s2);
```

Description

The **strstr** function locates the first occurrence in the string pointed to by **s1** of the sequence of characters (excluding the terminating null character) in the string pointed to by **s2**

Returns

The **strstr** function returns a pointer to the located string, or a null pointer if the string is not found. If **s2** points to a string with zero length, the function returns **s1**.

7.11.5.8 The `strtok` function

Synopsis

```
#include <string.h>
char *strtok(char *s1, const char *s2);
```

Description

A sequence of calls to the **strtok** function breaks the string pointed to by **s1** into a sequence of tokens, each of which is delimited by a character from the string pointed to by **s2**. The first call in the sequence has **s1** as its first argument, and is followed by calls with a null pointer as their first argument. The separator string pointed to by **s2** may be different from call to call.

The first call in the sequence searches the string pointed to by **s1** for the first character that is *not* contained in the current separator string pointed to by **s2**. If no such character is found, then there are no tokens in the string pointed to by **s1** and the **strtok** function returns a null pointer. If such a character is found, it is the start of the first token.

The **strtok** function then searches from there for a character that *is* contained in the current separator string. If no such character is found, the current token extends to the end of the string pointed to by **s1**, and subsequent searches for a token will return a null pointer. If such a character is found, it is overwritten by a null character, which terminates the current token. The

(7.11.5.1 The memchr function through 7.11.5.7 The strstr function, continued)

The foregoing program displays this output:

```
First match of 'a' found: a sample string.
Using memchr(), match of 'a' found: a sample string.
Last match of 'a' found: ample string.
Index of first 'a' is: 8, found at: a sample string.
First match of 'a' or 'm' found: a sample string.
Match of 'ple' found: ple string.
Index of first mismatch is: 8, found at: a sample string.
```

7.11.5.8 *The strtok function* This program illustrates the **strtok()** function:

```
/* This program demonstrates strtok(). */
#include <stdio.h>
#include <string.h>

char str[] = "One two, three. Four - five.";

void main(void)
{
  char *tok;

  /* tokenize the string in str */
  tok = strtok(str, " ,.-");
  while(tok) { /* so long as there are tokens */
    printf(" |%s| ", tok);
    tok = strtok(NULL, " ,.-");
  }
}
```

and has the following output:

```
|One|  |two|  |three|  |Four|  |five|
```

strtok function saves a pointer to the following character, from which the next search for a token will start.

Each subsequent call, with a null pointer as the value of the first argument, starts searching from the saved pointer and behaves as described above.

The implementation shall behave as if no library function calls the **strtok** function.

Returns

The **strtok** function returns a pointer to the first character of a token, or a null pointer if there is no token.

Example

```
#include <string.h>
static char str[] = "?a???b,,,#c";
char *t;

t = strtok(str, "?");    /* t points to the token "a" */
t = strtok(NULL, ",");   /* t points to the token "??b" */
t = strtok(NULL, "#,");  /* t points to the token "c" */
t = strtok(NULL, "?");   /* t is a null pointer */
```

7.11.6 Miscellaneous functions

7.11.6.1 The memset function

Synopsis

```
#include <string.h>
void *memset(void *s, int c, size_t n);
```

Description

The **memset** function copies the value of **c** (converted to an **unsigned char**) into each of the first **n** characters of the object pointed to by **s**.

Returns

The **memset** function returns the value of **s**.

7.11.6.2 The strerror function

Synopsis

```
#include <string.h>
char *strerror(int errnum);
```

Description

The **strerror** function maps the error number in **errnum** to an error message string.

The implementation shall behave as if no library function calls the **strerror** function.

Returns

The **strerror** function returns a pointer to the string, the contents of which are implementation-defined. The array pointed to shall not be modified by the program, but may be overwritten by a subsequent call to the **strerror** function.

7.11.6.1 The memset function The **memset()** function provides a convenient way to initialize a region of memory to a known value. Notice that although *c* is specified as an integer, only the low-order byte is used. The following fragment zeros 100 bytes of dynamically allocated memory:

```
char *p;

p = malloc(100);
if(p) memset(p, 0, 100);
```

7.11.6.2 The strerror function The **strerror()** function returns a pointer to the error message associated with the value passed in *errnum*. The value of *errnum* and of the message are implementation defined, and you will need to refer to your compiler's user manual for details. Notice that you must not modify the string pointed to by the return value of **strerror()**. Although not explicitly required by the standard, most compilers return a null pointer if no error message is associated with the value of *errnum*.

The following program displays the error messages associated with the values 0 through 9. (These may or may not be valid error messages for your compiler.)

```
/* This program demonstrates the strerror() function. */
#include <stdio.h>
#include <string.h>

#define MAX 10

void main(void)
{
  int i;

  for(i=0; i<MAX; i++)
    printf("%s\n", strerror(i));

}
```

The following output was produced by one of the compilers used by the author. Of course, your output may differ.

```
Error 0
Invalid function number
No such file or directory
Path not found
```

7.11.6.3 The `strlen` function

Synopsis

```
#include <string.h>
size_t strlen(const char *s);
```

Description

The **strlen** function computes the length of the string pointed to by **s**.

Returns

The **strlen** function returns the number of characters that precede the terminating null character.

*(**7.11.6.2** **The sterror function,** continued)*

```
Too many open files
Permission denied
Bad file number
Memory arena trashed
Not enough memory
Invalid memory block address
```

7.11.6.3 *The strlen function* The **strlen()** function returns the length of the string pointed to by *s* and does not count the null terminator. Thus, the value returned by **strlen()** is also the index of the null terminator of the string.

7.12 Date and time <time.h>

7.12.1 Components of time

The header <time.h> defines two macros, and declares four types and several functions for manipulating time. Many functions deal with a *calendar time* that represents the current date (according to the Gregorian calendar) and time. Some functions deal with *local time*, which is the calendar time expressed for some specific time zone, and with *Daylight Saving Time*, which is a temporary change in the algorithm for determining local time. The local time zone and Daylight Saving Time are implementation-defined.

The macros defined are **NULL** (described in 7.1.6); and

> **CLOCKS_PER_SEC**

which is the number per second of the value returned by the **clock** function.

The types declared are **size_t** (described in 7.1.6);

> **clock_t**

and

> **time_t**

which are arithmetic types capable of representing times; and

> **struct tm**

which holds the components of a calendar time, called the *broken-down time*. The structure shall contain at least the following members, in any order. The semantics of the members and their normal ranges are expressed in the comments.[137]

```
int tm_sec;     /* seconds after the minute — [0, 61] */
int tm_min;     /* minutes after the hour — [0, 59] */
int tm_hour;    /* hours since midnight — [0, 23] */
int tm_mday;    /* day of the month — [1, 31] */
int tm_mon;     /* months since January — [0, 11] */
int tm_year;    /* years since 1900 */
int tm_wday;    /* days since Sunday — [0, 6] */
int tm_yday;    /* days since January 1 — [0, 365] */
int tm_isdst;   /* Daylight Saving Time flag */
```

The value of **tm_isdst** is positive if Daylight Saving Time is in effect, zero if Daylight Saving Time is not in effect, and negative if the information is not available.

7.12.2 Time manipulation functions

7.12.2.1 The clock function

Synopsis

```
#include <time.h>
clock_t clock(void);
```

Description

The **clock** function determines the processor time used.

---

137 The range [0, 61] for **tm_sec** allows for as many as two leap seconds.

7.12.1   *Components of time*   The standard C *date and time functions* provide a complete and flexible system of managing the system date and time. They also furnish a means of timing certain run-time events, including the length of a program's execution. The date and time functions require that the host system maintain the date and time; otherwise, these functions are useless.

The date and time functions make use of two different date and time representations: the *calendar time* and the *broken-down time*. In essence, calendar time represents the date and time using an internal format; the calendar time is a value of type **time_t**. The broken-down time represents the date and time by their individual fields. The broken-down time is held in a structure of type **struct tm**.

The date and time functions are, for the most part, easy to understand. Following are a few additional points and some example programs.

7.12.2.1   *The clock function*   The **clock()** function returns the number of clock ticks since the program began execution (this value is of type **clock_t**). Dividing this number by the macro **CLOCKS_PER_SEC** converts it to seconds. The **clock()** function is particularly useful for timing events that occur within a program. For example, the following program illustrates the **clock()** function by timing a **for** loop:

Returns

The **clock** function returns the implementation's best approximation to the processor time used by the program since the beginning of an implementation-defined era related only to the program invocation. To determine the time in seconds, the value returned by the **clock** function should be divided by the value of the macro **CLOCKS_PER_SEC**. If the processor time used is not available or its value cannot be represented, the function returns the value **(clock_t)-1**.[138]

7.12.2.2 The **difftime** function

Synopsis

```
#include <time.h>
double difftime(time_t time1, time_t time0);
```

Description

The **difftime** function computes the difference between two calendar times: **time1 - time0**.

Returns

The **difftime** function returns the difference expressed in seconds as a **double**.

7.12.2.3 The **mktime** function

Synopsis

```
#include <time.h>
time_t mktime(struct tm *timeptr);
```

Description

The **mktime** function converts the broken-down time, expressed as local time, in the structure pointed to by **timeptr** into a calendar time value with the same encoding as that of the values returned by the **time** function. The original values of the **tm_wday** and **tm_yday** components of the structure are ignored, and the original values of the other components are not restricted to the ranges indicated above.[139] On successful completion, the values of the **tm_wday** and **tm_yday** components of the structure are set appropriately, and the other components are set to represent the specified calendar time, but with their values forced to the ranges indicated above; the final value of **tm_mday** is not set until **tm_mon** and **tm_year** are determined.

Returns

The **mktime** function returns the specified calendar time encoded as a value of type **time_t**. If the calendar time cannot be represented, the function returns the value **(time_t)-1**.

Example

What day of the week is July 4, 2001?

---

138 In order to measure the time spent in a program, the **clock** function should be called at the start of the program and its return value subtracted from the value returned by subsequent calls.

139 Thus, a positive or zero value for **tm_isdst** causes the **mktime** function to presume initially that Daylight Saving Time, respectively, is or is not in effect for the specified time. A negative value causes it to attempt to determine whether Daylight Saving Time is in effect for the specified time.

(7.12.2.1   The clock function, continued)

```
/* This program demonstrates the clock() function. */
#include <stdio.h>
#include <time.h>

void main(void)
{
  clock_t start, end;
  unsigned long i;

  /* time a for loop */
  start = clock();
  for(i=0; i<1000000; i++) ; /* delay */
  end = clock();

  printf("Starting time: %lf seconds\n",
         (double) start/CLOCKS_PER_SEC);
  printf("Ending time: %lf seconds\n",
         (double) end/CLOCKS_PER_SEC);

  printf("Duration: %lf seconds",
         (double) (end-start) / CLOCKS_PER_SEC);
}
```

Sample output from the program is shown below; of course, times will vary with processor speed and compiler implementation.

```
Starting time: 0.000000 seconds
Ending time: 0.329670 seconds
Duration: 0.329670 seconds
```

```
#include <stdio.h>
#include <time.h>
static const char *const wday[] = {
        "Sunday", "Monday", "Tuesday", "Wednesday",
        "Thursday", "Friday", "Saturday", "-unknown-"
};
struct tm time_str;
/*...*/
time_str.tm_year  = 2001 - 1900;
time_str.tm_mon   = 7 - 1;
time_str.tm_mday  = 4;
time_str.tm_hour  = 0;
time_str.tm_min   = 0;
time_str.tm_sec   = 1;
time_str.tm_isdst = -1;
if (mktime(&time_str) == -1)
        time_str.tm_wday = 7;
printf("%s\n", wday[time_str.tm_wday]);
```

7.12.2.4 The time function

Synopsis

```
#include <time.h>
time_t time(time_t *timer);
```

Description

The **time** function determines the current calendar time. The encoding of the value is unspecified.

Returns

The **time** function returns the implementation's best approximation to the current calendar time. The value (**time_t**)-1 is returned if the calendar time is not available. If **timer** is not a null pointer, the return value is also assigned to the object it points to.

7.12.3 Time conversion functions

Except for the **strftime** function, these functions return values in one of two static objects: a broken-down time structure and an array of **char**. Execution of any of the functions may overwrite the information returned in either of these objects by any of the other functions. The implementation shall behave as if no other library functions call these functions.

7.12.3.1 The asctime function

Synopsis

```
#include <time.h>
char *asctime(const struct tm *timeptr);
```

Description

The **asctime** function converts the broken-down time in the structure pointed to by **timeptr** into a string in the form

```
Sun Sep 16 01:03:52 1973\n\0
```

using the equivalent of the following algorithm.

7.12.2.4 The time function The **time()** function obtains the current system date and time, represented in their calendar (internal) format. Once you have obtained the system time, it can be converted into various other formats using other date and time functions.

Notice that **time()** "returns" the current date and time in two ways: First, it returns the current date and time. Second, if **time()** is called with a pointer to a variable of type **time_t**, then that variable is also assigned the current date and time. If **time()** is called with a null pointer, then the argument is ignored.

The following program displays the current system date and time and shows the step-by-step process of each conversion involved:

```
/* This program displays the current system
   date and time. */
#include <stdio.h>
#include <time.h>

void main(void)
{
  time_t systime;
  struct tm tmtime;

  systime = time(NULL); /* get encoded system time */
  tmtime = *localtime(&systime); /* get broken-down time */
  printf(asctime(&tmtime)); /* display time as string */
}
```

Although the foregoing program is correct as an illustration, it can be simplified, as shown here, using the **ctime()** function:

```
/* This program displays the current system
   date and time using a shorter method. */
#include <stdio.h>
#include <time.h>

void main(void)
{
  time_t systime;

  systime = time(NULL); /* get encoded system time */
  printf(ctime(&systime)); /* display time as string */
}
```

```
char *asctime(const struct tm *timeptr)
{
        static const char wday_name[7][3] = {
                "Sun", "Mon", "Tue", "Wed", "Thu", "Fri", "Sat"
        };
        static const char mon_name[12][3] = {
                "Jan", "Feb", "Mar", "Apr", "May", "Jun",
                "Jul", "Aug", "Sep", "Oct", "Nov", "Dec"
        };
        static char result[26];

        sprintf(result, "%.3s %.3s%3d %.2d:%.2d:%.2d %d\n",
                wday_name[timeptr->tm_wday],
                mon_name[timeptr->tm_mon],
                timeptr->tm_mday, timeptr->tm_hour,
                timeptr->tm_min, timeptr->tm_sec,
                1900 + timeptr->tm_year);
        return result;
}
```

Returns

The **asctime** function returns a pointer to the string.

7.12.3.2 The ctime function

Synopsis

```
#include <time.h>
char *ctime(const time_t *timer);
```

Description

The **ctime** function converts the calendar time pointed to by **timer** to local time in the form of a string. It is equivalent to

```
asctime(localtime(timer))
```

Returns

The **ctime** function returns the pointer returned by the **asctime** function with that broken-down time as argument.

Forward references: the **localtime** function (7.12.3.4).

7.12.3.3 The gmtime function

Synopsis

```
#include <time.h>
struct tm *gmtime(const time_t *timer);
```

Description

The **gmtime** function converts the calendar time pointed to by **timer** into a broken-down time, expressed as Coordinated Universal Time (UTC).

Returns

The **gmtime** function returns a pointer to that object, or a null pointer if UTC is not available.

(7.12.2.4 *The time function,* *continued*)

It is possible to use the broken-down form of the date and time directly, without converting it to a string, as shown in the following program:

```
/* This program displays the current system
   date and time using the broken-down form. */
#include <stdio.h>
#include <time.h>

void main(void)
{
  time_t systime;
  struct tm tmtime;

  systime = time(NULL); /* get encoded system time */
  tmtime = *localtime(&systime); /* get broken-down time */

  /* use broken-down time */
  printf("Time: %d:%02d\n", tmtime.tm_hour, tmtime.tm_min);
  printf("Date: %d/%d/%d\n", tmtime.tm_mon, tmtime.tm_mday,
         tmtime.tm_year);
}
```

7.12.3.4 The `localtime` function

Synopsis

```
#include <time.h>
struct tm *localtime(const time_t *timer);
```

Description

The **localtime** function converts the calendar time pointed to by **timer** into a broken-down time. expressed as local time.

Returns

The **localtime** function returns a pointer to that object.

7.12.3.5 The `strftime` function

Synopsis

```
#include <time.h>
size_t strftime(char *s, size_t maxsize,
        const char *format, const struct tm *timeptr);
```

Description

The **strftime** function places characters into the array pointed to by **s** as controlled by the string pointed to by **format**. The format shall be a multibyte character sequence. beginning and ending in its initial shift state. The **format** string consists of zero or more conversion specifiers and ordinary multibyte characters. A conversion specifier consists of a **%** character followed by a character that determines the behavior of the conversion specifier. All ordinary multibyte characters (including the terminating null character) are copied unchanged into the array. If copying takes place between objects that overlap. the behavior is undefined. No more than **maxsize** characters are placed into the array. Each conversion specifier is replaced by appropriate characters as described in the following list. The appropriate characters are determined by the **LC_TIME** category of the current locale and by the values contained in the structure pointed to by **timeptr**.

%a   is replaced by the locale's abbreviated weekday name.

%A   is replaced by the locale's full weekday name.

%b   is replaced by the locale's abbreviated month name.

%B   is replaced by the locale's full month name.

%c   is replaced by the locale's appropriate date and time representation.

%d   is replaced by the day of the month as a decimal number (**01-31**).

%H   is replaced by the hour (24-hour clock) as a decimal number (**00-23**).

%I   is replaced by the hour (12-hour clock) as a decimal number (**01-12**).

%j   is replaced by the day of the year as a decimal number (**001-366**).

%m   is replaced by the month as a decimal number (**01-12**).

%M   is replaced by the minute as a decimal number (**00-59**).

%p   is replaced by the locale's equivalent of the AM/PM designations associated with a 12-hour clock.

%S   is replaced by the second as a decimal number (**00-61**).

%U   is replaced by the week number of the year (the first Sunday as the first day of week 1) as a decimal number (**00-53**).

%w   is replaced by the weekday as a decimal number (**0-6**). where Sunday is **0**.

%W   is replaced by the week number of the year (the first Monday as the first day of week 1) as a decimal number (**00-53**).

%x   is replaced by the locale's appropriate date representation.

%X   is replaced by the locale's appropriate time representation.

%y   is replaced by the year without century as a decimal number (**00-99**).

%Y   is replaced by the year with century as a decimal number.

7.12.3.5 *The strftime function* The **strftime()** function—one of the most over-looked functions in the C standard library—provides complete date and time formatting capabilities. It works a little like **sprintf()** in two ways: First, it formats the date and time as specified by conversion specifiers, which begin with the percentage sign. Second, it puts the formatted output into a string. Notice that the case of the conversion specifiers is important; for instance, **%M** and **%m** are different. If you will be working frequently with the date and time in a program, you may find this function very useful.

The description of **strftime()** states that the string pointed to by *format* consists of *multibyte* characters. Don't be confused by this. Remember, the definition of a multibyte character includes the basic (single-byte) character set.

The following program demonstrates **strftime()**:

```c
/* This program demonstrates the strftime() function. */
#include <stdio.h>
#include <time.h>

void main(void)
{
  time_t systime;
  struct tm tmtime;
  char ftime[80];

  systime = time(NULL); /* get encoded system time */
  tmtime = *localtime(&systime); /* get broken-down time */

  /* format a date and time string */
  strftime(ftime, sizeof ftime,
           "It is %H:%M on %A the %d, %Y.\n",
           &tmtime);

  printf(ftime); /* display time as string */
}
```

Here is an example of the output produced by the foregoing program:

```
It is 09:57 on Saturday the 29, 1993.
```

%Z   is replaced by the time zone name or abbreviation, or by no characters if no time zone is determinable.

%%   is replaced by **%**.

If a conversion specifier is not one of the above, the behavior is undefined.

Returns

If the total number of resulting characters including the terminating null character is not more than **maxsize**, the **strftime** function returns the number of characters placed into the array pointed to by **s** not including the terminating null character. Otherwise, zero is returned and the contents of the array are indeterminate.

There are no annotations for page 175.

7.13 Future library directions

The following names are grouped under individual headers for convenience. All external names described below are reserved no matter what headers are included by the program.

7.13.1 Errors <errno.h>

Macros that begin with **E** and a digit or **E** and an uppercase letter (followed by any combination of digits, letters, and underscore) may be added to the declarations in the <**errno.h**> header.

7.13.2 Character handling <ctype.h>

Function names that begin with either **is** or **to**, and a lowercase letter (followed by any combination of digits, letters, and underscore) may be added to the declarations in the <**ctype.h**> header.

7.13.3 Localization <locale.h>

Macros that begin with **LC_** and an uppercase letter (followed by any combination of digits, letters, and underscore) may be added to the definitions in the <**locale.h**> header.

7.13.4 Mathematics <math.h>

The names of all existing functions declared in the <**math.h**> header, suffixed with **f** or **l**, are reserved respectively for corresponding functions with **float** and **long double** arguments and return values.

7.13.5 Signal handling <signal.h>

Macros that begin with either **SIG** and an uppercase letter or **SIG_** and an uppercase letter (followed by any combination of digits, letters, and underscore) may be added to the definitions in the <**signal.h**> header.

7.13.6 Input/output <stdio.h>

Lowercase letters may be added to the conversion specifiers in **fprintf** and **fscanf**. Other characters may be used in extensions.

7.13.7 General utilities <stdlib.h>

Function names that begin with **str** and a lowercase letter (followed by any combination of digits, letters, and underscore) may be added to the declarations in the <**stdlib.h**> header.

7.13.8 String handling <string.h>

Function names that begin with **str**, **mem**, or **wcs** and a lowercase letter (followed by any combination of digits, letters, and underscore) may be added to the declarations in the <**string.h**> header.

7.13 *Future library directions* The material on this page of the standard is important because it reserves certain names, prefixes, and suffixes that may be used by future versions of the standard. You may wish to avoid using these names, prefixes, and suffixes in your own programs, to prevent future problems.

Annex A
(informative)
Bibliography

1. "The C Reference Manual" by Dennis M. Ritchie, a version of which was published in *The C Programming Language* by Brian W. Kernighan and Dennis M. Ritchie, Prentice-Hall, Inc., (1978). Copyright owned by AT&T.

2. *1984 /usr/group Standard* by the /usr/group Standards Committee, Santa Clara, California, USA, November 1984.

3. ANSI X3/TR-1-82 (1982), *American National Dictionary for Information Processing Systems*, Information Processing Systems Technical Report.

4. ANSI/IEEE 754-1985, *American National Standard for Binary Floating-Point Arithmetic*.

Annex B
(informative)
Language syntax summary

Note — The notation is described in the introduction to clause 3 (Language).

B.1   Lexical grammar

B.1.1   Tokens

(6.1) *token:*
> *keyword*
> *identifier*
> *constant*
> *string-literal*
> *operator*
> *punctuator*

(6.1) *preprocessing-token:*
> *header-name*
> *identifier*
> *pp-number*
> *character-constant*
> *string-literal*
> *operator*
> *punctuator*
> each non-white-space character that cannot be one of the above

B.1.2   Keywords

(6.1.1) *keyword:* one of

auto	double	int	struct
break	else	long	switch
case	enum	register	typedef
char	extern	return	union
const	float	short	unsigned
continue	for	signed	void
default	goto	sizeof	volatile
do	if	static	while

B.1.3   Identifiers

(6.1.2) *identifier:*
> *nondigit*
> *identifier nondigit*
> *identifier digit*

(6.1.2) *nondigit:* one of

```
_   a   b   c   d   e   f   g   h   i   j   k   l   m
    n   o   p   q   r   s   t   u   v   w   x   y   z
    A   B   C   D   E   F   G   H   I   J   K   L   M
    N   O   P   Q   R   S   T   U   V   W   X   Y   Z
```

(6.1.2) *digit:* one of

```
0   1   2   3   4   5   6   7   8   9
```

B.1.4 Constants

(6.1.3) *constant:*
> *floating-constant*
> *integer-constant*
> *enumeration-constant*
> *character-constant*

(6.1.3.1) *floating-constant:*
> *fractional-constant exponent-part$_{opt}$ floating-suffix$_{opt}$*
> *digit-sequence exponent-part floating-suffix$_{opt}$*

(6.1.3.1) *fractional-constant:*
> *digit-sequence$_{opt}$. digit-sequence*
> *digit-sequence .*

(6.1.3.1) *exponent-part:*
> **e** *sign$_{opt}$ digit-sequence*
> **E** *sign$_{opt}$ digit-sequence*

(6.1.3.1) *sign:* one of
> **+   –**

(6.1.3.1) *digit-sequence:*
> *digit*
> *digit-sequence digit*

(6.1.3.1) *floating-suffix:* one of
> **f   l   F   L**

(6.1.3.2) *integer-constant:*
> *decimal-constant integer-suffix$_{opt}$*
> *octal-constant integer-suffix$_{opt}$*
> *hexadecimal-constant integer-suffix$_{opt}$*

(6.1.3.2) *decimal-constant:*
> *nonzero-digit*
> *decimal-constant digit*

(6.1.3.2) *octal-constant:*
> **0**
> *octal-constant octal-digit*

(6.1.3.2) *hexadecimal-constant:*
> **0x** *hexadecimal-digit*
> **0X** *hexadecimal-digit*
> *hexadecimal-constant hexadecimal-digit*

(6.1.3.2) *nonzero-digit:* one of
> **1   2   3   4   5   6   7   8   9**

(6.1.3.2) *octal-digit:* one of
> **0   1   2   3   4   5   6   7**

(6.1.3.2) *hexadecimal-digit:* one of
> **0   1   2   3   4   5   6   7   8   9**
> **a   b   c   d   e   f**
> **A   B   C   D   E   F**

(6.1.3.2) *integer-suffix:*
        unsigned-suffix long-suffix$_{opt}$
        long-suffix unsigned-suffix$_{opt}$

(6.1.3.2) *unsigned-suffix:* one of
        u   U

(6.1.3.2) *long-suffix:* one of
        l   L

(6.1.3.3) *enumeration-constant:*
        identifier

(6.1.3.4) *character-constant:*
        ' c-char-sequence'
        L' *c-char-sequence'*

(6.1.3.4) *c-char-sequence:*
        c-char
        c-char-sequence c-char

(6.1.3.4) *c-char:*
        any member of the source character set except
            the single-quote *'*, backslash **, or new-line character
        escape-sequence

(6.1.3.4) *escape-sequence:*
        simple-escape-sequence
        octal-escape-sequence
        hexadecimal-escape-sequence

(6.1.3.4) *simple-escape-sequence:* one of
        **\\'   \\"   \\?   **
        \\a   \\b   \\f   \\n   \\r   \\t   \\v

(6.1.3.4) *octal-escape-sequence:*
        **** *octal-digit*
        **** *octal-digit octal-digit*
        **** *octal-digit octal-digit octal-digit*

(6.1.3.4) *hexadecimal-escape-sequence:*
        \\x *hexadecimal-digit*
        hexadecimal-escape-sequence hexadecimal-digit

B.1.5 String literals

(6.1.4) *string-literal:*
        "*s-char-sequence*$_{opt}$**"**
        L"*s-char-sequence*$_{opt}$**"**

(6.1.4) *s-char-sequence:*
        s-char
        s-char-sequence s-char

(6.1.4) *s-char:*
        any member of the source character set except
            the double-quote *"*, backslash **, or new-line character
        escape-sequence

B.1.6 Operators

(6.1.5) *operator:* one of

```
    [  ]  (  )  .  ->
    ++  --  &  *  +  -  ~  !  sizeof
    /  %  <<  >>  <  >  <=  >=  ==  !=  ^  |  &&  ||
    ?  :
    =  *=  /=  %=  +=  -=  <<=  >>=  &=  ^=  |=
    ,  #  ##
```

B.1.7 Punctuators

(6.1.6) *punctuator:* one of

```
    [  ]  (  )  {  }  *  ,  :  =  ;  ...  #
```

B.1.8 Header names

(6.1.7) *header-name:*

> <*h-char-sequence*>
> "*q-char-sequence*"

(6.1.7) *h-char-sequence:*

> *h-char*
> *h-char-sequence h-char*

(6.1.7) *h-char:*

> any member of the source character set except
> the new-line character and >

(6.1.7) *q-char-sequence:*

> *q-char*
> *q-char-sequence q-char*

(6.1.7) *q-char:*

> any member of the source character set except
> the new-line character and "

B.1.9 Preprocessing numbers

(6.1.8) *pp-number:*

> *digit*
> . *digit*
> *pp-number digit*
> *pp-number nondigit*
> *pp-number* ● *sign*
> *pp-number* E *sign*
> *pp-number* .

B.2 Phrase structure grammar

B.2.1 Expressions

(6.3.1) *primary-expression:*
>   *identifier*
>   *constant*
>   *string-literal*
>   **(** *expression* **)**

(6.3.2) *postfix-expression:*
>   *primary-expression*
>   *postfix-expression* **[** *expression* **]**
>   *postfix-expression* **(** *argument-expression-list*$_{opt}$ **)**
>   *postfix-expression* **.** *identifier*
>   *postfix-expression* **->** *identifier*
>   *postfix-expression* **++**
>   *postfix-expression* **--**

(6.3.2) *argument-expression-list:*
>   *assignment-expression*
>   *argument-expression-list* **,** *assignment-expression*

(6.3.3) *unary-expression:*
>   *postfix-expression*
>   **++** *unary-expression*
>   **--** *unary-expression*
>   *unary-operator cast-expression*
>   **sizeof** *unary-expression*
>   **sizeof** **(** *type-name* **)**

(6.3.3) *unary-operator:* one of
>   **&   *   +   -   ~   !**

(6.3.4) *cast-expression:*
>   *unary-expression*
>   **(** *type-name* **)** *cast-expression*

(6.3.5) *multiplicative-expression:*
>   *cast-expression*
>   *multiplicative-expression* ***** *cast-expression*
>   *multiplicative-expression* **/** *cast-expression*
>   *multiplicative-expression* **%** *cast-expression*

(6.3.6) *additive-expression:*
>   *multiplicative-expression*
>   *additive-expression* **+** *multiplicative-expression*
>   *additive-expression* **-** *multiplicative-expression*

(6.3.7) *shift-expression:*
>   *additive-expression*
>   *shift-expression* **<<** *additive-expression*
>   *shift-expression* **>>** *additive-expression*

(6.3.8) *relational-expression:*
>> *shift-expression*
>> *relational-expression* **<** *shift-expression*
>> *relational-expression* **>** *shift-expression*
>> *relational-expression* **<=** *shift-expression*
>> *relational-expression* **>=** *shift-expression*

(6.3.9) *equality-expression:*
>> *relational-expression*
>> *equality-expression* **==** *relational-expression*
>> *equality-expression* **!=** *relational-expression*

(6.3.10) *AND-expression:*
>> *equality-expression*
>> *AND-expression* **&** *equality-expression*

(6.3.11) *exclusive-OR-expression:*
>> *AND-expression*
>> *exclusive-OR-expression* **^** *AND-expression*

(6.3.12) *inclusive-OR-expression:*
>> *exclusive-OR-expression*
>> *inclusive-OR-expression* **|** *exclusive-OR-expression*

(6.3.13) *logical-AND-expression:*
>> *inclusive-OR-expression*
>> *logical-AND-expression* **&&** *inclusive-OR-expression*

(6.3.14) *logical-OR-expression:*
>> *logical-AND-expression*
>> *logical-OR-expression* **||** *logical-AND-expression*

(6.3.15) *conditional-expression:*
>> *logical-OR-expression*
>> *logical-OR-expression* **?** *expression* **:** *conditional-expression*

(6.3.16) *assignment-expression:*
>> *conditional-expression*
>> *unary-expression assignment-operator assignment-expression*

(6.3.16) *assignment-operator:* one of
>> **=   *=   /=   %=   +=   -=   <<=   >>=   &=   ^= |=**

(6.3.17) *expression:*
>> *assignment-expression*
>> *expression* **,** *assignment-expression*

(6.4) *constant-expression:*
>> *conditional-expression*

B.2.2 Declarations

(6.5) *declaration:*
>> *declaration-specifiers init-declarator-list$_{opt}$* **;**

(6.5) *declaration-specifiers:*
>> *storage-class-specifier declaration-specifiers$_{opt}$*
>> *type-specifier declaration-specifiers$_{opt}$*
>> *type-qualifier declaration-specifiers$_{opt}$*

(6.5) *init-declarator-list:*
> *init-declarator*
> *init-declarator-list , init-declarator*

(6.5) *init-declarator:*
> *declarator*
> *declarator = initializer*

(6.5.1) *storage-class-specifier:*
> **typedef**
> **extern**
> **static**
> **auto**
> **register**

(6.5.2) *type-specifier:*
> **void**
> **char**
> **short**
> **int**
> **long**
> **float**
> **double**
> **signed**
> **unsigned**
> *struct-or-union-specifier*
> *enum-specifier*
> *typedef-name*

(6.5.2.1) *struct-or-union-specifier:*
> *struct-or-union identifier$_{opt}$ { struct-declaration-list }*
> *struct-or-union identifier*

(6.5.2.1) *struct-or-union:*
> **struct**
> **union**

(6.5.2.1) *struct-declaration-list:*
> *struct-declaration*
> *struct-declaration-list struct-declaration*

(6.5.2.1) *struct-declaration:*
> *specifier-qualifier-list struct-declarator-list ;*

(6.5.2.1) *specifier-qualifier-list:*
> *type-specifier specifier-qualifier-list$_{opt}$*
> *type-qualifier specifier-qualifier-list$_{opt}$*

(6.5.2.1) *struct-declarator-list:*
> *struct-declarator*
> *struct-declarator-list , struct-declarator*

(6.5.2.1) *struct-declarator:*
> *declarator*
> *declarator$_{opt}$: constant-expression*

(6.5.2.2) *enum-specifier:*
> **enum** *identifier$_{opt}$ { enumerator-list }*
> **enum** *identifier*

(6.5.2.2) *enumerator-list:*
> *enumerator*
> *enumerator-list , enumerator*

(6.5.2.2) *enumerator:*
> *enumeration-constant*
> *enumeration-constant* **=** *constant-expression*

(6.5.3) *type-qualifier:*
> **const**
> **volatile**

(6.5.4) *declarator:*
> *pointer*$_{opt}$ *direct-declarator*

(6.5.4) *direct-declarator:*
> *identifier*
> **(** *declarator* **)**
> *direct-declarator* **[** *constant-expression*$_{opt}$ **]**
> *direct-declarator* **(** *parameter-type-list* **)**
> *direct-declarator* **(** *identifier-list*$_{opt}$ **)**

(6.5.4) *pointer:*
> ***** *type-qualifier-list*$_{opt}$
> ***** *type-qualifier-list*$_{opt}$ *pointer*

(6.5.4) *type-qualifier-list:*
> *type-qualifier*
> *type-qualifier-list type-qualifier*

(6.5.4) *parameter-type-list:*
> *parameter-list*
> *parameter-list* **, ...**

(6.5.4) *parameter-list:*
> *parameter-declaration*
> *parameter-list , parameter-declaration*

(6.5.4) *parameter-declaration:*
> *declaration-specifiers declarator* .
> *declaration-specifiers abstract-declarator*$_{opt}$

(6.5.4) *identifier-list:*
> *identifier*
> *identifier-list , identifier*

(6.5.5) *type-name:*
> *specifier-qualifier-list abstract-declarator*$_{opt}$

(6.5.5) *abstract-declarator:*
> *pointer*
> *pointer*$_{opt}$ *direct-abstract-declarator*

(6.5.5) *direct-abstract-declarator:*
> **(** *abstract-declarator* **)**
> *direct-abstract-declarator*$_{opt}$ **[** *constant-expression*$_{opt}$ **]**
> *direct-abstract-declarator*$_{opt}$ **(** *parameter-type-list*$_{opt}$ **)**

(6.5.6) *typedef-name:*
> *identifier*

(6.5.7) *initializer:*
> *assignment-expression*
> { *initializer-list* }
> { *initializer-list* , }

(6.5.7) *initializer-list:*
> *initializer*
> *initializer-list* , *initializer*

B.2.3 Statements

(6.6) *statement:*
> *labeled-statement*
> *compound-statement*
> *expression-statement*
> *selection-statement*
> *iteration-statement*
> *jump-statement*

(6.6.1) *labeled-statement:*
> *identifier* : *statement*
> **case** *constant-expression* : *statement*
> **default** : *statement*

(6.6.2) *compound-statement:*
> { *declaration-list*$_{opt}$ *statement-list*$_{opt}$ }

(6.6.2) *declaration-list:*
> *declaration*
> *declaration-list declaration*

(6.6.2) *statement-list:*
> *statement*
> *statement-list statement*

(6.6.3) *expression-statement:*
> *expression*$_{opt}$;

(6.6.4) *selection-statement:*
> **if** (*expression*) *statement*
> **if** (*expression*) *statement* **else** *statement*
> **switch** (*expression*) *statement*

(6.6.5) *iteration-statement:*
> **while** (*expression*) *statement*
> **do** *statement* **while** (*expression*) ;
> **for** (*expression*$_{opt}$; *expression*$_{opt}$; *expression*$_{opt}$) *statement*

(6.6.6) *jump-statement:*
> **goto** *identifier* ;
> **continue** ;
> **break** ;
> **return** *expression*$_{opt}$;

B.2.4 External definitions

(6.7) *translation-unit:*
> *external-declaration*
> *translation-unit external-declaration*

(6.7) *external-declaration:*
> *function-definition*
> *declaration*

(6.7.1) *function-definition:*
> *declaration-specifiers$_{opt}$ declarator declaration-list$_{opt}$ compound-statement*

B.3 Preprocessing directives

(6.8) *preprocessing-file:*
> *group$_{opt}$*

(6.8) *group:*
> *group-part*
> *group group-part*

(6.8) *group-part:*
> *pp-tokens$_{opt}$ new-line*
> *if-section*
> *control-line*

(6.8.1) *if-section:*
> *if-group elif-groups$_{opt}$ else-group$_{opt}$ endif-line*

(6.8.1) *if-group:*
> **# if**   *constant-expression new-line group$_{opt}$*
> **# ifdef**   *identifier new-line group$_{opt}$*
> **# ifndef** *identifier new-line group$_{opt}$*

(6.8.1) *elif-groups:*
> *elif-group*
> *elif-groups elif-group*

(6.8.1) *elif-group:*
> **# elif**   *constant-expression new-line group$_{opt}$*

(6.8.1) *else-group:*
> **# else**   *new-line group$_{opt}$*

(6.8.1) *endif-line:*
> **# endif**   *new-line*

control-line:

(6.8.2)	**# include**	*pp-tokens new-line*
(6.8.3)	**# define**	*identifier replacement-list new-line*
(6.8.3)	**# define**	*identifier lparen identifier-list$_{opt}$) replacement-list new-line*
(6.8.3)	**# undef**	*identifier new-line*
(6.8.4)	**# line**	*pp-tokens new-line*
(6.8.5)	**# error**	*pp-tokens$_{opt}$ new-line*
(6.8.6)	**# pragma**	*pp-tokens$_{opt}$ new-line*
(6.8.7)	**#**	*new-line*

(6.8.3) *lparen:*
> the left-parenthesis character without preceding white space

(6.8.3) *replacement-list:*
    pp-tokens$_{opt}$

(6.8) *pp-tokens:*
    preprocessing-token
    pp-tokens preprocessing-token

(6.8) *new-line:*
    the new-line character

Annex C
(informative)
Sequence points

The following are the sequence points described in 5.1.2.3.

— The call to a function, after the arguments have been evaluated (6.3.2.2).

— The end of the first operand of the following operators: logical AND **&&** (6.3.13); logical OR **||** (6.3.14); conditional **?** (6.3.15); comma **,** (6.3.17).

— The end of a full expression: an initializer (6.5.7); the expression in an expression statement (6.6.3); the controlling expression of a selection statement (**if** or **switch**) (6.6.4); the controlling expression of a **while** or **do** statement (6.6.5); each of the three expressions of a **for** statement (6.6.5.3); the expression in a **return** statement (6.6.6.4).

Annex D
(informative)
Library summary

D.1 Errors <errno.h>

    EDOM
    ERANGE
    errno

D.2 Common definitions <stddef.h>

    NULL
    offsetof(type, member-designator)
    ptrdiff_t
    size_t
    wchar_t

D.3 Diagnostics <assert.h>

    NDEBUG
    void assert(int expression);

D.4 Character handling <ctype.h>

    int isalnum(int c);
    int isalpha(int c);
    int iscntrl(int c);
    int isdigit(int c);
    int isgraph(int c);
    int islower(int c);
    int isprint(int c);
    int ispunct(int c);
    int isspace(int c);
    int isupper(int c);
    int isxdigit(int c);
    int tolower(int c);
    int toupper(int c);

D.5 Localization <locale.h>

    LC_ALL
    LC_COLLATE
    LC_CTYPE
    LC_MONETARY
    LC_NUMERIC
    LC_TIME
    NULL
    struct lconv
    char *setlocale(int category, const char *locale);
    struct lconv *localeconv(void);

D.6 Mathematics <`math.h`>

```
HUGE_VAL
double acos(double x);
double asin(double x);
double atan(double x);
double atan2(double y, double x);
double cos(double x);
double sin(double x);
double tan(double x);
double cosh(double x);
double sinh(double x);
double tanh(double x);
double exp(double x);
double frexp(double value, int *exp);
double ldexp(double x, int exp);
double log(double x);
double log10(double x);
double modf(double value, double *iptr);
double pow(double x, double y);
double sqrt(double x);
double ceil(double x);
double fabs(double x);
double floor(double x);
double fmod(double x, double y);
```

D.7 Nonlocal jumps <`setjmp.h`>

```
jmp_buf
int setjmp(jmp_buf env);
void longjmp(jmp_buf env, int val);
```

D.8 Signal handling <`signal.h`>

```
sig_atomic_t
SIG_DFL
SIG_ERR
SIG_IGN
SIGABRT
SIGFPE
SIGILL
SIGINT
SIGSEGV
SIGTERM
void (*signal(int sig, void (*func)(int)))(int);
int raise(int sig);
```

D.9   Variable arguments <stdarg.h>

```
va_list
void va_start(va_list ap, parmN);
type va_arg(va_list ap, type);
void va_end(va_list ap);
```

D.10   Input/output <stdio.h>

```
_IOFBF
_IOLBF
_IONBF
BUFSIZ
EOF
FILE
FILENAME_MAX
FOPEN_MAX
fpos_t
L_tmpnam
NULL
SEEK_CUR
SEEK_END
SEEK_SET
size_t
stderr
stdin
stdout
TMP_MAX
int remove(const char *filename);
int rename(const char *old, const char *new);
FILE *tmpfile(void);
char *tmpnam(char *s);
int fclose(FILE *stream);
int fflush(FILE *stream);
FILE *fopen(const char *filename, const char *mode);
FILE *freopen(const char *filename, const char *mode,
      FILE *stream);
void setbuf(FILE *stream, char *buf);
int setvbuf(FILE *stream, char *buf, int mode, size_t size);
int fprintf(FILE *stream, const char *format, ...);
int fscanf(FILE *stream, const char *format, ...);
int printf(const char *format, ...);
int scanf(const char *format, ...);
int sprintf(char *s, const char *format, ...);
int sscanf(const char *s, const char *format, ...);
int vfprintf(FILE *stream, const char *format, va_list arg);
int vprintf(const char *format, va_list arg);
int vsprintf(char *s, const char *format, va_list arg);
int fgetc(FILE *stream);
char *fgets(char *s, int n, FILE *stream);
int fputc(int c, FILE *stream);
int fputs(const char *s, FILE *stream);
int getc(FILE *stream);
int getchar(void);
char *gets(char *s);
int putc(int c, FILE *stream);
```

```
int putchar(int c);
int puts(const char *s);
int ungetc(int c, FILE *stream);
size_t fread(void *ptr, size_t size, size_t nmemb,
    FILE *stream);
size_t fwrite(const void *ptr, size_t size, size_t nmemb,
    FILE *stream);
int fgetpos(FILE *stream, fpos_t *pos);
int fseek(FILE *stream, long int offset, int whence);
int fsetpos(FILE *stream, const fpos_t *pos);
long int ftell(FILE *stream);
void rewind(FILE *stream);
void clearerr(FILE *stream);
int feof(FILE *stream);
int ferror(FILE *stream);
void perror(const char *s);
```

D.11   General utilities <stdlib.h>

```
EXIT_FAILURE
EXIT_SUCCESS
MB_CUR_MAX
NULL
RAND_MAX
div_t
ldiv_t
size_t
wchar_t
double atof(const char *nptr);
int atoi(const char *nptr);
long int atol(const char *nptr);
double strtod(const char *nptr, char **endptr);
long int strtol(const char *nptr, char **endptr, int base);
unsigned long int strtoul(const char *nptr, char **endptr,
      int base);
int rand(void);
void srand(unsigned int seed);
void *calloc(size_t nmemb, size_t size);
void free(void *ptr);
void *malloc(size_t size);
void *realloc(void *ptr, size_t size);
void abort(void);
int atexit(void (*func)(void));
void exit(int status);
char *getenv(const char *name);
int system(const char *string);
void *bsearch(const void *key, const void *base,
      size_t nmemb, size_t size,
      int (*compar)(const void *, const void *));
void qsort(void *base, size_t nmemb, size_t size,
      int (*compar)(const void *, const void *));
int abs(int j);
div_t div(int numer, int denom);
long int labs(long int j);
ldiv_t ldiv(long int numer, long int denom);
int mblen(const char *s, size_t n);
int mbtowc(wchar_t *pwc, const char *s, size_t n);
int wctomb(char *s, wchar_t wchar);
size_t mbstowcs(wchar_t *pwcs, const char *s, size_t n);
size_t wcstombs(char *s, const wchar_t *pwcs, size_t n);
```

D.12 String handling `<string.h>`

```
NULL
size_t
void *memcpy(void *s1, const void *s2, size_t n);
void *memmove(void *s1, const void *s2, size_t n);
char *strcpy(char *s1, const char *s2);
char *strncpy(char *s1, const char *s2, size_t n);
char *strcat(char *s1, const char *s2);
char *strncat(char *s1, const char *s2, size_t n);
int memcmp(const void *s1, const void *s2, size_t n);
int strcmp(const char *s1, const char *s2);
int strcoll(const char *s1, const char *s2);
int strncmp(const char *s1, const char *s2, size_t n);
size_t strxfrm(char *s1, const char *s2, size_t n);
void *memchr(const void *s, int c, size_t n);
char *strchr(const char *s, int c);
size_t strcspn(const char *s1, const char *s2);
char *strpbrk(const char *s1, const char *s2);
char *strrchr(const char *s, int c);
size_t strspn(const char *s1, const char *s2);
char *strstr(const char *s1, const char *s2);
char *strtok(char *s1, const char *s2);
void *memset(void *s, int c, size_t n);
char *strerror(int errnum);
size_t strlen(const char *s);
```

D.13 Date and time `<time.h>`

```
CLOCKS_PER_SEC
NULL
clock_t
time_t
size_t
struct tm
clock_t clock(void);
double difftime(time_t time1, time_t time0);
time_t mktime(struct tm *timeptr);
time_t time(time_t *timer);
char *asctime(const struct tm *timeptr);
char *ctime(const time_t *timer);
struct tm *gmtime(const time_t *timer);
struct tm *localtime(const time_t *timer);
size_t strftime(char *s, size_t maxsize,
      const char *format, const struct tm *timeptr);
```

Annex E
(informative)
Implementation limits

The contents of a header **<limits.h>** are given below, in alphabetic order. The minimum magnitudes shown shall be replaced by implementation-defined magnitudes with the same sign. The values shall all be constant expressions suitable for use in **#if** preprocessing directives. The components are described further in 5.2.4.2.1.

```
#define CHAR_BIT                            8
#define CHAR_MAX      UCHAR_MAX or SCHAR_MAX
#define CHAR_MIN              0 or SCHAR_MIN
#define INT_MAX                        +32767
#define INT_MIN                        -32767
#define LONG_MAX                  +2147483647
#define LONG_MIN                  -2147483647
#define MB_LEN_MAX                          1
#define SCHAR_MAX                        +127
#define SCHAR_MIN                        -127
#define SHRT_MAX                       +32767
#define SHRT_MIN                       -32767
#define UCHAR_MAX                         255
#define UINT_MAX                        65535
#define ULONG_MAX                  4294967295
#define USHRT_MAX                       65535
```

The contents of a header **<float.h>** are given below. The value of **FLT_RADIX** shall be a constant expression suitable for use in **#if** preprocessing directives. Values that need not be constant expressions shall be supplied for all other components. The components are described further in 5.2.4.2.2.

```
#define FLT_ROUNDS
```

The values given in the following list shall be replaced by implementation-defined expressions that shall be equal or greater in magnitude (absolute value) to those shown, with the same sign:

```
#define DBL_DIG                            10
#define DBL_MANT_DIG
#define DBL_MAX_10_EXP                    +37
#define DBL_MAX_EXP
#define DBL_MIN_10_EXP                    -37
#define DBL_MIN_EXP
#define FLT_DIG                             6
#define FLT_MANT_DIG
#define FLT_MAX_10_EXP                    +37
#define FLT_MAX_EXP
#define FLT_MIN_10_EXP                    -37
#define FLT_MIN_EXP
#define FLT_RADIX                           2
#define LDBL_DIG                           10
#define LDBL_MANT_DIG
#define LDBL_MAX_10_EXP                   +37
#define LDBL_MAX_EXP
#define LDBL_MIN_10_EXP                   -37
#define LDBL_MIN_EXP
```

The values given in the following list shall be replaced by implementation-defined expressions that shall be equal to or greater than those shown:

```
#define DBL_MAX                    1E+37
#define FLT_MAX                    1E+37
#define LDBL_MAX                   1E+37
```

The values given in the following list shall be replaced by implementation-defined expressions that shall be equal to or less than those shown:

```
#define DBL_EPSILON                1E-9
#define DBL_MIN                    1E-37
#define FLT_EPSILON                1E-5
#define FLT_MIN                    1E-37
#define LDBL_EPSILON               1E-9
#define LDBL_MIN                   1E-37
```

Annex F
(informative)
Common warnings

An implementation may generate warnings in many situations, none of which is specified as part of this International Standard. The following are a few of the more common situations.

— A block with initialization of an object that has automatic storage duration is jumped into (6.1.2.4).

— An integer character constant includes more than one character or a wide character constant includes more than one multibyte character (6.1.3.4).

— The characters **/*** are found in a comment (6.1.7).

— An implicit narrowing conversion is encountered, such as the assignment of a **long int** or a **double** to an **int**, or a pointer to **void** to a pointer to any type other than a character type (6.2).

— An "unordered" binary operator (not comma, **&&** or **||**) contains a side-effect to an lvalue in one operand, and a side-effect to, or an access to the value of, the identical lvalue in the other operand (6.3).

— A function is called but no prototype has been supplied (6.3.2.2).

— The arguments in a function call do not agree in number and type with those of the parameters in a function definition that is not a prototype (6.3.2.2).

— An object is defined but not used (6.5).

— A value is given to an object of an enumeration type other than by assignment of an enumeration constant that is a member of that type, or an enumeration variable that has the same type, or the value of a function that returns the same enumeration type (6.5.2.2).

— An aggregate has a partly bracketed initialization (6.5.7).

— A statement cannot be reached (6.6).

— A statement with no apparent effect is encountered (6.6).

— A constant expression is used as the controlling expression of a selection statement (6.6.4).

— A function has **return** statements with and without expressions (6.6.6.4).

— An incorrectly formed preprocessing group is encountered while skipping a preprocessing group (6.8.1).

— An unrecognized **#pragma** directive is encountered (6.8.6).

Annex G
(informative)
Portability issues

This annex collects some information about portability that appears in this International Standard.

G.1 Unspecified behavior

The following are unspecified:

— The manner and timing of static initialization (5.1.2).

— The behavior if a printable character is written when the active position is at the final position of a line (5.2.2).

— The behavior if a backspace character is written when the active position is at the initial position of a line (5.2.2).

— The behavior if a horizontal tab character is written when the active position is at or past the last defined horizontal tabulation position (5.2.2).

— The behavior if a vertical tab character is written when the active position is at or past the last defined vertical tabulation position (5.2.2).

— The representations of floating types (6.1.2.5).

— The order in which expressions are evaluated — in any order conforming to the precedence rules, even in the presence of parentheses (6.3).

— The order in which side effects take place (6.3).

— The order in which the function designator and the arguments in a function call are evaluated (6.3.2.2).

— The alignment of the addressable storage unit allocated to hold a bit-field (6.5.2.1).

— The layout of storage for parameters (6.7.1).

— The order in which **#** and **##** operations are evaluated during macro substitution (6.8.3.3).

— Whether **errno** is a macro or an external identifier (7.1.4).

— Whether **setjmp** is a macro or an external identifier (7.6.1.1).

— Whether **va_end** is a macro or an external identifier (7.8.1.3).

— The value of the file position indicator after a successful call to the **ungetc** function for a text stream, until all pushed-back characters are read or discarded (7.9.7.11).

— The details of the value stored by the **fgetpos** function on success (7.9.9.1).

— The details of the value returned by the **ftell** function for a text stream on success (7.9.9.4).

— The order and contiguity of storage allocated by the **calloc**, **malloc**, and **realloc** functions (7.10.3).

— Which of two elements that compare as equal is returned by the **bsearch** function (7.10.5.1).

— The order in an array sorted by the **qsort** function of two elements that compare as equal (7.10.5.2).

— The encoding of the calendar time returned by the **time** function (7.12.2.3).

G.2 Undefined behavior

The behavior in the following circumstances is undefined:

— A nonempty source file does not end in a new-line character, ends in new-line character immediately preceded by a backslash character, or ends in a partial preprocessing token or comment (5.1.1.2).

— A character not in the required character set is encountered in a source file, except in a preprocessing token that is never converted to a token, a character constant, a string literal, a header name, or a comment (5.2.1).

— A comment, string literal, character constant, or header name contains an invalid multibyte character or does not begin and end in the initial shift state (5.2.1.2).

— An unmatched ′ or ″ character is encountered on a logical source line during tokenization (6.1).

— The same identifier is used more than once as a label in the same function (6.1.2.1).

— An identifier is used that is not visible in the current scope (6.1.2.1).

— Identifiers that are intended to denote the same entity differ in a character beyond the minimal significant characters (6.1.2).

— The same identifier has both internal and external linkage in the same translation unit (6.1.2.2).

— The value stored in a pointer that referred to an object with automatic storage duration is used (6.1.2.4).

— Two declarations of the same object or function specify types that are not compatible (6.1.2.6).

— An unspecified escape sequence is encountered in a character constant or a string literal (6.1.3.4).

— An attempt is made to modify a string literal of either form (6.1.4).

— A character string literal token is adjacent to a wide string literal token (6.1.4).

— The characters ′, \, ″, or /* are encountered between the < and > delimiters or the characters ′, \, or /* are encountered between the ″ delimiters in the two forms of a header name preprocessing token (6.1.7).

— An arithmetic conversion produces a result that cannot be represented in the space provided (6.2.1).

— An lvalue with an incomplete type is used in a context that requires the value of the designated object (6.2.2.1).

— The value of a void expression is used or an implicit conversion (except to **void**) is applied to a void expression (6.2.2.2).

— An object is modified more than once, or is modified and accessed other than to determine the new value, between two sequence points (6.3).

— An arithmetic operation is invalid (such as division or modulus by 0) or produces a result that cannot be represented in the space provided (such as overflow or underflow) (6.3).

— An object has its stored value accessed by an lvalue that does not have one of the following types: the declared type of the object, a qualified version of the declared type of the object, the signed or unsigned type corresponding to the declared type of the object, the signed or unsigned type corresponding to a qualified version of the declared type of the object, an aggregate or union type that (recursively) includes one of the aforementioned types among its members, or a character type (6.3).

— An argument to a function is a void expression (6.3.2.2).

— For a function call without a function prototype, the number of arguments does not agree with the number of parameters (6.3.2.2).

— For a function call without a function prototype, if the function is defined without a function prototype, and the types of the arguments after promotion do not agree with those of the parameters after promotion (6.3.2.2).

— If a function is called with a function prototype and the function is not defined with a compatible type (6.3.2.2).

— A function that accepts a variable number of arguments is called without a function prototype that ends with an ellipsis (6.3.2.2).

— An invalid array reference, null pointer reference, or reference to an object declared with automatic storage duration in a terminated block occurs (6.3.3.2).

— A pointer to a function is converted to point to a function of a different type and used to call a function of a type not compatible with the original type (6.3.4).

— A pointer to a function is converted to a pointer to an object or a pointer to an object is converted to a pointer to a function (6.3.4).

— A pointer is converted to other than an integral or pointer type (6.3.4).

— A pointer that does not behave like a pointer to an element of an array object is added to or subtracted from (6.3.6).

— Pointers that do not behave as if they point to the same array object are subtracted (6.3.6).

— An expression is shifted by a negative number or by an amount greater than or equal to the width in bits of the expression being shifted (6.3.7).

— Pointers are compared using a relational operator that do not point to the same aggregate or union (6.3.8).

— An object is assigned to an overlapping object (6.3.16.1).

— An identifier for an object is declared with no linkage and the type of the object is incomplete after its declarator, or after its init-declarator if it has an initializer (6.5).

— A function is declared at block scope with a storage-class specifier other than **extern** (6.5.1).

— A structure or union is defined as containing only unnamed members (6.5.2.1).

— A bit-field is declared with a type other than **int**, **signed int**, or **unsigned int** (6.5.2.1).

— An attempt is made to modify an object with const-qualified type by means of an lvalue with non-const-qualified type (6.5.3).

— An attempt is made to refer to an object with volatile-qualified type by means of an lvalue with non-volatile-qualified type (6.5.3).

— The value of an uninitialized object that has automatic storage duration is used before a value is assigned (6.5.7).

— An object with aggregate or union type with static storage duration has a non-brace-enclosed initializer, or an object with aggregate or union type with automatic storage duration has either a single expression initializer with a type other than that of the object or a non-brace-enclosed initializer (6.5.7).

— The value of a function is used, but no value was returned (6.6.6.4).

— An identifier with external linkage is used but there does not exist exactly one external definition in the program for the identifier (6.7).

— A function that accepts a variable number of arguments is defined without a parameter type list that ends with the ellipsis notation (6.7.1).

— An identifier for an object with internal linkage and an incomplete type is declared with a tentative definition (6.7.2).

— The token **defined** is generated during the expansion of a **#if** or **#elif** preprocessing directive (6.8.1).

— The **#include** preprocessing directive that results after expansion does not match one of the two header name forms (6.8.2).

— A macro argument consists of no preprocessing tokens (6.8.3).

— There are sequences of preprocessing tokens within the list of macro arguments that would otherwise act as preprocessing directive lines (6.8.3).

— The result of the preprocessing operator **#** is not a valid character string literal (6.8.3.2).

— The result of the preprocessing concatenation operator **##** is not a valid preprocessing token (6.8.3.3).

— The **#line** preprocessing directive that results after expansion does not match one of the two well-defined forms (6.8.4).

— One of the following identifiers is the subject of a **#define** or **#undef** preprocessing directive: **defined**, **__LINE__**, **__FILE__**, **__DATE__**, **__TIME__**, or **__STDC__** (6.8.8).

— An attempt is made to copy an object to an overlapping object by use of a library function other than **memmove** (clause 7).

— The effect if a standard header is included within an external definition; is included for the first time after the first reference to any of the functions or objects it declares, or to any of the types or macros it defines; or is included while a macro is defined with a name the same as a keyword (7.1.2).

— The effect if the program redefines a reserved external identifier (7.1.3).

— A macro definition of **errno** is suppressed to obtain access to an actual object (7.1.4).

— The parameter *member-designator* of an **offsetof** macro is an invalid right operand of the **.** operator for the *type* parameter or designates bit-field member of a structure (7.1.6).

— A library function argument has an invalid value, unless the behavior is specified explicitly (7.1.7).

— A library function that accepts a variable number of arguments is not declared (7.1.7).

— The macro definition of **assert** is suppressed to obtain access to an actual function (7.2).

— The argument to a character handling function is out of the domain (7.3).

— A macro definition of **setjmp** is suppressed to obtain access to an actual function (7.6).

— An invocation of the **setjmp** macro occurs in a context other than as the controlling expression in a selection or iteration statement, or in a comparison with an integral constant expression (possibly as implied by the unary **!** operator) as the controlling expression of a selection or iteration statement, or as an expression statement (possibly cast to **void**) (7.6.1.1).

— An object of automatic storage class that does not have volatile-qualified type has been changed between a **setjmp** invocation and a **longjmp** call and then has its value accessed (7.6.2.1).

— The **longjmp** function is invoked from a nested signal routine (7.6.2.1).

— A signal occurs other than as the result of calling the **abort** or **raise** function, and the signal handler calls any function in the standard library other than the **signal** function itself or refers to any object with static storage duration other than by assigning a value to a static storage duration variable of type **volatile sig_atomic_t** (7.7.1.1).

— The value of **errno** is referred to after a signal occurs other than as the result of calling the **abort** or **raise** function and the corresponding signal handler calls the **signal** function such that it returns the value **SIG_ERR** (7.7.1.1).

— The macro **va_arg** is invoked with the parameter **ap** that was passed to a function that invoked the macro **va_arg** with the same parameter (7.8).

— A macro definition of **va_start**, **va_arg**, or **va_end** or a combination thereof is suppressed to obtain access to an actual function (7.8.1).

— The parameter *parmN* of a **va_start** macro is declared with the **register** storage class, or with a function or array type, or with a type that is not compatible with the type that results after application of the default argument promotions (7.8.1.1).

— There is no actual next argument for a **va_arg** macro invocation (7.8.1.2).

— The type of the actual next argument in a variable argument list disagrees with the type specified by the **va_arg** macro (7.8.1.2).

— The **va_end** macro is invoked without a corresponding invocation of the **va_start** macro (7.8.1.3).

— A return occurs from a function with a variable argument list initialized by the **va_start** macro before the **va_end** macro is invoked (7.8.1.3).

— The stream for the **fflush** function points to an input stream or to an update stream in which the most recent operation was input (7.9.5.2).

— An output operation on an update stream is followed by an input operation without an intervening call to the **fflush** function or a file positioning function, or an input operation on an update stream is followed by an output operation without an intervening call to a file positioning function (7.9.5.3).

— The format for the **fprintf** or **fscanf** function does not match the argument list (7.9.6).

— An invalid conversion specification is found in the format for the **fprintf** or **fscanf** function (7.9.6).

— A **%%** conversion specification for the **fprintf** or **fscanf** function contains characters between the pair of **%** characters (7.9.6).

— A conversion specification for the **fprintf** function contains an **h** or **l** with a conversion specifier other than **d**, **i**, **n**, **o**, **u**, **x**, or **X**, or an **L** with a conversion specifier other than **e**, **E**, **f**, **g**, or **G** (7.9.6.1).

— A conversion specification for the **fprintf** function contains a **#** flag with a conversion specifier other than **o**, **x**, **X**, **e**, **E**, **f**, **g**, or **G** (7.9.6.1).

— A conversion specification for the **fprintf** function contains a **0** flag with a conversion specifier other than **d**, **i**, **o**, **u**, **x**, **X**, **e**, **E**, **f**, **g**, or **G** (7.9.6.1).

— An aggregate or union, or a pointer to an aggregate or union is an argument to the **fprintf** function, except for the conversion specifiers **%s** (for an array of character type) or **%p** (for a pointer to **void**) (7.9.6.1).

— A single conversion by the **fprintf** function produces more than 509 characters of output (7.9.6.1).

— A conversion specification for the **fscanf** function contains an **h** or **l** with a conversion specifier other than **d**, **i**, **n**, **o**, **u**, or **x**, or an **L** with a conversion specifier other than **e**, **f**, or **g** (7.9.6.2).

— A pointer value printed by **%p** conversion by the **fprintf** function during a previous program execution is the argument for **%p** conversion by the **fscanf** function (7.9.6.2).

— The result of a conversion by the **fscanf** function cannot be represented in the space provided, or the receiving object does not have an appropriate type (7.9.6.2).

— The result of converting a string to a number by the **atof**, **atoi**, or **atol** function cannot be represented (7.10.1).

— The value of a pointer that refers to space deallocated by a call to the **free** or **realloc** function is referred to (7.10.3).

— The pointer argument to the **free** or **realloc** function does not match a pointer earlier returned by **calloc**, **malloc**, or **realloc**, or the object pointed to has been deallocated by a call to **free** or **realloc** (7.10.3).

— A program executes more than one call to the **exit** function (7.10.4.3).

— The result of an integer arithmetic function (**abs**, **div**, **labs**, or **ldiv**) cannot be represented (7.10.6).

— The shift states for the **mblen**, **mbtowc**, and **wctomb** functions are not explicitly reset to the initial state when the **LC_CTYPE** category of the current locale is changed (7.10.7).

— An array written to by a copying or concatenation function is too small (7.11.2, 7.11.3).

— An invalid conversion specification is found in the format for the **strftime** function (7.12.3.5).

G.3 Implementation-defined behavior

Each implementation shall document its behavior in each of the areas listed in this subclause. The following are implementation-defined:

G.3.1 Translation

— How a diagnostic is identified (5.1.1.3).

G.3.2 Environment

— The semantics of the arguments to **main** (5.1.2.2.1).

— What constitutes an interactive device (5.1.2.3).

G.3.3 Identifiers

— The number of significant initial characters (beyond 31) in an identifier without external linkage (6.1.2).

— The number of significant initial characters (beyond 6) in an identifier with external linkage (6.1.2).

— Whether case distinctions are significant in an identifier with external linkage (6.1.2).

G.3.4 Characters

— The members of the source and execution character sets, except as explicitly specified in this International Standard (5.2.1).

— The shift states used for the encoding of multibyte characters (5.2.1.2).

— The number of bits in a character in the execution character set (5.2.4.2.1).

— The mapping of members of the source character set (in character constants and string literals) to members of the execution character set (6.1.3.4).

— The value of an integer character constant that contains a character or escape sequence not represented in the basic execution character set or the extended character set for a wide character constant (6.1.3.4).

— The value of an integer character constant that contains more than one character or a wide character constant that contains more than one multibyte character (6.1.3.4).

— The current locale used to convert multibyte characters into corresponding wide characters (codes) for a wide character constant (6.1.3.4).

— Whether a "plain" **char** has the same range of values as **signed char** or **unsigned char** (6.2.1.1).

G.3.5 Integers

— The representations and sets of values of the various types of integers (6.1.2.5).

— The result of converting an integer to a shorter signed integer, or the result of converting an unsigned integer to a signed integer of equal length, if the value cannot be represented (6.2.1.2).

— The results of bitwise operations on signed integers (6.3).

— The sign of the remainder on integer division (6.3.5).

— The result of a right shift of a negative-valued signed integral type (6.3.7).

G.3.6 Floating point

— The representations and sets of values of the various types of floating-point numbers (6.1.2.5).

— The direction of truncation when an integral number is converted to a floating-point number that cannot exactly represent the original value (6.2.1.3).

— The direction of truncation or rounding when a floating-point number is converted to a narrower floating-point number (6.2.1.4).

G.3.7 Arrays and pointers

— The type of integer required to hold the maximum size of an array — that is, the type of the **sizeof** operator, **size_t** (6.3.3.4, 7.1.1).

— The result of casting a pointer to an integer or vice versa (6.3.4).

— The type of integer required to hold the difference between two pointers to elements of the same array, **ptrdiff_t** (6.3.6, 7.1.1).

G.3.8 Registers

— The extent to which objects can actually be placed in registers by use of the **register** storage-class specifier (6.5.1).

G.3.9 Structures, unions, enumerations, and bit-fields

— A member of a union object is accessed using a member of a different type (6.3.2.3).

— The padding and alignment of members of structures (6.5.2.1). This should present no problem unless binary data written by one implementation are read by another.

— Whether a "plain" **int** bit-field is treated as a **signed int** bit-field or as an **unsigned int** bit-field (6.5.2.1).

— The order of allocation of bit-fields within a unit (6.5.2.1).

— Whether a bit-field can straddle a storage-unit boundary (6.5.2.1).

— The integer type chosen to represent the values of an enumeration type (6.5.2.2).

G.3.10 Qualifiers

— What constitutes an access to an object that has volatile-qualified type (6.5.5.3).

G.3.11 Declarators

— The maximum number of declarators that may modify an arithmetic, structure, or union type (6.5.4).

G.3.12 Statements

— The maximum number of **case** values in a **switch** statement (6.6.4.2).

G.3.13 Preprocessing directives

— Whether the value of a single-character character constant in a constant expression that controls conditional inclusion matches the value of the same character constant in the execution character set. Whether such a character constant may have a negative value (6.8.1).

— The method for locating includable source files (6.8.2).

— The support of quoted names for includable source files (6.8.2).

— The mapping of source file character sequences (6.8.2).

— The behavior on each recognized **#pragma** directive (6.8.6).

— The definitions for **__DATE__** and **__TIME__** when respectively, the date and time of translation are not available (6.8.8).

G.3.14 Library functions

— The null pointer constant to which the macro **NULL** expands (7.1.6).

— The diagnostic printed by and the termination behavior of the **assert** function (7.2).

— The sets of characters tested for by the **isalnum**, **isalpha**, **iscntrl**, **islower**, **isprint**, and **isupper** functions (7.3.1).

— The values returned by the mathematics functions on domain errors (7.5.1).

— Whether the mathematics functions set the integer expression **errno** to the value of the macro **ERANGE** on underflow range errors (7.5.1).

— Whether a domain error occurs or zero is returned when the **fmod** function has a second argument of zero (7.5.6.4).

— The set of signals for the **signal** function (7.7.1.1).

— The semantics for each signal recognized by the **signal** function (7.7.1.1).

— The default handling and the handling at program startup for each signal recognized by the **signal** function (7.7.1.1).

— If the equivalent of **signal(sig, SIG_DFL);** is not executed prior to the call of a signal handler, the blocking of the signal that is performed (7.7.1.1).

— Whether the default handling is reset if the **SIGILL** signal is received by a handler specified to the **signal** function (7.7.1.1).

— Whether the last line of a text stream requires a terminating new-line character (7.9.2).

— Whether space characters that are written out to a text stream immediately before a new-line character appear when read in (7.9.2).

— The number of null characters that may be appended to data written to a binary stream (7.9.2).

— Whether the file position indicator of an append mode stream is initially positioned at the beginning or end of the file (7.9.3).

— Whether a write on a text stream causes the associated file to be truncated beyond that point (7.9.3).

— The characteristics of file buffering (7.9.3).

— Whether a zero-length file actually exists (7.9.3).

— The rules for composing valid file names (7.9.3).

— Whether the same file can be open multiple times (7.9.3).

— The effect of the **remove** function on an open file (7.9.4.1).

— The effect if a file with the new name exists prior to a call to the **rename** function (7.9.4.2).

— The output for **%p** conversion in the **fprintf** function (7.9.6.1).

— The input for **%p** conversion in the **fscanf** function (7.9.6.2).

— The interpretation of a – character that is neither the first nor the last character in the scanlist for **%[** conversion in the **fscanf** function (7.9.6.2).

— The value to which the macro **errno** is set by the **fgetpos** or **ftell** function on failure (7.9.9.1, 7.9.9.4).

— The messages generated by the **perror** function (7.9.10.4).

— The behavior of the **calloc, malloc,** or **realloc** function if the size requested is zero (7.10.3).

— The behavior of the **abort** function with regard to open and temporary files (7.10.4.1).

— The status returned by the **exit** function if the value of the argument is other than zero, **EXIT_SUCCESS,** or **EXIT_FAILURE** (7.10.4.3).

— The set of environment names and the method for altering the environment list used by the **getenv** function (7.10.4.4).

— The contents and mode of execution of the string by the **system** function (7.10.4.5).

— The contents of the error message strings returned by the **strerror** function (7.11.6.2).

— The local time zone and Daylight Saving Time (7.12.1).

— The era for the **clock** function (7.12.2.1).

G.4 Locale-specific behavior

The following characteristics of a hosted environment are locale-specific:

— The content of the execution character set, in addition to the required members (5.2.1).

— The direction of printing (5.2.2).

— The decimal-point character (7.1.1).

— The implementation-defined aspects of character testing and case mapping functions (7.3).

— The collation sequence of the execution character set (7.11.4.4).

— The formats for time and date (7.12.3.5).

G.5 Common extensions

The following extensions are widely used in many systems, but are not portable to all implementations. The inclusion of any extension that may cause a strictly conforming program to become invalid renders an implementation nonconforming. Examples of such extensions are new keywords, or library functions declared in standard headers or predefined macros with names that do not begin with an underscore.

G.5.1 Environment arguments

In a hosted environment, the **main** function receives a third argument, **char *envp[]**, that points to a null-terminated array of pointers to **char**, each of which points to a string that provides information about the environment for this execution of the process (5.1.2.2.1).

G.5.2 Specialized identifiers

Characters other than the underscore _, letters, and digits, that are not defined in the required source character set (such as the dollar sign **$**, or characters in national character sets) may appear in an identifier (6.1.2).

G.5.3 Lengths and cases of identifiers

All characters in identifiers (with or without external linkage) are significant and case distinctions are observed (6.1.2).

G.5.4 Scopes of identifiers

A function identifier, or the identifier of an object the declaration of which contains the keyword **extern**, has file scope (6.1.2.1).

G.5.5 Writable string literals

String literals are modifiable. Identical string literals shall be distinct (6.1.4).

G.5.6 Other arithmetic types

Other arithmetic types, such as **long long int**, and their appropriate conversions are defined (6.2.2.1).

G.5.7 Function pointer casts

A pointer to an object or to **void** may be cast to a pointer to a function, allowing data to be invoked as a function (6.3.4). A pointer to a function may be cast to a pointer to an object or to **void**, allowing a function to be inspected or modified (for example, by a debugger) (6.3.4).

G.5.8 Non-int bit-field types

Types other than **int**, **unsigned int**, or **signed int** can be declared as bit-fields, with appropriate maximum widths (6.5.2.1).

G.5.9 The fortran keyword

The **fortran** declaration specifier may be used in a function declaration to indicate that calls suitable for FORTRAN should be generated, or that different representations for external names are to be generated (6.5.4.3).

G.5.10 The `asm` keyword

The `asm` keyword may be used to insert assembly language code directly into the translator output. The most common implementation is via a statement of the form

> `asm` (*character-string-literal*) ;

(6.6).

G.5.11 Multiple external definitions

There may be more than one external definition for the identifier of an object, with or without the explicit use of the keyword `extern`. If the definitions disagree, or more than one is initialized, the behavior is undefined (6.7.2).

G.5.12 Empty macro arguments

A macro argument may consist of no preprocessing tokens (6.8.3).

G.5.13 Predefined macro names

Macro names that do not begin with an underscore, describing the translation and execution environments, may be defined by the implementation before translation begins (6.8.8).

G.5.14 Extra arguments for signal handlers

Handlers for specific signals may be called with extra arguments in addition to the signal number (7.7.1.1).

G.5.15 Additional stream types and file-opening modes

Additional mappings from files to streams may be supported (7.9.2), and additional file-opening modes may be specified by characters appended to the `mode` argument of the `fopen` function (7.9.5.3).

G.5.16 Defined file position indicator

The file position indicator is decremented by each successful call to the `ungetc` function for a text stream, except if its value was zero before a call (7.9.7.11).

Index

Only major references are listed.

The American National Standards Institute (ANSI)
The Center for Strategic Standardization

Achieving global competitiveness has become an imperative for survival in today's economic climate. Thus standardization has become a necessary and important tool in achieving global success. Over the past few years industry has realized the strategic importance of standardization and the role it can play in achieving success in the global marketplace. To achieve their goals, industry needs to establish strategies to deal with the impact of standardization on their business operations.

In the United States, providing leadership in strategic standardization activities is the work of the American National Standards Institute (ANSI). ANSI is a private not-for-profit membership organization that administers the private sector voluntary standards system in the U.S. Founded in 1918, it brings together groups from both the private and public sectors dedicated to furthering the U.S. consensus standards system and to creating and approving American National Standards. ANSI provides the means for the U.S. to influence global standardization activities and development of international standards. It is the dues paying member and sole U.S. representative of the two major non-treaty international standards organizations, the International Organization for Standardization (ISO) and the International Electrotechnical Commission (IEC), via the U.S. National Committee (USNC). ANSI's broad membership includes industry, standards developing organizations, trade associations, professional and technical societies, government, labor and consumer groups.

ANSI provides national and international recognition of standards for credibility and force in domestic commerce and world trade. It assists companies in reducing operating and purchasing costs and assures product quality and safety. It is the main source of national and international standards information essential for marketing worldwide. ANSI promotes a self-regulated and strong privately administered voluntary national and international standards system.

To learn more about ANSI and its services contact:
ANSI's Membership Department at 212 642-4948 or write to:
American National Standards Institute (ANSI)
Membership Department
11 West 42nd Street
New York, NY 10036